Import/Export Kit

FOR

DUMMIES®

2ND EDITION

Import/Export Kit

FOR

DUMMIES®

2ND EDITION

by John J. Capela

WILEY

John Wiley & Sons, Inc.

Import/Export Kit For Dummies,® 2nd Edition

Published by
John Wiley & Sons, Inc.
111 River St.
Hoboken, NJ 07030-5774
www.wiley.com

For general information on our other products and services, please contact our Customer Care Department within the U.S. at 877-762-2974, outside the U.S. at 317-572-3993, or fax 317-572-4002.

For technical support, please visit www.wiley.com/techsupport.

Wiley publishes in a variety of print and electronic formats and by print-on-demand. Some material included with standard print versions of this book may not be included in e-books or in print-on-demand. If this book refers to media such as a CD or DVD that is not included in the version you purchased, you may download this material at http://booksupport.wiley.com. For more information about Wiley products, visit us at www.wiley.com.

Library of Congress Control Number: 2012931721

ISBN 978-1-118-09515-7 (pbk); ISBN 978-1-118-20629-4 (ebk); ISBN 978-1-118-20630-0 (ebk); ISBN 978-1-118-20631-7 (ebk)

Manufactured in the United States of America

10 9 8 7 6 5 4 3 2

WILEY

About the Author

John Capela is an assistant professor of business at St. Joseph's College in New York, where he has taught marketing, management, and international business courses for the past 20 years.

Prior to becoming a faculty member at St. Joseph's, John was an assistant professor of management in the School of Management at the New York Institute of Technology, and a visiting professor of management at the Sy Syms School of Business of Yeshiva University. He has conducted numerous workshops and seminars throughout the New York metropolitan area on how to start an import/export business. He also was a coauthor of the *Dictionary of International Business Terms* (Barron's), initially published in 1994 and currently in its third edition.

Prior to teaching, John served as the director of international operations for one of the oldest and largest manufacturers and marketers of medical, surgical, and healthcare products. He directed the start-up of manufacturing operations in Puerto Rico and served as its chief operating executive.

He is president of CADE International, a firm that provides consulting and training in international business, specializing in communications, importing, exporting, licensing, and foreign investment. The firm serves both American and foreign exporters and importers.

Dedication

I would like to dedicate this book to those family members and friends who were always there to support me in my personal and professional endeavors. A special thanks to my parents, who are missed and will always be part of my life; my sons, John and Christopher; my "Cioci" Mary and Uncle Johnnie; my friend Kathleen; and my mentors, Fred and Greg, who guided me into my career in international business over 35 years ago.

I would finally like to add a special dedication to two new people who have become part of my life since the release of the first edition of this book in July 2008. They are Christopher's wife Tracey, who is the daughter I never had, and that extra special person Alexa Caroline, my first grandchild. After she came in to my life, I soon found out that a grandchild fills a space in your heart that you never knew was empty.

Author's Acknowledgments

I would like to again thank Mike Baker, the acquisitions editor at Wiley from the first edition of this book, for his efforts in finding me and providing me with the opportunity. He has since moved on to an assignment in the United Kingdom with the *For Dummies* brand of Wiley. I would also like to thank my new editor, Erin Calligan Mooney.

I have always had a passion for international business. I've been involved with importing or exporting since 1970, having started out as an export assistant, then an import assistant, an international traffic manager, director of international operations, an entrepreneur, a seminar leader, and a teacher. So writing this kind of book is truly something I've always wanted to do. If it weren't for Mike finding me, I would never have had the opportunity to complete something that was on my to-do list.

I would also like to express my thanks to the other members of the editorial staff at Wiley, including my project editor, Tim Gallan, who showed a great deal of patience in dealing with my many delays. Also, I would like to give a special thanks to copy editor Danielle Voirol, who made some great recommendations in the editing process, and I have to give her a special thanks for her comments for the section covering international negotiations. Many thanks to my good friend for many years, George Haber, who again served as the technical editor.

Finally, I would like to thank all those students who, over the past 20 years, have sat through my "Build and Start Your Own Import/Export Business" seminar. Their enthusiasm has always inspired me, and I have referred to them and many of their stories throughout this text.

Publisher's Acknowledgments

We're proud of this book; please send us your comments at http://dummies.custhelp.com. For other comments, please contact our Customer Care Department within the U.S. at 877-762-2974, outside the U.S. at 317-572-3993, or fax 317-572-4002.

Some of the people who helped bring this book to market include the following:

Acquisitions, Editorial, and Vertical Websites

Senior Project Editor: Tim Gallan

Acquisitions Editor: Erin Calligan Mooney

Senior Copy Editor: Danielle Voirol

Technical Reviewer: George Haber

Assistant Editor: David Lutton

Editorial Program Coordinator: Joe Niesen

Editorial Manager: Michelle Hacker

Editorial Assistants: Rachelle S. Amick, Alexa Koschier

Vertical Websites: Jenny Swisher

Cover Photos: © Stockphoto.com / Björn Meyer

Cartoons: Rich Tennant (www.the5thwave.com)

Composition Services

Project Coordinator: Katie Crocker

Layout and Graphics: Carrie A. Cesavice, Tim Detrick, Sennett Vaughan Johnson

Proofreaders: Cynthia Fields, Lauren Mandelbaum

Indexer: Ty Koontz

Publishing and Editorial for Consumer Dummies

    Kathleen Nebenhaus, Vice President and Executive Publisher

    Kristin Ferguson-Wagstaffe, Product Development Director

    Ensley Eikenburg, Associate Publisher, Travel

    Kelly Regan, Editorial Director, Travel

Publishing for Technology Dummies

    Andy Cummings, Vice President and Publisher

Composition Services

    Debbie Stailey, Director of Composition Services

Contents at a Glance

Table of Contents

Introduction

⋅ ⋅

*T*he global marketplace is a fast-growing and rapidly changing field. International business is exploding as a direct result of changes in technology, rapidly expanding economies, and international trade agreements — the United States imported $1.9 trillion and exported $1.277 trillion in goods in 2010. If you want to start your own international business or diversify the activities of your existing firms, you've come to the right place.

About This Book

Import/Export Kit For Dummies is a reference book — something you can keep on your desk and turn to when you have questions, as well as something you can read through from beginning to end if you like. Either way, this book helps you determine whether the business of international trade is for you. In this book, you

- ✔ Explore how to set up an office for international trade

- ✔ Find products to import and export

- ✔ Identify target markets and find customers

- ✔ Make sense of applicable rules and regulations

- ✔ Find out how to complete the necessary licensing application and shipping documents

- ✔ Understand the process of international negotiations and cultural differences

Finally, *Import/Export Kit For Dummies* gives you know-how and up-to-date info that you need in order to enter or advance in the challenging and highly rewarding world of importing and exporting.

Conventions Used in This Book

I don't use too many special conventions in this book, but you should be aware of the following:

✔ I use *italics* for emphasis and to highlight new words or terms, which I define shortly thereafter.

✔ I use **boldface** for key words in bulleted lists and to indicate the action part of numbered steps.

✔ I use `monofont` for e-mail and web addresses.

Note: When this book was printed, some web addresses may have needed to break across two lines of text. If that happened, rest assured that I haven't put in any extra characters (such as hyphens) to indicate the break. So when using one of these web addresses, just type in exactly what you see in this book, pretending as though the line break doesn't exist.

What You're Not to Read

The great thing about the *For Dummies* series is that you can choose what to read and what to skip. You aren't going to be quizzed on anything in this book.

If you're looking for guidance on exactly what the most skippable text is, keep this in mind:

✔ Sidebars (text in gray boxes) are for topics that are interesting but not essential to your understanding of the material, so if you're in a hurry, skip them.

✔ Anything marked with a Technical Stuff icon is safe to skip, too.

Foolish Assumptions

I don't make many assumptions about you as the reader of the book, but I do assume the following:

✔ You may be an entrepreneur or an owner of a small to medium-size business, and you're looking to get involved in importing and/or exporting.

✔ You may be an employee of a business that's planning to get involved in importing and exporting, and you want to be in the know.

✔ You have some business experience, but you may never have imported or exported before.

✔ You may be a college or business student taking an import/export course, and you want information in plain English.

How This Book Is Organized

I divide *Importing/Exporting For Dummies* into seven parts. You don't have to read all the parts, and you don't have to read them in order. Here's the low-down on what to expect.

Part I: Breaking into the Import/Export Business

Before you can put together a plan, you have to identify objectives and set goals. This part helps you determine how much money you need to invest and how much you can earn in an import/export business. I cover various approaches to import/export business opportunities. I also help you identify the rules and regulations that are applicable to firms importing products into or exporting products from the United States. Finally, every business owner must make decisions in setting up a business. Chapter 4 addresses issues such as trade names, forms of organization, registration, bank accounts, office equipment, addresses, telephone numbers, websites, and e-mail addresses.

Part II: Selecting Products and Suppliers

This part helps you select products and find firms to supply you with those products. I provide guidelines that enable you to narrow down your product choices and select the products you want to import or export. If you're already in business and want to go global with your product, skip Chapter 5 and head straight for Chapter 6 or Chapter 7.

Part III: Identifying Your Target Market and Finding Customers

In this part, I fill you in on selecting a target market and finding customers for the products that you've selected. I review the process of creating and delivering goods and services to customers. I share the importance of knowing your company's target customers' needs, demands, and wants; offering the products and services that will satisfy those needs, demands, and wants; and providing customers with quality, service, convenience, and value so that they continue being your customers. Then I help you develop a marketing plan that focuses on the customer and build a strategy leading to success for your business.

Part IV: Negotiating around the World

This part focuses on what you need to know when negotiating with anyone anywhere around the world. I begin by discussing how the international negotiation process works, including information on what you can negotiate about and ultimately how to close the deal. I then provide you with information on what makes negotiating around the world different and identify the cultural factors that affect global business negotiations.

The final chapter in this part focuses on seven different regions around the world. For each of these regions, I provide information on the business environment, specific cultural factors that affect the negotiating process, and detailed do's and don'ts for key countries within these regions.

Part V: Completing the Transaction: International Trade Procedures and Regulations

After you've identified the applicable rules and regulations, selected your products, identified your target markets, and developed a marketing plan, you need to deal with procedural issues, such as negotiating a price and arranging for payments.

This part identifies the various terms of sale that are used in all international transactions. I also cover the alternative methods of payments that are used when dealing with overseas suppliers or customers. Issues relating to documentation, logistics, insurance, packing, Customs brokers, and freight forwarders are also covered in this part.

I also include a general explanation of import requirements, in case you're interested in going into an importing business or you want to import something for personal use and not for resale. Chapter 19 provides info on the process and documents required to import goods into the United States, the methods used in determining the dutiable value for the goods being imported, and what Customs is looking for when it examines the goods.

In addition, this part covers import quotas, which can limit your ability to import specific products from specific countries. Finally, I focus on the role of international trade agreements and their effect on import/export business opportunities.

Part VI: The Part of Tens

In the Part of Tens, I give you reminders, hints, observations, and warnings about what to do and not to do as you strive to be a successful importer and/or exporter.

Part VII: Appendixes

This part is all about references. You can find a multilingual cross-reference list and resources that can help you in the import/export business.

Icons Used in This Book

Icons are those little images in the left-hand margins of the book, designed to draw your attention to certain kinds of information. Here's what they mean:

When you see the Tip icon, you can be sure to find a helpful piece of information that'll save you time or money or just make your life as an importer/exporter easier.

Ouch! You may get burned if you don't heed these warnings.

You don't have to memorize this book, but occasionally, I tell you something that bears repeating or that you'll want to commit to memory. When I do, I flag the info with this icon.

Sometimes I tell you more information than you really need on a particular subject, and when I do, I flag that info with this icon. If you just want the basics, skip anything marked with this icon.

Where to Go from Here

If you're the kind of person who never missed a homework assignment in your life and did every extra credit assignment possible, you've probably already read the copyright information and table of contents. In that case, keep on reading until you hit the very last page of the book, and you'll be happy.

If you're more interested in getting the information you need, the table of contents and index are your new best friends. Use them to locate just the information you need, without having to read anything you don't need.

Still not sure where to go? Here's a quick guide: If you're trying to decide whether importing/exporting is right for you and how doing business internationally is different, turn to Chapter 1. If you're interested in finding out whether you need a license or permit before you can import or export a product, turn to Chapter 3. If you want to find suppliers, turn to Chapters 6 and 7. If you want to find customers, turn to Chapters 11 and 12. If you want tips on negotiating around the world, check out Chapter 15. If you want to figure out how to pay or get paid from individuals or firms from other countries, turn to Chapter 17. And if you want to clear a shipment through U.S. Customs, turn to Chapter 19.

Part I
Breaking into the Import/Export Business

The 5th Wave   By Rich Tennant

"Business here is good, but the weak dollar is killing my overseas markets!"

In this part . . .

1 fill you in on the different environmental forces that you encounter when doing business with other countries. I explain the various approaches to exporting and importing, together with some of the qualities that you need in order to be successful. I help you consider your motivations for wanting to start your own import/export business and tell you why someone with an existing business may consider moving into the international business arena.

I offer guidelines that you can use to determine how much money you need to invest and how much you can earn. I tell you who to contact to identify the rules and regulations when importing goods into, or exporting goods from, the United States. Finally, I help you organize for your export and import operations.

Chapter 1

Introducing Import/Export

In This Chapter

▶ Finding out what the import/export business is all about

▶ Looking at the environmental forces you can control — and those you can't

I can't imagine a more exciting time for international trade than the present. The opportunities for exporting and importing are growing at an impressive rate — and with those opportunities come challenges. Many factors have contributed to this growth: the establishment of the World Trade Organization (WTO), the implementation of trade agreements such as the North American Free Trade Agreement (NAFTA) and the CAFTA-DR (Dominican Republic–Central America–United States Free Trade Agreement), the continued economic integration of Europe, and the growth of emerging markets such as India, China, Turkey, and more.

You're living in an exciting time! In the past, opportunities for many small businesses ended within the borders of their own country, and international trade was only for large multinational corporations. Today, the global marketplace provides opportunities not just for the multinational corporation but also for small upstart companies. The Internet, affordable changes in technology, and increased access to information have all made it easier for firms of all sizes to engage in international trade.

In this chapter, I introduce you to the wonderful and exciting world of importing and exporting. You discover various approaches to doing business internationally and the environmental forces that make doing business with other countries different.

Defining the Import/Export Business

Most companies begin their initial involvement in international business by exporting or importing. *Exporting* is sending goods out of your country in order to sell them in another country. *Importing* is bringing goods into your country from another country in order to sell them.

Both of these approaches require minimal investment and are, for the most part, free of major risks. They provide individuals and companies with a way of getting into international business without the commitment of significant financial resources, like the kind required to actually set up shop overseas. In this section, I introduce you to the main forms of importing and exporting.

Exporting: Do you want what I've got?

Exporting comes in two major forms:

- **Direct exporting:** Direct exporting is a business activity occurring between an exporter and an importer without the intervention of a third party. This option is good for existing businesses that are looking for ways to expand their operations.

- **Indirect exporting:** Indirect exporting is easier than direct exporting. It involves exporting goods through various intermediaries in the producer's country. Indirect exporting doesn't require any expertise or major cash expenditures, and it's the type of exporting used most often by companies that are new to exporting.

As you gain experience in doing business internationally, you may want to move from indirect exporting to direct exporting. You'll have greater control over the sales and distribution of your products.

Looking at types of indirect exporting

Indirect exporting can include the use of an export management company or something called *piggyback exporting,* both of which I cover in this section.

Dedicated exporting: Export management companies

An *export management company* (EMC) is a private company based in the United States that serves as the export department for several manufacturers, soliciting and transacting export business on behalf of its clients. EMCs normally take title to the goods and assume all the risks associated with doing business in other countries. Using an EMC is helpful when you're new to exporting or you don't have a distributor or agent in a foreign country.

Entrepreneurs not interested in manufacturing can get involved in exporting by setting up an EMC. An EMC usually specializes in a product category. If you have a network of overseas contacts, some general product knowledge, and a desire to start an export business, contact American manufacturers who aren't actively exporting and offer your services.

For example, when I was employed in the healthcare industry selling goods internationally, I identified customers in various countries. With that knowledge in hand, I decided to establish an EMC. So I contacted domestic medical-products manufacturers who had products that would be of interest to my clients but who weren't actively involved in exporting. I offered my services to these firms and found that they wanted to open up new markets, but they'd been hesitant because they didn't want to deal with many exporting issues (payment, documentation, shipping, and so on). My EMC was able to handle those issues for them.

Piggyback exporting: Having another manufacturer export your related goods

Piggyback exporting is a foreign distribution operation in which your products are sold along with those of another manufacturer. Companies that have related or complementary but noncompetitive products use this form of exporting.

For example, say that you have a company that manufactures hairbrushes. You're not yet exporting, but you're interested in selling your hairbrushes in Italy. You just don't want to assume any risks or deal with major headaches. Across town is a company that makes shampoos. It's a well-established manufacturer and exporter of a line of shampoo products — and it's currently selling its entire product line in the Italian marketplace. In piggyback exporting, you approach the shampoo company and offer to let that company represent and sell your hairbrushes in Italy.

Why would the shampoo company be interested in such a deal? Because this setup lets the shampoo company offer a more complete line of products to its distributors with little to no additional investment. The shampoo company profits either by purchasing the hairbrushes and adding on a markup or by coordinating a commission arrangement with you.

Doing direct exporting

In *direct exporting,* you do your own exporting. Companies usually export directly only after having exported indirectly for a while. If you're interested in direct exporting, you can choose one of three routes:

- ✔ **Use an agent.** An *agent* is a company that acts as an intermediary but, unlike an EMC, doesn't take title to the goods (see the earlier section "Dedicated exporting: Export management companies" for info on EMCs). You appoint an agent in each market (or country), and the agent solicits orders, with goods and payment for the goods happening directly between you and the customer in the other country.

✔ **Appoint a distributor.** You can appoint a distributor in another country; the distributer purchases goods, takes title, and serves the customers on your behalf.

✔ **Set up an overseas sales office.** You can go to another country, perhaps rent a warehouse, set up an office, and distribute the goods to customers. In practice, you're exporting to *yourself* overseas.

Importing: Can I sell what you have?

Importers purchase goods in foreign markets and sell them domestically. An importer can be a small company that buys goods from distributors and manufacturers in foreign markets or it can be a global corporation for which importing components and raw materials valued at millions of dollars is just one of its functions.

Because businesses face intense price competition, more companies are looking to the global marketplace to source products. Many nations have a well-educated and skilled workforce that earns salaries that are less than those of comparable workers in the United States. To remain competitive, U.S. companies import goods from suppliers in countries where costs are lower than they are domestically. This is true for both low-cost items and luxury items.

To determine whether the item you want to import is produced in foreign markets and, if so, where to find it, look for similar products that are being sold in your country. Examining the product can tell you where it's made and, often, by whom. The U.S. Customs service requires that all goods be labeled with the country of origin on each product or on its container if product-marking isn't feasible. You can then use many of the resources in this book to identify suppliers — see Chapter 6 and Appendix A for details.

Environmental Forces That Make International Business Different

Doing business in a global environment is very different from doing business domestically. When you cross borders, you have to deal with a variety of dynamic *environmental forces*, conditions that have an impact on the operations of a company. Environmental forces are either internal (within the company) or external (outside the company). *Internal forces* are the ones you can control, and *external forces* are the ones you can't.

I'll start off with the good news: When you're in business — any business, whether domestic or international — certain factors *are* within your control. Internal forces include things such as

- ✔ Availability of capital
- ✔ Finances
- ✔ Personnel
- ✔ Production and marketing capabilities
- ✔ Raw materials

Your job is to coordinate these controllable forces so that you can adapt to the uncontrollable forces.

You'll be way ahead of the competition if you recognize what you *can't* control and figure out a way to adapt. In this section, I cover the main forces in international business.

Looking at economic and socioeconomic conditions

Other countries' economic and socioeconomic conditions — which include factors such as population size, income levels, growth and recessions, and so on — are definitely factors you have no control over. And yet, when you're considering doing business internationally, you have to examine those conditions closely because they may affect the attractiveness of the market. If you want to export goods, a potential market must have enough people with the means to purchase your products. If you want to import goods, you need to understand the country's labor costs.

Even after you've decided to do business in a particular country, the country's exchange rate, inflation, and interest rates — all of which change over time — can impact your business.

Considering geography and other physical factors

The impact of geography and natural resources is an important factor to consider. You need to be aware of the country's location, size, topography, and climate. The location of a country also explains many of its trading relationships and political alliances.

Paying attention to political and legal conditions

When you're importing or exporting, the primary political considerations are those having to do with the stability of the governments and their attitudes toward free trade. A friendly political atmosphere permits businesses to grow even if the country is poor in natural resources. The opposite is also true: Some countries blessed with natural resources are poor because of government instability or hostility.

Regulations in other countries can be quite different from those in the domestic market. When you're evaluating business opportunities around the world, determine whether the country is governed by the rule of law and eliminate countries that are political dictatorships. Look at a country's laws and how the country interprets and enforces them. You can find more information at www.export.gov and in Chapter 9.

Before finalizing any purchase or sale agreement, make sure you understand the warranties and service included. You and the company you're doing business with must agree on how to handle defective or unsold products. Confirm who will register trademarks, copyrights, and patents, if applicable, and in whose name they'll be. Finally, make sure that any agreement includes a provision for termination and settlement of disputes.

When you conduct business in the United States, domestic laws cover all transactions. However, questions of the appropriate law and courts of jurisdiction may arise in cases involving different countries. When a commercial dispute arises between individuals from two different countries, each person would prefer to have the matter adjudicated in his own courts and under his own laws. Insert a clause in any agreement stating that each party agrees that the laws of a particular country — preferably, the United States — govern.

Considering culture

If you're reading this book, you have at least some interest in doing business in a country other than your own. But importing/exporting isn't just about business — you also need to study the cultures of the countries you want to work with.

Culture affects all business functions, including marketing, human resource management, production, and finance. *Culture* is the total of the beliefs, values, rules, techniques, and institutions that characterize populations. In other words, culture is the thing that makes individual groups different. In this section, I cover the aspects of culture that are especially important to international businesspeople.

For information on the uniqueness of cultures around the world and how to apply the skills of cultural understanding to become more successful in the global business environment, go to www.cyborlink.com and www.executiveplanet.com.

Aesthetics

Aesthetics is a society's sense of beauty and good taste. In particular, you want to pay attention to color and the messages that different colors may convey. Color can mean different things in different cultures. For example, black is the color of mourning in the United States and Mexico, white is the color of mourning in Asia, and purple is the color of mourning in Brazil. Green is the color of good luck in the Islamic world, so any item featuring green is looked upon favorably there.

Attitudes and beliefs

Attitudes and beliefs include predispositions — either favorable or unfavorable — toward someone, someplace, or something. Attitudes and beliefs influence most aspects of human behavior because they bring order to a society and its individuals. The better you understand differing attitudes and beliefs, the better you'll be able to work with people from other countries.

Here's an example: Although Americans tend to think that time equals money, people from the Middle East, Asia, and Latin America may feel just the opposite — they'd rather get to know you before discussing business. Arabs typically dislike deadlines, and when faced with one, an Arab may feel as though he's being backed into a corner.

Religion

Religion is one of the most important elements of culture. An awareness of some of the basic beliefs of the major religions of the world can help you understand why attitudes vary from country to country. As an importer/exporter, keep in mind that religion influences all aspects of business. If you don't understand and adapt to a culture's religious beliefs, you'll fail — that's the bottom line.

For example, a company called American White Cross manufactured a variety of first-aid products and sold them throughout the United States and around the world. Because its corporate logo and packaging included a cross, it was unable to market its product line in the Islamic world because the cross is a symbol representing Christianity.

Material culture

Material culture consists of technology (how people make things) and economics (who makes what and why). The aspects of technology and economics apply not just to production but also to marketing, finance, and management. If you want to do business with other countries and you're using new production methods and products, that may require changes in people's beliefs and lifestyle — and change is never easy.

Language

Language is probably the most obvious cultural distinction that newcomers to international business face. Even though many businesspeople throughout the world speak English, your ability to communicate in the local language gives you an advantage and conveys a sense of respect to your potential associates.

Although knowing the local language is a positive, you can always use a translator. And not speaking the local language isn't a reason to avoid doing business somewhere.

Nonverbal communication is often as important as written or spoken language. Gestures can have different meanings from one country to the next. For example, Americans and most Europeans understand the thumbs-up gesture to mean that everything is all right; however, in southern Italy and Greece, it conveys the message for which Americans reserve the middle finger. Making a circle with the thumb and forefinger is the *okay* sign in the United States, but it's a vulgar sexual invitation in Greece and Turkey.

Noting currencies and exchange rates: Financial conditions

Values of currencies do not remain fixed — they change, sometimes rapidly, as currencies are traded in the world's financial centers. Fluctuating currency values can result in major losses if a currency trader's timing is wrong, so you need to have a keen awareness of exchange rates and use them as a factor in deciding when and where to do business.

Make sure you're able to read and understand foreign exchange quotations and to recognize and understand currency exchange risks. Many newspapers list the foreign exchange table in their finance sections. You may see a quote like the one in Table 1-1.

Table 1-1	An Example Currency Quotation			
	US$ Equivalent		**Currency per US$**	
Country	*Monday*	*Friday*	*Monday*	*Friday*
United Kingdom (£)	1.8412	1.8498	0.5431	0.5406
1 month forward	1.8422	1.8508	0.5429	0.5403
3 months forward	1.8448	1.8534	0.5421	0.5395
6 months forward	1.8483	1.8571	0.5410	0.5385

The table shows that at close of business on Monday, the British pound cost in U.S. dollars was 1.8412, and at the same time on Friday, the pound cost in U.S. dollars was 1.8498. The table also shows that at close of business on Monday, the U.S. dollar was valued at 0.5431 British pounds, and at the same time Friday, the U.S. dollar was valued at 0.5406 British pounds.

The *spot rate* is the exchange rate between two currencies quoted for delivery within two business days. The *forward rate* is for delivery in the future, usually 30, 60, 90, or 180 days down the road.

Suppose that 1 U.S. dollar equals 100 Japanese yen. If you sell an item to a client in Japan for US$10,000, the item would cost the client in Japan ¥1,000,000. If the rate of exchange fluctuates to ¥125 to the dollar, the same item would now cost your client ¥1,250,000.

In this example, the dollar is getting stronger. It's making your product more expensive and, hence, more difficult for you to export. On the other hand, a strong dollar enables you to import more goods, because the dollar has a stronger buying power.

Importers like a strong currency, and exporters like a weak currency. As the value of a currency *increases* in relation to another country's currency, exports decrease and imports increase. On the other hand, as the value of the currency *decreases* in relation to the other country's currency, imports increase and exports decrease.

The risk due to the fluctuation in the exchange rate is always assumed by the individual who's either making or receiving the payment in a foreign currency. In other words, if you don't want any risks as an exporter, invoice your client in U.S. dollars; as an importer, always request that the supplier quote you in U.S. dollars. For much more information on currencies and how currency trading works, check out *Currency Trading For Dummies,* 2nd Edition, by Brian Dolan (Wiley).

Chapter 2

Figuring Out Your Role in the Import/Export Business

In This Chapter

▶ Looking at why you want to get involved in import/export

▶ Explaining trade agreements and their impact on business

▶ Going global with your small business

▶ Determining how much money you need to invest

▶ Figuring out how much money you can expect to earn

*P*eople get involved in international trade for a variety of reasons:

- ✔ **Foreign goods are everywhere.** Next time you're in a store, take a look around: Almost everything is made overseas. Looking overseas can help your business be more competitive.

- ✔ **The U.S. dollar is weak.** The value of the dollar is (as of this writing) at a very low point, and a weak dollar is positive for exports because it makes U.S. products cheaper in foreign markets.

- ✔ **The U.S. dollar is strong.** The dollar has been very strong in the past, and it'll likely be strong again in the future. When the dollar is strong, that's a plus for imports because it makes foreign products cheaper in the United States.

- ✔ **What happens in one part of the world has an immediate impact on the rest of the world.** Technological advancements, advancing economies, and trade agreements have combined to make this the case.

In this chapter, you identify why you're interested in import/export, see what you can get out of adding import/export to your business, and determine the costs — and rewards! — that you can expect.

The Benefits of Import/Export

Existing businesses go abroad for one or both of the following reasons:

- ✔ To increase profits and sales
- ✔ To protect themselves from being eroded by competition

Some businesses make their initial entry into a foreign market by exporting. Then they set up foreign sales companies. Finally, if the sales volume warrants it, they establish foreign production facilities.

Other businesses decide to get involved in importing to take advantage of lower manufacturing costs, to protect themselves from lower-priced imports being sold in the U.S., and to remain competitive with other companies that do business in the U.S.

Most businesses that are *not* exporting to sell products, importing to reduce costs, and competing on a global basis will have difficulty surviving.

In this section, I cover the benefits of going global with your existing business.

Increasing sales and profits

Managers are under constant pressure to increase sales and make their companies more profitable. After a while, most businesses reach a point where they can only sell so much — the market is *saturated* with the product. When a business reaches this point, it needs to look for new people to sell its products to. Businesses often begin looking for ways to sell their products overseas.

You can earn greater profits either by generating additional revenues or by decreasing your cost of goods sold. Exporting gives you the opportunity to increase sales and generate additional revenues, and importing gives you access to low-cost sources of supply.

Taking advantage of expanding international economies

New foreign markets are appearing and, in some instances, are growing at a faster rate than U.S. markets. Today, U.S. businesses are seeing increases in exports to developing countries, especially in Latin America, Central Europe, Eastern Europe, the Middle East, and Asia. Companies also go overseas to obtain the lower manufacturing costs available in nations with expanding economies.

If you want to be an importer, start by looking at China, Mexico, Malaysia, Thailand, and Brazil, because they're the largest exporters of goods to the U.S. If you want to be an exporter, look at China, Mexico, Malaysia, Thailand, India, and Turkey, the largest importers of American products.

Economies expand because

✔ They offer a favorable business climate.

✔ Regulations to do business there are not insurmountable.

✔ They have an established transportation infrastructure.

✔ They've earned foreign exchange (money) by exporting their products. As countries grow and export more goods to the U.S., they have more money that they can use to purchase goods from the U.S.

Countries with trade agreements with the U.S.

The U.S. has trade agreements with the following countries:

✔ **North America:** Canada and Mexico, under the North American Free Trade Agreement (NAFTA)

✔ **Central America and the Caribbean:** Costa Rica, Dominican Republic, El Salvador, Guatemala, Honduras, and Nicaragua, under the Dominican Republic–Central America–United States Free Trade Agreement (CAFTA-DR); Panama, under the United States–Panama Free Trade Agreement

✔ **South America:** Chile, under the United States–Chile Free Trade Agreement; Colombia, under the United States–Colombia Trade Promotion Agreement; Peru, under the United States–Peru Trade Promotion Agreement

✔ **Australia:** Australia, under the United States–Australia Free Trade Agreement

✔ **Asia:** Singapore, under the United States–Singapore Trade Agreement

✔ **Middle East/North Africa:** Bahrain, under the United States–Bahrain Free Trade Agreement; Israel, under the United States–Israel Free Trade Agreement; Jordan, under the United States–Jordan Free Trade Agreement; Morocco, under the United States–Morocco Free Trade Agreement; Oman, under the United States–Oman Free Trade Agreement

You can access complete details on these trade agreements at www.export.gov/fta/index.asp or www.ustr.gov/trade-agreements/free-trade-agreements. Or if you'd like additional information on exporting to any FTA partner country, contact the Trade Information Center at 800-872-8723.

Making use of trade agreements

Trade agreements involve a small group of countries getting together to establish a free-trade area among themselves while maintaining trade restrictions with all other nations. These agreements provide improved market access for consumer, industrial, and agricultural products from the U.S.

Trade agreements also can help your business enter and compete more easily in the global marketplace. They help level the international playing field and encourage foreign governments to adopt open rule-making procedures, as well as laws and regulations that don't discriminate. Free-trade agreements (FTAs) help strengthen business climates by eliminating or reducing tariff rates, improving intellectual property regulations, opening government procurement opportunities, and easing investment rules.

These agreements provide the following benefits to small and medium-size exporters:

- ✔ They reduce high tariffs on U.S. exports, which lowers the cost of selling to customers overseas.

- ✔ They maximize small-business resources by eliminating inconsistent Customs procedures and improving and reducing burdensome paperwork.

- ✔ They minimize risks in foreign markets by providing certainty and predictability for U.S. small-business owners and investors.

- ✔ They enforce intellectual property rights.

- ✔ They promote the rule of law so that small businesses know what the rules are and that they'll be applied fairly and consistently.

U.S. importers also benefit from such trade agreements. Just as the countries with whom the U.S. has a trade agreement have to provide improved market access for American goods, the U.S. must provide similar considerations to the countries with which the U.S. has an agreement. So if you're an importer and you deal with the countries the U.S. has agreements with, you'll also experience the elimination or reduction of tariff rates.

In order for an importer to take advantage of the preferential duty rates offered by free-trade agreements, the following conditions must apply:

- ✔ The goods must be imported directly from the beneficiary country (the country that has signed and is part of the agreement) to the U.S.

- ✔ The goods must be manufactured in the beneficiary country. This condition is met if the goods are wholly produced or manufactured in the country *or* if the goods have been substantially transformed into a new article in the country.

Getting out of diaper duty with the CAFTA-DR

Here's an example of how a trade agreement created an opportunity to sell American goods abroad. Softee Supreme Diaper Corporation, located in Decatur, Georgia, is a manufacturer and marketer of quality disposable baby diapers. The Commercial Service in Central America and the Atlanta Export Assistance Center helped introduce the company to potential buyers in the CAFTA-DR region — El Salvador, Guatemala, Honduras, Nicaragua, and the Dominican Republic (and, as of 2009, Costa Rica).

Softee Supreme has benefited from the tariff reductions as a result of CAFTA-DR — the 15 percent tariff in Central America for baby diapers was eliminated immediately for some countries and is being phased out for the rest. In 2006, Softee had export sales of several hundred thousand dollars to distributors in CAFTA-DR markets.

In order for an item to change its country of origin, the value added in the beneficiary country needs to be 35 percent. For example, say a company in Mexico imports absorbent gauze from China. Upon receipt of the gauze, the Mexican company cuts the gauze into pieces and sews the pieces into medical sponges used in the operating room. Then the Mexican company washes, wraps, and sterilizes the sponges. Now, even though the initial gauze came from China, it has been redefined as a product from Mexico — as long as someone can show that at least 35 percent of the sponges' value was added during the production process in Mexico. A U.S. importer of those sponges would then be able to benefit from preferential duty rates.

Lowering manufacturing costs

Most businesses go overseas to obtain lower manufacturing costs and protect themselves from lower-priced imports being sold in their own country. There are many arguments for and against sourcing goods from overseas suppliers. Sourcing products from overseas can give you the following advantages:

- ✔ **Lower costs:** A company can go abroad and enjoy the benefits of lower labor and material costs.

- ✔ **Access to products and technologies not available domestically:** Overseas suppliers may provide access to products that aren't readily available from a domestic supplier.

- ✔ **More product variety:** A foreign supplier may offer a greater variety because she has lower carrying costs (lower warehousing and storage costs) and can keep a more extensive product line in stock.

- ✔ **Better-quality products:** In some instances, the perception of many buyers is that foreign products are of a higher quality.

- ✔ **The ability to overcome domestic shortages:** Having alternative sources of supply is important in case domestic suppliers can't satisfy your requirements (for example, because of labor or equipment problems).

- ✔ **Less dependency on a limited domestic supplier base:** At times, the number of domestic suppliers for a particular good may be limited. Sourcing from overseas can not only give you better prices but also serve as a backup and put you in a better situation when negotiating with your domestic supplier.

Starting from scratch: The entrepreneurial approach

What if you haven't yet started a business and you're interested in import/export? You stand to gain all the benefits that an existing business gains by going global. And you don't have to be a huge business to make a go of importing or exporting; according to the U.S. Department of Commerce, big companies make up about 4 percent of U.S. exporters, which means that 96 percent of exporters are small or mid-size companies.

Still, starting a new business — *any* new business — is a challenge. Throw in the complexities of international trade, and you're in for an even bigger challenge. If you're up for the challenge, here's what you need:

- ✔ **Knowledge:** In addition to finding out what it takes to start a business, you need to be up on everything from documentation and shipping to communications and government regulations. I cover all these issues in this book, but you'll also want to check out books like *Small Business For Dummies,* 3rd Edition, by Eric Tyson and Jim Schell, and *Business Plans Kit For Dummies,* 3rd Edition, by Steven D. Peterson, Peter E. Jaret, and Barbara Findlay Schenck (Wiley).

- ✔ **Enthusiasm:** You need to be an enthusiastic salesperson, someone who likes to spend time tracking things like invoices and shipping receipts. You need to get excited at the thought of seeing where new ideas and products will take you. And you need to enjoy working with people from different cultures. Your enthusiasm will carry you through some of the challenges along the way, so the more enthusiasm you have, the better.

- ✔ **Consideration:** Establishing a solid relationship with your supplier or buyer is important in *any* business, but it's even more important in the import/export business. Cultural differences play a huge part in buying or selling and in establishing ongoing relationships. The hard sell that's effective in the U.S. may not produce the same results in foreign markets.

- ✔ **Commitment:** You won't be successful in *any* venture unless you're personally committed to its success. As with most businesses, you'll encounter peaks and valleys, good times and bad. People who are successful in the import/export business are willing to work their way through the valleys.

Importing is not without risks. If you're considering importing as a way to lower your manufacturing costs, keep the following in mind:

- ✔ Currency exchange rates fluctuate. What may work in your favor today because of the exchange rate may not work in your favor next year. *Remember:* Importers benefit from a strong U.S. dollar, which makes foreign products cheaper in the U.S. market.

- ✔ Trade barriers in the form of tariffs may make importing difficult or impossible.

- ✔ Goods can arrive late or damaged.

- ✔ Negotiations can fail or be delayed because of language and cultural barriers.

Determining Your Place in the Food Chain: Import, Export, or Both?

You know you're ready for international trade, but do you know whether you want to import or export? The answer that's right for you depends, in large part, on why you want to go global in the first place.

Importing makes sense when

- ✔ The value of the U.S. dollar is strong — the stronger the dollar, the cheaper purchasing goods overseas is.

- ✔ You're faced with increased competition, and the only way to remain competitive is to source goods at lower costs for suppliers overseas.

- ✔ You want to identify new products or expand your existing product line.

- ✔ You can't access products or technologies from domestic suppliers.

- ✔ Another country can produce a product more efficiently because of available resources.

- ✔ You're a good negotiator and enjoy selling.

Exporting makes sense when

- ✔ The value of the dollar is weak — the weaker the dollar, the cheaper your U.S.-manufactured products are.

- ✔ You want to increase sales and profits. Rising income levels in many developing countries are creating opportunities for more people to purchase goods.

- ✔ You want to serve a market that has nonexistent or limited production facilities.

✔ Before your business invests in a production facility overseas, you want to test whether the foreign market accepts your product.

✔ You want to use your excess production capacity to lower per-unit fixed costs.

✔ You want to extend your product's life cycle by exporting to markets that are currently not being served.

✔ You enjoy selling and dealing with people from other countries and cultures.

Being both an importer and an exporter makes sense when

✔ Countries have negotiated preferential trading arrangements.

✔ You want to remain price-competitive at home. Many businesses import labor-intensive components produced in foreign countries or export components for assembly in countries where labor is less expensive and then import the finished product.

✔ You enjoy buying and selling, dealing with people from different cultures, and traveling.

✔ You're comfortable dealing with the numerous uncontrollable environmental forces involved in importing and exporting. (See Chapter 1 for details on these factors.)

Deciding Whether to Become a Distributor or an Agent

After you've decided to get into the import/export business, you have to decide how you want to set up your business. You have two options:

✔ **Be a distributor (an intermediary who purchases and takes title to the goods).** For example, you purchase sweaters from a manufacturer in Japan and import them into the U.S. If you're a distributor, you take title to the sweaters, store them, and then look for customers, eventually selling them to Macy's, Bloomingdale's, Nordstrom, and so on.

✔ **Be an agent (a firm that brings two parties together but doesn't take title to the goods).** For example, you know the sweater manufacturer in Japan and you know that Macy's, Bloomingdale's, and Nordstrom are interested in buying the sweaters. You can bring the sweater manufacturer and the U.S. department stores together, without ever taking title to the goods.

In both cases, you're involved in setting up an import/export business. The choice that's right for you depends on how much money you have to invest and the amount that you hope to earn. A distributor has higher risks and greater expenses than an agent has, but a distributor also has more control over the process.

In this section, I explain what distributors and agents are and help you decide which path is right for you.

Understanding distributors

A *distributor* is an independently owned business that is primarily involved in wholesaling and takes title to the goods that it's distributing. A distributor is a middleman who handles consumer or business goods that may be manufactured or not manufactured (such as agricultural products), imported or exported, and then sold. Figure 2-1 illustrates the distributor's relationship to the seller and buyer.

Figure 2-1:
The dis-
tributor is a
middleman,
working
with the
supplier and
buyer.

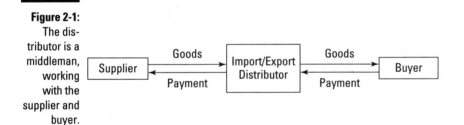

Distributors typically purchase goods on their own account and resell them at a higher price, accepting the risks and the rights that come with ownership of the goods. For example, ABC Importing in New York imports women's sweaters from XYZ International in Japan. If ABC Importing is acting as a distributor, it purchases the goods from XYZ in Japan and arranges to have the goods transported to New York and cleared through Customs. After the goods are cleared, ABC stores the goods in its warehouse and makes arrangements to sell and deliver them to its customers, including Big-Name Department Store.

A distributor

- ✔ Is independently owned

- ✔ Takes title to the goods it's distributing (ownership passes from the seller to the buyer upon purchase)

- ✔ Is often classified by product line (such as medical, hardware, or electronics products)

In the import/export business, there are two main types of distributors:

- ✔ **Full-service distributors:** A full-service distributor provides the following services to its customers and suppliers:

  - **Buying:** The distributor acts as a purchasing intermediary for its customers.

  - **Creating assortments:** The distributor purchases goods from a variety of suppliers and maintains an inventory that meets the needs of its customers.

  - **Breaking bulk:** The distributor purchases in large quantities and resells to its customers in smaller quantities.

  - **Selling:** The distributor provides a sales force to its suppliers.

  - **Storing:** The distributor serves in a warehousing capacity for its customers, delivering the goods to its customers at the customers' request.

  - **Transporting:** The distributor arranges for delivery of goods to its customers.

  - **Financing:** The distributor provides credit terms to its customers.

- ✔ **Drop-shipping distributors:** A drop shipper is a distributor who sells merchandise for delivery directly from the supplier to the customer and does not physically handle the product. The distributor *does* take title to the goods before delivery to its customer, however.

If you're an importer and you've received a significant order from one of your customers, shipping the goods to the client directly from the overseas supplier may be more efficient because of the size of the order. In this case, you're acting as a drop shipper. For example, ABC Importing in New York receives an order for 300 dozen sweaters from its customer Big-Name Department Store. ABC Importing purchases the sweaters from XYZ International in Japan. The 300 dozen sweaters will be enough product to fill a complete 20-foot shipping container. When ABC places the order, it provides shipping instructions to XYZ International, telling XYZ that when the goods are ready for shipment, they should be placed into the container, invoiced to ABC Importing, and shipped directly to Big-Name Department Store.

If you're concerned about the possibility of future direct contact between the supplier and customer, you can instruct the supplier to have the goods packed in neutral shipping containers, have the complete shipment sent to a shipping agent (a Customs broker), and give the shipping agent the specific delivery instructions.

Both situations offer pros and cons. When you're operating as a full-service distributor, you have a greater level of control. On the downside, you have a greater level of risk and need for working capital because of the significant additional expenses.

Understanding agents

An agent is similar to a distributor in that he's a middleman. However, an *agent* does not take title to the goods and provides fewer services than a distributor does. The agent's role is to get orders and (usually) earn a commission for his services. Figure 2-2 illustrates the relationship among the agent, the supplier, and the buyer.

Figure 2-2:
An agent is similar to a distributor but has fewer responsibilities.

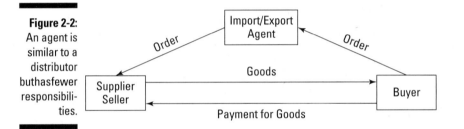

For example, suppose CADE International is an import/export agent headquartered in New York. CADE is aware that XYZ International is a manufacturer of quality women's sweaters in Japan and that Big-Name Department Store is interested in acquiring sweaters to sell to its customers. CADE is a middleman, bringing the seller and buyer together but not taking title to the goods and not providing any of the services that a distributor may perform.

REMEMBER

An agent

- ✔ Is independently owned
- ✔ Does not take title to the products being purchased and sold
- ✔ Is actively involved in the negotiations for either the sale or purchase of the products

Understanding types of agents

The import/export business has two main types of agents:

✔ **Traditional import-export agents:** An export agent works in the country where the product is produced. For example, you may identify a producer in the U.S. and work toward representing that producer (the seller) in foreign markets as the export agent. Or you may work as an import agent based in the country where the product will be sold, in which case you represent the buyers. For example, you may know a company in the U.S. that's looking to buy a certain kind of product overseas. You'd identify sellers of that product overseas and represent the buyer in foreign markets as the import agent.

✔ **Brokers:** A broker is an independent agent who brings buyers and sellers together. For the most part, brokers work for sellers, although some brokers do represent buyers. A broker differs from the traditional import/export agent in that she doesn't usually *represent* a company. Instead, she's traditionally hired to bring together one-of-a-kind or non-recurring deals.

For example, a broker is contacted and advised that Company A in New York has an excess inventory of a soon-to-be-discontinued product. This is a one-time deal, because as soon as the goods are purchased, they'll no longer be available. The broker identifies Singapore Electronics, a potential customer in Singapore, for these items. So the broker brings Company A and Singapore Electronics together for this one-time deal, and in return for her effort, the broker receives a commission from Company A.

Looking at the benefits and challenges of being an agent

Some of the benefits of the agent option are the reduced start-up costs and the limited working capital you need. The initial investment and costs of doing business as an agent are significantly lower than those that come along with operating as a distributor.

On the downside, when you're doing business as an agent, you run the risk that the parties will bypass your firm and deal directly with each other on any future transactions.

To minimize the risk of being eliminated from future transactions, remember that an agent is not someone who makes a call and brings people together just to earn a commission. The key is to develop a sound relationship with your connection and continually work toward increasing sales and improving the relationship.

Representing clients and getting commissions

The rate of commission when working as an agent depends on the nature and type of product, the nature of the market you're selling to, and the level of competition. (See "Pondering Profit Potential," later in this chapter, for info on typical commission rates.)

If you bring a buyer from one country together with a seller from another country, can you earn a commission from both parties? The answer is *no.* Why? Because as an agent, you're representing someone. If you represent the seller, you have an obligation to sell that company's products at the *highest* possible price. On the other hand, if you're representing the buyer, you have an obligation to secure the products for the buyer at the *lowest* possible price. Obviously, drawing a commission from both parties would create an ethical dilemma. Think of an import-export agent like a real estate agent: The buyer has an agent, and the seller has an agent, but the same agent doesn't represent both the buyer and the seller.

If you choose to set up your business working as an agent, decide who you're going to represent and then work at nurturing that relationship. The greater the effort you make in developing that relationship and representing the company, the more likely that company will be to maintain the relationship.

Analyzing Start-Up Costs

Capital is the money that you need to start and run your import/export business. Here are three types of capital:

- ✔ **Initial/fixed capital:** This is the money you use to purchase *fixed* (permanent) assets, such as office space, equipment, machinery, furniture, and so on, plus any money you need to start the business. You need funds to cover initial legal fees, deposits with public utility companies, licenses, permits, office equipment, advances for rental of premises, and so on. Finally, you need to allocate funds for your opening promotion, which are sometimes referred to as *promotional capital.*

- ✔ **Operating/working capital:** This is your business's temporary funds. It's the money you use to support the business's day-to-day operations, such as salaries, office supplies, utility expenses, and so on.

- ✔ **Growth/reserve capital:** This is the money you need, as an existing business, in order to expand or change the primary direction of the business, as well as to cover your personal living expenses.

When trying to figure out how much money you need to get started, you need to forecast the sales volume you expect your business to reach during your initial year of doing business. This forecast helps you determine your overall capital requirements. Make your forecast as accurate as possible, and make sure it's a fair appraisal of what you anticipate sales will actually total.

Forecasting is a projection — it's an educated guess. If you want information on sales forecasting, check out *Excel Sales Forecasting For Dummies,* by Conrad Carlberg (Wiley).

With your projected sales volume and any information you can secure from trade associations and competitors (such as market potential and market factors), you can project other information, such as operating expenses, size of the facility required, and miscellaneous overhead expenses. *Market potential* is the total sales volume that all companies can project to sell during a period of time in an industry under normal situations. *Market factors* are related to demand for the product (for example, birth rate is related to the demand for baby cribs).

Whether you're an importer or exporter affects your capital requirements in the import/export business. The capital requirements for being a distributor are higher, so the profit potential also needs to be higher. An agent, because he doesn't take title to the goods, has lower operating expenses.

Pondering Profit Potential

Profits in importing and exporting reflect your choice between operating as an agent and operating as a distributor. If you want to work as a distributor, your profit potential has to be higher because you have higher operating expenses. A full-service distributor has significantly more expenses than an agent — including warehousing, inventory, financing, transportation, and so on.

Your final profit level is based on your expenses, but as a general rule, the gross margin as a percentage of sales is at least 40 percent. To get the gross margin as a percentage of sales, start with this formula:

Sales – Cost of goods sold = Gross margin dollars

Then divide by sales to get the gross margin as a percentage of sales:

Gross margin dollars ÷ Sales = Gross margin as a percentage of sales

Say you have $250 in sales, and the cost of goods sold was $150. That makes your gross margin $100. Take your gross margin ($100) and divide that by your sales ($250) and you get 0.40, or 40 percent.

An agent earns a commission. Because the agent doesn't take title to the goods, he has lower operating expenses, but he also has a limit on profit potential. If an item is high-volume with a low unit price (such as a convenience good), then the rate of commission can be in the 4 to 5 percent range. On the other hand, if the item has a high unit price and low volume of sales (such as medical equipment), that rate of commission can range from, say, 12 to 15 percent. If the product falls somewhere in the middle (something that's purchased every few years but not regularly and that has a moderate unit price), the commission would be between 6 percent and 7 percent.

Chapter 3

Rules and Regulations to Consider Before You Get Started

*W*hether you're looking for a way to start your own import/export business or you're thinking about expanding the operations of your existing business, this chapter is important. You need to determine whether you need a license, permit, or authorization before you import a product into or export a product out of the United States.

If you want to import ceramic cookie jars from China, the first question in your mind should be, "Do I need someone's permission or authorization to get cookie jars from China into the country?" What about wine from Italy? Are the rules different for importing Italian wine? What if you want to export adhesive bandages to Saudi Arabia?

Before you can import or export *anything,* you need to find out whether you're required to secure an authorization from someone before those items can be shipped. In this chapter, I help you answer these questions.

For the most part, import and export rules and regulations are fairly straightforward. Developing an understanding of the requirements before you spend too much time on your project is a good idea. In this chapter, I help you identify the applicable rules and regulations, and I also provide you with resources where you can find answers to questions regarding your particular product and market.

If You're Exporting

Before you start exporting, you need to consider things like licensing and other regulations. No one likes thinking about these technicalities, but if you don't address these issues now, you'll run into problems later. In this section, I fill you in on the initial issues that anyone wanting to export needs to consider.

Export licensing

An *export* is any item that is sent from one country (in this case, the U.S.) to a foreign destination. An item can be a commodity, computer software, or technology. How you transport the item to the other country (via ocean vessel, air cargo, mail, and so on) doesn't matter. An export could be a set of schematics sent via fax, software uploaded or downloaded from a website, or information transmitted via e-mail. All these items can be considered exports, and they may be subject to export licensing requirements.

Export licensing is a basic and important first step in exporting. It may initially appear complex and confusing, but in most cases, the process is very simple and straightforward. A product can fall into only one of two categories:

- ✔ No license required (NLR)
- ✔ Validated export license required

The vast majority of items exported from the United States do *not* require a validated export license.

Previously, the U.S. government controlled the export and re-export of goods by granting two types of licenses (which you may still occasionally run into):

- ✔ **General license:** A broad grant of authority by the government to exporters for certain categories of products that don't require a formal application
- ✔ **Individually validated license (IVL):** A specific grant of authority from the government for a particular exporter to export a specific product to a specific country

The Bureau of Industry and Security (BIS) in the U.S. Department of Commerce is responsible for implementing and enforcing the Export Administration Regulations (EAR), which regulate the export and re-export of the majority of commercial items. If you have questions about these regulations, you can contact your local U.S. Department of Commerce official for assistance.

The starting point for these requirements is the Office of Export Services, Outreach and Educational Services Division of the BIS (www.bis.doc.gov). Or you can find info at www.export.gov. You can reach export counselors in Washington, DC, by phone at 202-482-4811 or in California at 949-660-0144.

Determining whether you need a license

Violations of licensing regulations carry both civil and criminal penalties, so you can't assume that your product doesn't require an export license — you need to do your homework. Some exporters have been sentenced to fines totaling more than $125,000, several years' probation with a period of home detention, and dozens of hours of community service after being found guilty of exporting without a license. The exporter is responsible for determining that the item to be exported is properly designated as an NLR (no license required).

The percentage of items being exported requiring an export license issued by the BIS is very small. The U.S. issues export licenses for reasons of national security, foreign policy, or short supply. In determining whether an item requires an export license, consider the questions in the following sections.

What are you exporting?

The key in determining whether an export license is required from the U.S. Department of Commerce for a given product is whether the item has a specific Export Control Classification Number (ECCN), which is simply a five-digit classification code.

You have three options in determining whether a given item has an ECCN:

- **Figure it out yourself.** You can find these codes listed in the Commerce Control List (CCL) available at www.gpo.gov/bis. (This list is in the supplement to Part 774 of Title 15: Commerce and Foreign Trade.)

- **Ask the manufacturer.** The manufacturer may know whether the product has an ECCN if the company has exported the item in the past.

- **Get an official classification from the BIS.** You can make this request through the Simplified Network Application Process Redesign (SNAP-R), the electronic licensing system. When filing electronically, you must obtain a personal identification number (PIN) before submitting this request. You can get a PIN by visiting www.bis.doc.gov or calling 202-482-4811.

What will the item you're exporting be used for?

The items that the BIS regulates are classified as *dual-use* items because they have both commercial and military applications. For example, if you want to export polygraphs, arms, ammunition, gas masks, telecommunication equipment, navigational equipment, and so on, you have to secure a license before exporting these goods.

The EAR (Export Administration Regulations) also makes an allowance for commodities in short supply, making them subject to export licensing. These restrictions are supposed to protect the economy in the United States from an excessive drain of scarce materials and to reduce any inflationary impact due to satisfying foreign demand.

As of this writing, products on this list include petroleum and petroleum products, unprocessed western red cedar, and horses exported by sea for slaughter. (You can find information on licensing requirements for your product at www.export.gov; click Licenses & Regulations for updated information on products and country restrictions.)

Where are you exporting to?

Restrictions vary from country to country and from item to item. The principal restricted destinations are embargoed countries and those designated as supporting terrorist activities. As of this writing, the list includes Cuba, Iran, North Korea, Sudan, and Syria.

To make sure that exports from the U.S. go only to legally authorized destinations, the U.S. government requires a destination control statement on all shipping documents. The *destination control statement* is important because it's a notification to the carrier and all foreign parties that these goods can't be diverted to another country, contrary to U.S. law.

Exporters must place the destination control statement on commercial invoices and bills of lading for most export sales. The only exception to the use of this statement is shipments to Canada that are intended for consumption in Canada.

Violations of the destination restrictions may be subject to both criminal and administrative penalties. Criminal penalties can reach up to ten years' imprisonment and $1 million per violation. Administrative penalties can reach $11,000 per violation, and certain cases involving national security issues can reach $120,000 per violation.

Who will receive your item?

Certain individuals and organizations are also prohibited from receiving U.S. exports, and others may receive goods only if the exporter has received a license. This restriction may also apply to goods that don't normally require a license. You can access the list from the BIS website (www.bis.doc.gov/complianceandenforcement/liststocheck.htm). Included in this list are people engaging in the development of weapons of mass destruction and those involved in terrorism or drug trafficking.

Applying for a license

If you determine that an export license is required for your product, the fastest and easiest way to submit your application for a license is to use the online system SNAP-R. You can get information on signing up to be a SNAP-R user by visiting https://snapr.bis.doc.gov.

You can also take the hard-copy approach to submitting an application by using Form BIS-748P, the Multipurpose Application Form. You can request a copy of this form by phone at 202-482-4811, by fax at 202-219-9179, or online at www.bis.doc.gov.

If you submit the form by mail (express mail or a commercial courier service like FedEx or DHL is recommended), be sure to avoid some common errors that may delay the processing of your application, such as

- ✔ Forgetting to sign the application.

- ✔ Hand-writing the application instead of typing it.

- ✔ Inadequately responding to Section 21 of the application, which asks the exporter to describe in detail the specific end use of the product; if you aren't specific, the application process will likely be delayed, or the application may be rejected.

- ✔ Inadequately responding to Section 22(j) of the application, which calls for a detailed description of the item being exported (to avoid this problem, attach any available additional material to fully explain the product).

You can follow up on your export license application via an automated voice-response system by contacting the BIS System for Tracking Export License Applications (STELA) at 202-482-2752.

Other export regulations

Licensing isn't the only regulation that you need to consider when you first enter the world of exporting. You also need to consider anti-boycott requirements, the Foreign Corrupt Practices Act, and regulations related to food, drugs, and the environment.

Anti-boycott requirements

The U.S. has a policy of opposing restrictive trade practices that countries impose against other countries friendly to the U.S. The Arab League boycott of Israel is the principal foreign economic boycott that U.S. companies have to be concerned with today.

So what does this mean to you? You'd be in violation of these laws if you agreed *not* to do business with Israel as a precondition to doing business with another country.

The following are a few examples of boycott requests or conditions that would be in violation of U.S. law if you agreed to the terms. (For more information on the export documents in question, see Chapter 18.)

- ✔ "In the case of overseas suppliers, this order is placed subject to the suppliers' not being on the Israel boycott list published by the central Arab League." You may see this language on a purchase order.

- ✔ "Goods of Israeli origin not acceptable." You may see this language on the importer's purchase order.

- ✔ "We hereby certify that the beneficiaries, manufacturers, exporters, and transferees of this credit are neither blacklisted nor have any connection with Israel and that the terms and conditions of this credit in no way contravene the law pertaining to the boycott of Israel and the decisions issued by the Israel Boycott Office." You may see this language on a letter of credit.

These are just some examples of the kind of language that, if you agreed to the terms, would get you in trouble.

Want a real-world example? On May 20, 1999, the U.S. Department of Commerce imposed a $5,000 civil penalty on the SABRE Group, a Texas provider of travel-related products and services. This penalty settled allegations that, in a 1998 contract with a company in Pakistan, SABRE agreed to refuse to subcontract any work to Israeli-based businesses or individuals. Additionally, the Commerce Department alleged that SABRE failed to promptly report its receipt of the request to make this agreement. SABRE voluntarily disclosed the transaction that led to the allegations and fully cooperated with the department's investigation.

Anti-bribery measures: The Foreign Corrupt Practices Act

Under the Foreign Corrupt Practices Act (FCPA), it's illegal for a U.S. company to offer, pay, or promise to pay money or anything of value to any foreign official for the purpose of securing or retaining business.

Here's a case study for you: In January 2009, after 27 years in the U.S. Secret Service, Patrick Caldwell became head of sales and marketing for Protective Products of America, Inc. (PPA), a Florida firm that sells body armor to federal and state agencies. Five months later, he was approached to help equip the presidential guard of an African country for about $15 million. The offer came from two undercover FBI agents posing as the sales broker and representative of an African defense minister in meetings at Miami's Mandarin Oriental hotel and at Clyde's restaurant in Washington, DC. During negotiations, Caldwell was advised that a 20 percent commission needed to be tacked on to the real price as a kickback for the two men.

The defendants were told that half of that "commission" would be paid directly to the minister of defense. The defendants allegedly agreed to create two price quotations in connection with the deals, with one quote representing the true cost of the goods and the second quote representing the true cost plus the 20 percent "commission." The defendants also allegedly agreed to engage in a small "test" deal to show the minister of defense that he would personally receive the 10 percent bribe.

Caldwell agreed to the commission, and after $18,000 was wired to a PPA bank account as a test purchase, the first batch of 50 body-armor plates (from a total order of 3,600) was shipped off — on July 16, the same day Caldwell was promoted to CEO. Caldwell had a very short stint as PPA chief: He was arrested in January 2011, along with 21 executives of other law-enforcement and military-supply companies.

Food and drug requirements

Through regulations, the U.S. Food and Drug Administration (FDA) assures American consumers that foods are pure and wholesome and that drugs, medical devices, and cosmetics are safe. The FDA requires U.S. manufacturers to go through rigorous testing and inspection.

Many countries have their own versions of the FDA. If you're exporting products covered by the regulations of the FDA, you must also comply with the laws of the country to which the goods are being shipped and make sure that the product is properly labeled and meets the specifications of the foreign purchaser.

Ultimately, the importer is responsible for complying with his local regulations; otherwise, he won't be able to clear the goods through his country's Customs organization.

Environmental Protection Agency notification requirements

The Environmental Protection Agency's involvement in exports is limited to hazardous waste, pesticides, and toxic chemicals. The EPA can't prohibit the export of these substances, but a notification process has been established to inform the receiving foreign government that these materials will be entering their country.

Exporters of hazardous waste should contact the EPA's Office of Compliance, Import/Export Program at 202-564-2280 or the Resource Conservation and Recovery Act (RCRA) hotline at 800-424-9346 or 703-412-9810 (www.epa.gov/rcraonline/).

Customs benefits available to exporters

As an exporter, you need to be aware of the U.S. Customs benefits that are available to you. These benefits are designed to encourage U.S. exporters by enabling them to be competitive in other countries without having to include in their sales price any duties paid on imported items.

Here's a rundown of the benefits you may be able to take advantage of:

- ✔ **Drawback of Customs duties:** *Drawback* is a form of tax reduction in which duties collected on imported goods are refunded to the importer if these goods are exported from the United States. The refund is on all duties paid on the imported goods, less 1 percent to cover Customs costs.

  Note: Drawback restricts the ability of NAFTA (North American Free Trade Agreement) countries to provide export incentives, such as refunds of import duties in connection with exports to other NAFTA countries. This restriction also impacts all other free trade agreements in place or to be negotiated in the future.

- ✔ **U.S. Foreign-Trade Zones (FTZs):** FTZs are sites in the United States that are considered outside the United States for Customs purposes. As long as the goods remain in the FTZ, they aren't subject to payment of any Customs duties. While in the zone, the goods may or may not be processed; after the goods leave the zone, they're subject to duties. If the goods are exported out of the country, no duty payments are required.

  For a list of the contact information for each FTZ project, go to http://ia.ita.doc.gov/ftzpage/resources.html. You can also get information on FTZs by calling 202-482-2862 or e-mailing ftz@trade.gov.

- ✔ **Foreign free port and free trade zones:** These are similar to the U.S. Foreign-Trade Zones (see the preceding bullet), but they're located in foreign countries, usually in or near seaports and airports. U.S. companies use these ports or zones for receiving shipments of goods that are reshipped in smaller lots to customers in the surrounding areas.

✔ **Bonded warehouses:** These public warehouses, which are under the supervision of the U.S. Customs Service, are located in many different places around the U.S. Goods can be stored in them with no assessment of duties, but after the goods are released, they're subject to Customs duties.

The difference between a bonded warehouse and an FTZ is that bonded warehouses are simply used to store goods prior to exporting them, whereas goods can be stored and can undergo some manufacturing process in an FTZ.

Bonded warehouses are privately owned. For details on how they work, go to www.cbp.gov/linkhandler/cgov/newsroom/publications/ trade/bond_warehouses.ctt/bonded_20wh2.pdf at the U.S. Customs and Border Protection website.

If You're Importing

You need to be aware of licensing requirements, restrictions, prohibitions, standards, and procedures when importing specific products. In this section, I fill you in on importing rules and regulations.

Import licensing, restrictions, and prohibitions

As a general rule, the U.S. Customs Service doesn't require an importer to have a license or permit to import goods into the U.S. However, you may be required to have a license, permit, or other certification, depending on the commodity.

The importation of certain classes of merchandise may be prohibited or restricted. These prohibitions and restrictions have been put in place by U.S. Customs and specific government agencies (such as the U.S. Department of Agriculture, the FDA, and so on) to protect the economy and security of the U.S., protect American consumers, and preserve plant and animal life. Some items are also subject to quantity limits on imports (called *quotas*) or trade agreements.

A diamond may not be a girl's best friend

Conflict diamonds are rough diamonds sold by rebel, military, and terrorist groups (or their allies) in parts of Africa to finance insurrections against legitimate, internationally recognized governments. Conflict diamonds are so-called because of the atrocities committed on civilian populations during these insurrections.

The U.S. played a key role in forging an international consensus to curb this trade and has therefore strongly supported the Kimberley Process Certification Scheme (KPCS), an international initiative aimed at breaking the link between the legitimate diamond trade and trade in conflict diamonds. This initiative involves documenting and tracking all rough diamonds that enter participating KPCS countries and shipping diamonds in tamper-resistant containers.

Conflict diamonds were behind the primary story line of the movie *Blood Diamond* (2006), starring Leonardo DiCaprio, Jennifer Connelly, and Djimon Hounsou.

I couldn't publish this book at a thousand pages, so I don't have room to list each product. But in the following list, I provide various *classes* of articles for which you need a license or permit from the responsible agency. (You can find the name of the responsible agency by talking to commodity specialist teams — see the next section for details.)

- Agricultural products
  - Alcohol and alcoholic beverages
  - Cheese, milk, and dairy products
  - Fruits, vegetables, and nuts
  - Insects
  - Livestock and animals
  - Meat, poultry, and egg products
  - Plants and plant products
  - Seeds
  - Tobacco-related products
  - Wood packing materials
- Arms, ammunition, and radioactive material
- Conflict diamonds
- Consumer products — energy conservation
  - Commercial and industrial equipment
  - Household appliances

- ✔ Consumer products — safety
    - Art materials (which may be toxic or flammable)
    - Bicycles and bicycle helmets
    - Cigarette lighters and multipurpose lighters
    - Fireworks
    - Flammable fabrics
    - Lead in paint
    - Toys and children's articles
- ✔ Electronic products
    - Radiation and sonic radiation-producing products
    - Radio frequency devices
- ✔ Food, drugs, cosmetics, and medical devices
- ✔ Gold, silver, currency, and stamps
- ✔ Pesticides and toxic and hazardous substances
- ✔ Textile, wool, and fur products
- ✔ Trademarks, trade names, and copyrights
- ✔ Wildlife and pets

Products such as textiles, clothing, automobiles, boats, radios, television sets, and medical devices are subject to special standards, declarations, certifications, marking, or labeling requirements, even if restrictions and prohibitions aren't in place. Additionally, merchandise can be inspected for fitness of use or freedom from contamination, and items can be subject to quotas. For more information, turn to Chapter 19.

Getting import help from commodity specialist teams

U.S. Customs has groups of import specialists who can help you get started in importing. Import specialists are organized according to *commodity specialist teams,* which are assigned specific types of goods and are available to respond to any questions you have about U.S. importing rules and regulations. Import specialists provide information about the proper classification of goods for the purpose of charging duties as well as information regarding specific agency permits, licenses, or certifications. Table 3-1 lists each commodity specialist team and its corresponding types of goods.

Table 3-1	Commodity Specialist Teams
Commodity Specialist Team Number	*Products*
201	Animals, meat, fish, dairy, trees, plants, vegetables, fruits, nuts, cereals, prepared foods, sugars, cocoa, raw hides, skins, fur skins, and articles of fur
202	Animal products, coffee, tea, lac, gum, resins, vegetable products, fats, oils, edible preparations, beverages, feed, and tobacco
203	Wood, paper, books, furniture, lighting, art, antiques, stones, ceramics, glass, salt, sulfur, lime, cement, minerals, fuels, glassware, and nonmetallic minerals
204	Toys, games, sporting goods, musical instruments, arms, and ammunition
206	Footwear
207	Gemstones, jewelry, coins; optical products; photographic, cinematographic, measuring, checking, precision, medical or surgical instruments and apparatus; musical instruments and parts and accessories thereof; clocks and watches and parts thereof
208	Reactors, machinery, heating and cooling apparatus, machine tools, office machines, valves, bearings, and computers
209	Transportation products, vehicles (automobiles, trucks, and so on), aircraft, pleasure boats, and civil aircraft equipment
210	Electrical machinery and devices, consumer electronics, televisions, radios, and tape recorders
211	Chemicals and chemical products; photographic supplies
212	Plastics and rubber products
220	Silk yarn fabric, wool yarn fabric, cotton yarn fabric, other vegetable textile fiber fabric, felt non-woven special yarns, cordage carpets, textile fibers, yarns, cordage, non-woven fabrics, textile furnishings, and miscellaneous textile products
221	Special wovens, lace, trimmings, embroideries, knitted fabrics
223	All underwear, nightshirts, nightdresses, pajamas, and head wear
224	Menswear apparel, boys' apparel in sizes 8 to 20
225	Women's knit apparel
226	Leather articles, travel goods, gloves, mittens and mitts, umbrellas, walking sticks, feathers and down, artificial flowers, and wigs
227	Iron, steel, articles of iron or steel, copper, nickel, aluminum, tin, lead, zinc, other metals, ores, slag, ash, tools, implements, cutlery, and tableware

Each district Customs office throughout the U.S. has a division set up with commodity specialists assigned for each group. (Appendix A has contact information for each district Customs office.)

Suppose you're interested in importing seafood from Thailand. Looking at this list, you'd contact team 201. But if you want to import paper clips from South Korea, you may look through the list and say, "Great — there's no team for paper clips or office supplies."

If you can't find your item on the list of commodity specialist teams, determine what the primary component of the item is. If the paper clips you want to import are made of steel, you'd contact team 227, which handles articles of iron or steel. On the other hand, if the paper clips are plastic, you'd contact team 212, because it handles plastic and rubber products.

When talking to the commodity specialist team, make sure you provide the complete product description and the country where the goods are coming from. The same product coming from different countries can have different rates of duty and different rules and regulations.

Figuring out the tariff classification of your imports

When goods arrive at the port, Customs and Border Protection (CBP) makes its decision as to the *dutiable status* of the merchandise — the appropriate tariff classification code, as found in the Harmonized Tariff Schedule of the United States (HTSUS). The HTSUS is the primary resource for determining duty classifications. You can use the HTSUS to determine the appropriate tariff classification number, Customs duty (tariff), and any applicable rules or regulations for the item you're importing.

Most importers want to know the dutiable status of their products before the products arrive at the port. You have two options for finding this information — informal tariff classifications and binding decisions. I cover these options next.

Informal tariff classifications

Every item entering the U.S. has been assigned a *tariff classification number,* which is the basis for all decisions relating to that item. Here are some ways to identify the tariff classification number of your product:

✔ Discuss the product with a commodity specialist. See the earlier section "Getting import help from commodity specialist teams."

✔ Access the HTSUS online at www.usitc.gov/tata/hts/bychapter/ index.htm.

> ✔ Contact the port director where your merchandise will be entered.
>
> ✔ Write to U.S. Customs and Border Protection. The address is Director, National Commodity Specialist Division, U.S. Customs and Border Protection, 1 Penn Plaza, 11th Floor, New York, NY 10119.

The information from any of these sources is informal and not binding.

Binding decisions

A *binding ruling* enables you to get binding pre-entry classification decisions prior to importing a product and filing entries with CBP. A binding ruling also allows you to get binding guidance about other CBP regulations pertaining to marking the country of origin.

Only the Office of Regulations and Rulings can give you binding classification info. You simply submit a letter to Director, National Commodity Specialist Division, U.S. Customs and Border Protection, Attention: CIE/Ruling Request, 1 Penn Plaza, 10th Floor, New York, NY 10119. You generally get a response within 30 days.

The following information is required in ruling requests:

> ✔ The names, addresses, and other identifying information of all interested parties
>
> ✔ The name(s) of the port(s) at which the merchandise will be entered
>
> ✔ A description of the transaction (for example, "A prospective importation of paper clips from South Korea")
>
> ✔ A statement that there are, to your knowledge, no issues on the commodity pending before CBP or any court
>
> ✔ A statement on whether you've previously sought classification advice from a CBP officer, and if so, who responded and what the advice was

A request for a tariff classification should include the following information:

> ✔ A complete description of the goods; send samples (if practical), sketches, diagrams, or other illustrative materials that will be useful in supplementing the written description
>
> ✔ Cost breakdowns of component materials and their respective quantities shown in percentages if possible

✔ A description of the principal use of the goods (as a class or kind of merchandise) in the U.S.

✔ Information about commercial, scientific, or common designations, as may be applicable

✔ Any other information that may be pertinent or required for the purpose of tariff classification

Tariff classifications are binding, but duty rates are not. The classification program promotes compliance, uniformity, and accuracy, and you can rely on it when placing or accepting orders or for making any other business-related decisions.

Chapter 4

Organizing for Import and Export Operations

*A*fter you decide to start your import/export business, one of the first things you have to do is decide on a name and a form of ownership. Choosing the form of ownership affects you and how your business will operate. There's no single best form of ownership. To pick the right form for you, you need to understand the characteristics of each — I discuss them here.

In this chapter, I also fill you in on the appropriate state or local agencies that you need to contact to register your business. I end the chapter with a review of your options regarding your office's location and its mailing address, telephone, e-mail address, fax number, and website.

Selecting a Company Name

One of the first decisions you'll make (and one that you can have a little fun with) is finding the right name for your business. You may spend a lot of time deliberating about potential names for your business. Choosing a name is one of the more challenging aspects of starting your new import/export business — and you have to do it without the help of all those name books that new parents have!

Your company name will serve as your initial identification to your customers. If you don't have a business name, you come across as inexperienced. No matter what you name your business (no matter how good or bad the name is), just having a name establishes that you're a company, and people will be more interested in dealing with you. That said, you want to choose a name that has some kind of meaning to you and that projects the right image to your customers. The name you choose automatically becomes a tool you can use in marketing your business.

When deciding on a business name, focus on the product or service that you'll be selling and on your intended customer. You may want to include words like *international, trading, import, export,* or *global* in your name.

On the other hand, you may want to wait to finalize your business name if you tend to deal with a specific product or category of products (see Chapter 5). After all, including a product in your name may work against you as your business grows.

When you're thinking about names, check phone books and do an Internet search to see whether any other U.S. businesses are using a name similar to the one you're considering. Finding another company using the same name in a similar business may create problems if you want to register or trademark your company name.

Here are some of the desirable characteristics for an effective company name:

- ✔ The name suggests something about the company, its products, or its services.

- ✔ The name is easy to spell and pronounce. Your customers should be able to remember it and spell it correctly.

- ✔ The name can be registered. What's the point of starting any company or marketing campaign if you can't have full rights in the name? Your best defense against having someone else use the name you've selected is a registered trademark (designed by ® in the name), which only the U.S. Patent and Trademark Office (USPTO) can issue. The USPTO won't issue a registration certificate if it judges the name to be generic or if someone else is already using the name. Be sure to trademark your business name through the USPTO and register it through the secretary of state where your business is located.

If your business operates online, be aware that domain names are not registered through state or local governments. Just registering your domain name (such as mybusinessname.com) is not enough to protect your great business name. (For more on domain names, see "Registering your domain name," later in this chapter.)

Choosing a Form of Organization

Every business owner must choose a form of organization for her business. The owner has three basic choices — sole proprietorship, partnership, or corporation —with two other variations: the S corporation and the limited liability company (LLC).

Each option has advantages and disadvantages. Prior to choosing a form of organization, ask the following questions:

✔ How much revenue do you anticipate this business to generate?

✔ How much money will you need to invest? What are the startup and future capital requirements?

✔ Do you lack any skills or experience in the operations of the business?

✔ Are you willing to share your ideas and profits with others?

✔ What are the tax implications for the various organization options? What do you envision as projected earnings?

✔ Do you have other sources of income?

✔ In the event of failure, to what extent do you want to be personally liable for the debts of the business?

Jot down your answers to these questions and refer back to them as you read this section.

Sole proprietorship

The sole proprietorship is the simplest of the three primary forms of organization and the form used by the majority of new businesses. There are usually no setup costs if you decide to do business under your own name.

If you want to operate your business under a trade name, you need to register with your local county clerk office. The requirements differ from one place to the next, but most counties require you to complete and file a business certificate form, also referred to as a certificate of doing business under an assumed name (or just a DBA, *doing business as,* for short).

Pros

Here are some of the advantages to a sole proprietorship:

✔ **A sole proprietorship is easy to create.** If you choose to operate under your own or an assumed name, all you need to do is complete a form similar to the one in Figure 4-1. Each county has its own form, and you can get the form you need from your county clerk's office. You have to sign the form and get it notarized; then it has to be certified by the office of the county clerk. You can do all this in one day.

✔ **A sole proprietorship is the least costly form of ownership.** You don't have to create or file any legal documents, as may be required with corporations. You just have to complete the form, visit the local office of the county clerk, and pay a nominal fee, which can range from $35 to $125, depending on where you live.

✔ **A sole proprietorship has a profit and tax incentive.** After expenses, you get to keep all the remaining profits. You report the net income on Schedule C of IRS Form 1040, and the income is then taxed at your personal tax rate. This form of organization doesn't require the business to pay any separate taxes. Because you're self-employed, this income is also subject to the self-employment tax, which is currently 15.3 percent.

✔ **A sole proprietor has decision-making authority.** Because you're the sole owner, you have complete control over any decision, giving you the ability to respond immediately to any changes.

✔ **There are no special government regulations regarding sole proprietorships.** A sole proprietorship is the least-regulated form of business organization, although it does have to follow all laws that apply to the business.

✔ **You can easily dissolve a sole proprietorship.** You don't need the approval of co-owners or partners. However, you're still personally liable for any outstanding debts that the business hasn't paid.

Cons

Here are the disadvantages of a sole proprietorship:

✔ **Sole proprietors face unlimited personal liability.** You have no separation between personal and business assets. The company's debts are your debts. A creditor can force the sale of your personal assets — such as your house or car or other assets — to recover any unpaid or outstanding debt. This is the primary disadvantage of this form of organization.

✔ **A sole proprietorship is limited to whatever capital you've contributed or whatever you've personally borrowed.** A sole proprietorship may find it difficult to obtain additional funding because of lack of collateral. And a sole proprietorship pays higher interest rates because it's a greater risk than a corporation is.

✔ **The sole proprietor may lack the complete range of skills required to run a successful business.** You must be able to perform a wide variety of functions in areas such as management, marketing, finance, accounting, and human resources. If you can't do all this yourself, you'll need to hire employees to do it for you.

✔ **If you die or become incapacitated, the business ceases to exist.** For example, I have a sole proprietorship — I am John Capela doing business as CADE International. After I die (hopefully not for a long time), CADE will no longer exist. If my sons decide to continue the business, they'll have to set up their own DBA.

BUSINESS CERTIFICATE

Pursuant to **General Business Law § 130**, I hereby certify that I intend to or am conducting or transacting business in the State of New York within the County of _____ under the name or designation of

_____

at _____

_____

My full name is _____

and I reside at _____

I further certify that I am the successor in interest to _____ the person(s) previously using the name(s) specified above to carry on or conduct or transact business.

[Complete if applicable]

I am not less than eighteen years of age [I am less than eighteen years of age, to wit: ____ years of age].

IN WITNESS WHEREOF, I have signed this certificate on the _____ day of

_____

_____

[Signature]

Acknowledgment in New York State (RPL § 309-a)

STATE OF NEW YORK

COUNTY OF _____

On the _____ day of _____ in the year _____ before me, the undersigned, personally appeared _____ , personally known to me or proved to me on the basis of satisfactory evidence to be the individual(s) whose name(s) is (are) subscribed to the within instrument and acknowledged to me that he/she/they executed the same in his/her/their capacity(ies), and that by his/her/their signature(s) on the instrument, the individual(s), or the person upon behalf of which the individual(s) acted, executed the instrument.

_____

Notary Public

Figure 4-1:
A business certificate.

Partnership

If you can't come up with enough money to make your new business a success, or if you lack some of the skills needed, consider a partnership. A *partnership* is an association of two or more persons engaging in a profit-making business as co-owners. A partnership is similar in many respects to a sole proprietorship, with the exception of sharing responsibilities and profits.

Although a formal partnership agreement isn't a legal requirement, it's in the best interest of all partners to have an attorney develop one that clearly details the status and responsibilities of each partner. A standard partnership agreement should include the following:

✔ The name of the partnership

✔ The purpose of the business

✔ The *domicile* of the business (where the business will be located)

✔ The *duration* of the partnership (how long the agreement will be in effect)

✔ Names of all partners and their legal addresses

✔ Performance requirements of the partners (a statement of each partner's individual management role and duty)

✔ Contributions of each partner to the business (this includes each partner's investment in the business; you may also want to include contributions such as experience and sales contact)

✔ An agreement on how to distribute the profits or losses of the partnership

✔ An agreement on the salaries or drawing rights against profits for each partner (how much money each partner will take from the business as a salary)

✔ An agreement on how the partnership might expand through the addition of a new partner

✔ How the assets of the partnership will be distributed if the partners agree to dissolve the partnership

✔ The steps required if a partner wants to sell his interest in the partnership

✔ What happens if one of the partners is absent or disabled

✔ The procedures necessary to alter or modify the partnership agreement

In a partnership, a person can be classified as either a general partner or a limited partner. Each partnership agreement must have at least one *general partner,* who has unlimited personal liability and plays an active role in the management of the business. A *limited partner* has limited liability and can lose only the amount of money she's invested. There's no restriction on the number of limited partners, but they can't play an active role in the management of the business.

Pros

Here are the advantages of a partnership:

- ✔ **A partnership is easy and inexpensive to establish.** In most states, the owner must file a business certificate for partners (similar to the one in Figure 4-2) with the local authorities and obtain any necessary business licenses.

- ✔ **In a successful partnership, the skills and abilities of each partner usually complement each other.** This makes for a much stronger organization.

- ✔ **A partnership has access to a larger base of capital and credit.** Each partner's assets increase the available pool of capital, which enhances the ability to borrow funds.

- ✔ **A partnership is flexible.** Although a partnership isn't as flexible as a sole proprietorship, partners can generally react quickly to changes.

- ✔ **A partnership comes with certain tax incentives.** The partnership itself is not subject to federal taxation. As with a proprietorship, the profits or losses that a partnership earns or incurs are personal income, and taxes are paid on the partners' personal tax rates. Each partner must be provided with a Schedule K-1 from the partnership, showing his share of the income or losses. *Note:* Partners are required to pay taxes on the share, even if none of that income is distributed to them.

Cons

Here are the disadvantages of a partnership:

- ✔ **At least one partner faces unlimited liability.** Every partnership must have at least one general partner, and like a sole proprietor, a general partner has unlimited personal liability for the debts of the business. In addition, a general partner's liability is *joint and several,* which means that creditors can hold all general partners equally responsible for the partnership's debts, or they can collect the entire debt from just one partner. The limited partner doesn't face this disadvantage, because her liability is limited to the amount of money she's invested in the business.

- ✔ **A partnership is terminated when a partner dies or withdraws from the agreement.** The sale of a partnership interest has the same effect as the death or withdrawal of a partner. Coming up with a fair value for the business that everyone can agree on is usually difficult, but it's easier if the partnership agreement specifies a method of valuation.

- ✔ **In a partnership, the partners may have personality conflicts that affect the success of the partnership.** Even if you're best friends when you start the partnership, that may change as you work together. Conflicts between partners can be the undoing of an otherwise successful venture.

BUSINESS CERTIFICATE FOR PARTNERS

Pursuant to **General Business Law § 130**, the undersigned do hereby certify that they intend to or are conducting or transacting business as members of a partnership in the State of New York within the County of _____ under the name or designation of

_____

at _____.

The full names and residence addresses of all the members of the partnership including the age of any who may be infants under the age of eighteen years, are set forth below:

_____   _____

_____   _____

_____   _____

_____   _____

We do further certify that we are the successors in interest to _____
the person(s) previously using the name(s) to carry on or conduct or transact business.
[Complete if applicable]

IN WITNESS WHEREOF, we have signed this certificate on the _____ day of _____.

_____

_____

_____

_____

[Signature/s]

Acknowledgment in New York State (RPL § 309-a)
STATE OF NEW YORK
COUNTY OF _____

On the _____ day of _____ in the year _____ before me, the undersigned, personally appeared_____,
personally known to me or proved to me on the basis of satisfactory evidence to be the individual(s) whose name(s) is (are) subscribed to the within instrument and acknowledged to me that he/she/they executed the same in his/her/their capacity(ies), and that by his/her/their signature(s) on the instrument, the individual(s), or the person upon behalf of which the individual(s) acted, executed the instrument.

_____
Notary Public

Figure 4-2:
A business certificate for partners.

Corporations

A *corporation* exists as a separate entity apart from the owners and may engage in business, make contracts, and sue and be sued. The corporation pays its own taxes. Incorporation involves the filing of a charter or a certificate of incorporation with the secretary of state in the state where you want to transact business and where the principal office of the business is located, as well as payment of a fee.

A corporation can be publicly or privately owned. A public corporation is one whose stock is openly traded on public stock exchanges, and anyone can buy or sell shares of stock he owns in the company. A private corporation is owned by one or a few people who are actively involved in managing the company.

For details on what's required to incorporate in the state where you want to do business, go to `www.statelocalgov.net/50states-secretary-state.cfm` and select the state. You can find links to business organizations and find all the steps required to incorporate your business.

Typically, businesses hire an attorney when filing to form a corporation. However, several businesses online can process the paperwork necessary to form a corporation. Here are two worth looking at:

- ✔ The Company Corporation, 2711 Centerville Rd., Suite 400, Wilmington, DE 19808; phone 800-818-6082; website `www.corporate.com`

- ✔ My Corporation Business Services, Inc., 23586 Calabasas Rd., Suite 102, Calabasas, CA 91302; phone 877-692-6772 (877-MY-CORP-2); website `www.mycorporation.com`

For more information on corporations, check out *Incorporating Your Business For Dummies,* by The Company Corporation (Wiley).

Pros

The advantages of forming a corporation include the following:

- ✔ **Liability is limited.** Because a corporation exists as a separate entity, there's a distinct separation of the business assets and the shareholders' personal assets. If the business fails, the stockholders aren't personally responsible for the debts of the firm; their liability is limited to the amount of their initial investment.

- ✔ **Transfer of ownership is easy.** Ownership changes hands when stockholders sell or trade shares of stock.

- ✔ **A corporation can continue indefinitely.** The existence of the corporation doesn't depend on the fate of any one individual. Unlike a proprietorship or partnership, which ceases to exist on the death or withdrawal of an owner, a corporation has perpetual life.

Cons

Here are the disadvantages of a corporation:

✔ **The process of incorporation involves time and money.** Incorporating can require a variety of fees that aren't applicable when forming a sole proprietorship or partnership. Corporations are chartered by the state; the registration process is the responsibility of the office of the secretary of state, and fees can vary from one state to the next. Plus, maintaining the corporation can be costly and time-consuming.

✔ **Because a corporation is a separate legal entity, it's responsible for paying federal taxes and possibly state and local taxes on its net income.** These taxes are due on the amount of income even before any distribution of dividends. Earnings distributed to shareholders in the form of dividends are then also subject to taxation. In other words, the income of the business is taxed, and then the dividend is distributed to the shareholders; shareholders need to report their dividends as income on their personal taxes. So the profits of the business are taxed twice.

✔ **Corporations are subject to more requirements than either a sole proprietorship or a partnership.** These additional requirements are legal, reporting, and financial.

✔ **When shares of stock are sold in a corporation, the owners give up some control.** When you take on investors, you take their money and give them part of the company.

S corporations

An *S corporation* is a special form of corporation that allows the earnings of the corporation to be taxed only as individual income — the corporation does not pay taxes. Additionally, the S corporation also preserves the owners' right to limited liability.

A corporation can elect to be an S corporation under the following conditions:

✔ It must be a domestic corporation with only one class of stock, which means that all shares must share the same rights (dividends).

✔ It can have no more than 100 shareholders.

✔ It can't have a nonresident alien as a shareholder.

✔ It must be eligible for S status for the entire year.

✔ All shareholders must give the approval to the firm's choice of S corporation status.

✔ It must file a Form 2553 (Election of Small Business Corporation) with the IRS within the first 75 days of the corporation's fiscal year if the corporation wants to make the election of S status effective for the current tax year.

The majority of these restrictions aren't likely to be a concern for most small businesses, many of which have five or fewer individual shareholders. Note that S corporation earnings are not subject to the self-employment tax requirement of sole proprietorships or partnerships.

One potential problem with an S corporation is the way that profits and losses are allocated among owners for income-tax purposes. The IRS states that shareholders in an S corporation must pay taxes on profits in proportion to their stock ownership. So if you have five shareholders, each of whom holds 20 percent of the corporation, each shareholder must pay taxes on 20 percent of the corporation's profits.

Limited liability companies

A limited liability company (LLC) brings together two benefits that can be valuable to many business owners:

- ✔ **Limited liability:** The members of an LLC enjoy the same limits on their personal liability as a corporate shareholder does (see "Corporations," earlier in this chapter). They aren't personally liable for the company's debts.
- ✔ **Pass-through taxation:** The business entity itself pays no federal income tax. Instead, just as in a partnership or sole proprietorship, each member of an LLC simply pays tax on his share of the profits or uses his share of losses to offset other income.

An LLC is very similar to an S corporation. The significant advantage of the LLC is flexibility. An LLC permits its members to divide income (or losses) as they see fit, and the allocations don't have to be based on percentages of ownership as they are with an S corporation.

For more information on limited liability companies, check out *Limited Liability Companies For Dummies,* 2nd Edition, by Jennifer Reuting (Wiley).

Setting Up Your Business

Setting up a business involves all kinds of little details that are easy to overlook. In this section, I cover everything you need to think about in the early days of your business, from registering it to setting up a phone line and more.

Registering your business

Depending on the type of business you operate, you need to take one or two steps for your business to be properly registered in most states:

1. **If your business is a legal entity such as a corporation, limited partnership, or limited liability company, you must file formation or authorization documents for the public record.**

   General partnerships and sole proprietorships are not subject to this step.

2. **You must register for tax purposes.**

To find the specific requirements in your state, go to www.statelocalgov. net/50states-secretary-state.cfm and click on the link for your state.

Opening a bank account

During the startup process, be sure to open a business checking account. When you're initiating your discussion with potential suppliers and customers, you'll need to pay by check, and it's far more professional if these transactions are completed using a company check rather than your personal checks with the cute kittens or pretty sunsets on them.

Selecting an office location

When you're starting a business, you need to choose a location. Most entrepreneurs initially look at starting a business from home. The cost of setting up a separate office can be far too costly, and the home-based option is a good alternative. Just be sure to look at your local community zoning requirements — depending on where you live and the kind of business you're running, you may not be able to operate your business out of your home.

If you decide to use your home, remember that you need to use it mostly for the administrative aspects of your business. If you choose the distributor approach (see Chapter 2), you need to arrange for outside warehousing or storage facilities.

As you begin the process of forming your own import/export business, consider which address you're going to put on your letterhead, business card, and so on. You may not be able to spend the money to rent an office. Furthermore, using a post office box can seem unprofessional, and you may be hesitant about using your home address. Another option is to get a mailbox at a UPS Store. The benefits of mailbox services at a UPS Store include the following:

✔ A street address (not a post office box), which provides a professional image for your business

✔ The ability to pick up your mail when it's convenient for you

✔ Someone to accept packages from all carriers and advise you of arrival so you don't have to be home to sign for them

✔ Someone to hold your packages in a secure location for pickup at your convenience or forward them to you, wherever you are

You can access information about this service from the UPS Store at www.theupsstore.com/products-services/mailbox/Pages/index.aspx.

Getting connected

Communication is important in any business. You need to be able to interact with potential suppliers and customers at all times. In my early days in importing and exporting, almost all communication was done using a telex (teletypewriter exchange) machine, which involved underwater cables. Today the process is easier and far more effective and efficient.

Telephone

When you're setting up your business, you need to create a sense of professionalism. Even during your early stages as you begin to explore ideas, search for product ideas, conduct market research, contact potential suppliers, and interact with prospective customers, you need to have a phone line that's separate and apart from your personal home number — even if you're running a home-based business.

When someone contacts you about your business, you need to be able to answer the phone in a professional manner — you don't want your 8-year-old picking it up, his mouth full of Oreos.

If you don't want to pay for an entirely new phone line, get a cellphone that you use only for business purposes, or use the distinctive ringing service provided by many telephone companies. In the latter, you have one phone line, but the phone company provides you with two phone numbers, each of which has a different ringing pattern so you can tell which phone line is ringing before you answer the call.

Internet and e-mail

Access to the Internet is a must. Today, dial-up Internet is virtually obsolete, especially when you're relying on the Internet to do research or conduct business. What you need is high-speed Internet access, either in the form of DSL (which runs through your phone line) or cable (which runs through the same kind of connection as your cable TV). Both of these options are available through numerous Internet service providers (ISPs), and which one you get really depends on what's available in your area and what the ISP charges.

After you have Internet access, set up an e-mail account. At a minimum, you should set up an account with a free service like Yahoo! Mail (`mail.yahoo.com`), Hotmail (`www.hotmail.com`), or Gmail (`mail.google.com`). The form for the address could look like this: `businessname@yahoo.com`. Another option is to set up an e-mail account through your company's website (see the following section); the advantage of this is that your e-mail address looks more professional: `yourname@businessname.com`, `sales@businessname.com`, and so on. Whatever option you choose, make sure your e-mail address focuses on a name and not something corny, like `muscleman@yahoo.com`.

In every e-mail you send, be sure to include your name, title, company name, mailing address, and phone number.

Opting for a Website

When you're deciding whether to set up a company website, look at the cost of setting up the site and the benefits you'll gain from the site. Then ask yourself whether that's the best use of your financial resources.

Web pages, like almost all promotional materials, are designed to communicate some specific message to a target audience. In this case, the target audience is either prospective suppliers or customers.

You may want to use the website to inform potential suppliers about your business operations. These can be suppliers in the United States for goods you want to export, or they can be suppliers from other countries for goods that you want to import into the United States. You can use the site as a marketing tool, giving prospective suppliers the information they need to decide whether they want to work with you.

You can also use the website to inform, persuade, influence, or remind your customers about your firm and the products that you're offering. Is the site going to be a tool for communication or an electronic brochure? Do you want to sell products through the site or just to educate people about your products?

You can use the site to sell or promote your services as either an export management company (see Chapter 1) or an import buying office, assisting business with limited resources in connecting with suppliers in other countries. Plus you can use the site to sell or promote a specific product to your target market (see Chapter 8).

Making your calls online

A number of programs allow you to make calls — with voice only or with video — through an Internet connection. Calls to other users of the same service are usually free, and you can make cheap international calls to phones through a monthly subscription or by paying by the minute. In terms of minutes, Skype's service accounted for 20 to 25 percent of international calls in 2010! Visit `www.skype.com/intl/en-us/business/` for information on Skype's business offerings.

In this section, I cover the basic issues you need to consider when opting for a website.

Planning for the kind of site you want

Before you hire a web designer, you need to know why you want a website and what your site will look like. A well-designed site takes your visitors where you want them to go and eventually convinces them to do business with you. Think about the following:

- ✔ **What is the purpose of the site?** To make a sale? To inform someone about your business?

- ✔ **Who are you attempting to reach?** You have to know your target audience so you can design the site to meet their needs.

- ✔ **What is the message of the site?** You may want to show visitors that you have the experience and knowledge to sell or represent their products. Or you may want to show off a product or service that you're trying to sell.

- ✔ **What information will you provide to gain visitors' attention?** The information you provide must be something that visitors want, and it must appear in a manner that's easy to follow.

Registering your domain name

Your domain name is your address on the Internet. For example, this book's publisher, Wiley, has the domain name *Wiley.com,* and the For Dummies series is at *Dummies.com* — both of those are domain names.

Put as much time and effort into coming up with your domain name as you put into coming up with your business name. Keep it short. It needs to be something people can remember and won't mind typing in. For example, the publisher of this book registered *Wiley.com,* not *JohnWileyandSonsIncorporated.com.*

After you find the domain name that you like, register it so that no one else can use it. You can check the availability of a particular domain name by visiting www.checkdomain.com.

Finding a web host

To publish a website online, you need a web host. The web host stores all the pages of your website and makes them available to computers connected to the Internet. In other words, the web host keeps your website up and running.

As you register your domain name at one of the myriad domain name registrars out there — such as Register.com (www.register.com) or Network Solutions (www.networksolutions.com) — you'll likely be given the option to sign up for web hosting. You usually have to pay a monthly fee that varies depending on how much disk space and bandwidth your site uses. Ongoing hosting fees can range from $30 to $100 per month. If you pay by the year instead of by the month, you can often get a discount.

Make sure the web host you choose offers technical support and has little or no downtime.

Considering content

The most obvious component of a successful website is its content. You want visitors to your site to get the maximum amount of information in as little time as possible. To do this, you need to make sure that all the content on your site is relevant, adds value to your site, and attracts visitors. The content needs to be consistent and credible. At the same time, you want to avoid communications overload — transmitting *too much* information.

Because visitors to your site may be from other countries, pay special attention to *semantics* (the different meanings of words) and etiquette. Check out www.cyborlink.com for information on international business etiquette and communication guidelines for countries around the world.

Working on web design

You need to make your site appealing and easy to find. Design issues include the look and feel of the site, how the information is presented, and how visitors will navigate the site. Web design includes the colors you use, the style of the text, the size and location of graphics, and so on.

Here's a list of website design resources:

- ✔ **Communication Arts** (www.commarts.com)**:** Identifies design trends and notes what does and does not work on the Internet.

- ✔ **Cool Home Pages** (www.coolhomepages.com)**:** Provides links to some of the better designed websites by category.

- ✔ **Page Resources** (www.pageresource.com)**:** A web development and tutorial site.

- ✔ **Web Pages That Suck** (www.webpagesthatsuck.com)**:** Provides examples of well-designed and poorly designed websites.

- ✔ **Web Style Guide** (www.webstyleguide.com)**:** Offers suggestions related to web page design, page layout, site organization, navigation, and content.

If you have the skills, time, expertise, and desire to design and develop your own site, go for it. But if you don't know enough about web design to make your site look professionally done, hire a professional. Having a poorly designed website can be worse than having no website at all.

If you decide to hire a designer, find someone whose other websites you like — and look at several examples of the person's work. Contact the people whose sites she's created and ask what it was like to work with the designer. Some designers are creative geniuses but aren't great at meeting deadlines. If time matters to you, you want someone who can do it all.

Promoting your site

A successful business uses every opportunity to reach out to its market and promote its website. Contact old clients and reach out to new ones, telling them about your new site. You can also use direct mail, postcards, e-mail, and so on.

Talk to your web designer about *search engine optimization,* setting up your site so that the most people find it. Designers can use the website structure, keywords, and other tools to make sure people find you online. If you want to look deeply into this topic, check out *Search Engine Optimization For Dummies,* 3rd Edition, by Peter Kent (Wiley).

Part II
Selecting Products and Suppliers

The 5th Wave   By Rich Tennant

"I guess we have to ask ourselves how much marketing synergy we want between our snack cake and rat poison product lines."

In this part . . .

1 cover the products you can deal in and how to find and negotiate with suppliers. I start by explaining why any initial movement into the import/export business requires a focus on a specific product category, and that the more product-focused you are, the more likely you'll be to succeed.

I also show you how to use various websites, periodicals, and foreign trade offices to identify suppliers from other countries for goods that can be imported into the United States. I show you how to use online and library resources to identify firms in the United States for products that you may want to export.

I explain how to approach a supplier with your proposal, and I provide you with a checklist covering the key points of agreement to be included when negotiating a purchase contract.

Chapter 5

Selecting the Right Products

. . . .

. . . .

*Y*our business exists to satisfy customers while making a profit, and the product that you choose to import or export has to fulfill this dual purpose. Choosing the right product is critical to your success.

In this chapter, I fill you in on the keys to selecting the right product. Two paths diverge in the woods: One leads toward being a generalist, and the other leads toward being a specialist. Which path is your best bet? I tell you the answer and give you three criteria that need to be met with whatever product you're thinking about selling.

Choosing Whether to Be a Generalist or a Specialist

The number of products that can be imported into or exported from the United States seems infinite. The key to success is to identify your niche or area of specialization. Most individuals starting an import/export business stand a better chance of succeeding if they specialize in a particular area instead of trying to make it as a generalist. The more specific you can be about what you want to sell, the greater are your odds of communicating clearly to your customers and making a sale.

Say you're interested in being an exporter, and you have a contact in another country. You call the contact and say one of the following; which will give you the best results?

> ✔ "I'm the owner of ABC International, an export management company. If you tell me what you want, I can arrange to get it."
>
> ✔ "I'm the owner of ABC International, an export management company that works with a variety of manufacturers of disposable medical supplies. If you're interested, I should be able to find products of interest for you."

The second statement is the one that'll help you reap the greatest rewards in the form of customers.

Introducing the Three E's of Product Selection

When you're selecting a product, you need to be personally and emotionally committed to its success. Begin the selection process by asking yourself the following questions:

> ✔ **Do you like the product that you're planning to offer for sale?** If you don't like it, you'll have a hard time selling it.
>
> ✔ **Can you see yourself getting excited about it?** Sometimes you choose a product based on data. If you can't see yourself getting jazzed about the product, move on to another one.
>
> ✔ **Would you buy and use it yourself?** If you wouldn't buy and use the product, what makes you think other people will buy and use it?
>
> ✔ **Would you sell this product to an immediate family member or friend?** If you don't think the product is good enough for your family and friends, it's not good enough for your customers, either.
>
> ✔ **Who would you sell this product to? Who would be your target market?** If you can't identify your target market for this product, go back to the drawing board.
>
> ✔ **Is there a real need for the product in today's market?** If the market doesn't need the product, you don't want to be selling it.
>
> ✔ **What are the product's advantages and disadvantages as compared to similar products in the market?** No product is perfect. Even if you're excited about the product, you need to be honest with yourself about its pros and cons so you can properly position it in the marketplace.

After you've answered these preliminary questions, you're ready to look at the three E's of product selection: experience, education, and enthusiasm. The three E's can help you narrow that infinite set of product options to a manageable list and eventually to a successful business venture. I cover the three E's in this section.

Experience

One key to being successful with a product is having experience with that product. The more you know about the product, the greater the chances that you'll be successful.

When I left the corporate setting and decided to form my import/export trading company, I decided to focus initially on health and beauty aids and disposable medical supplies. I made this choice because of my experience in the industry — I had just spent ten years working in that area, and it was something that I knew a lot about.

When choosing a product, start by reviewing your background. Look for areas in which you have some specific experience. This experience can come from your employment background, a family contact in another country, or simply a hobby.

The key when trying to introduce a product into a market is knowledge, and experience is the link that provides you with the knowledge that you need to be successful.

Education

There will always be new things to learn, and the sooner you understand that, the more successful you'll be. Product knowledge is important, and education is the key to gaining that knowledge.

Use education to expand and develop your base of experience. Reading this book is a good place to start, but don't stop here. Take business classes, visit the country you're interested in exporting to or importing from, and meet with your prospective customers. You can never have too much education or too much information about your product and your business.

Enthusiasm

You must enjoy selling your product. If you aren't enthusiastic about your product, you'll have a hard time convincing someone else that she should buy it. You can have the experience and use education to fill in the blanks, but if you aren't enthusiastic about the product, selling that product simply won't work.

One of my colleagues was awarded a one-year academic fellowship in the Czech Republic. While he and his family were abroad, his wife became interested in crystal giftware items that were designed and produced there. She used her time overseas to meet with manufacturers, select a category that she was particularly fond of, and negotiate some prices and selling agreements.

After the family returned to the U.S., she continued to express her interest in starting her own business importing this line of crystal glassware. Her next step was to learn about the process of importing and figure out what she needed to do to set up such a business. She attended my seminar and learned the specifics of dealing with suppliers, customers, and U.S. Customs regulations.

Working on her own, she started to realize that she enjoyed meeting and introducing clients to the products that she really loved. She enjoyed sharing the stories of her visits to the factories and the devotion that many of these craftsmen had toward the quality of their products. She enjoyed the challenge.

She had the experience (product knowledge). She used education wisely. And she had enthusiasm, the final key in evaluating and selecting a product.

Assessing a Product's Potential

Whether you're assessing a product you plan to sell in your hometown or one you hope to sell halfway around the world, the product has to match the needs of the market. So how can you tell what your product's potential is?

When you're importing, look at how the product is doing in international markets to try to gauge whether it could be successful in the U.S. If the product is successful overseas, it may also do well in the U.S., as long as the U.S. has similar needs and conditions. That last point is key — there may be a huge market for snowshoes in Siberia, but if your target market is Florida, you probably won't find many buyers.

If you're exporting, one way to gauge overseas market potential is to look at sales in the domestic market. If a product is selling well in the U.S., it may do well abroad in a market that has similar needs and conditions. For more info on gauging market potential in other countries, check out Chapter 11.

Even if the sales of a product in the U.S. are declining, you may still find a growing international market. This is especially true if the product is losing U.S. sales due to advances in technology. A developing country may not require state-of-the-art products. For example, sales of brooms in the U.S. may decline as vacuum cleaner sales rise, but a country where electricity isn't as widespread may have a huge market for high-quality brooms.

Because of economic, cultural, environmental, political, legal, and financial differences, some products offer limited potential in some markets. For details, turn to Chapter 1, where I discuss why international business is different from domestic business.

For more information on assessing a market for exporting, turn to Chapter 9; for importing, turn to Chapter 10.

Chapter 6

Connecting with Overseas Suppliers for Your Imports

In This Chapter

▶ Figuring out which countries have the products you want to import

▶ Finding the names of prospective suppliers of products from other countries

▶ Requesting samples and testing products

▶ Coming to agreement with an overseas supplier

After you decide on a product to import (see Chapter 5), the next step is to find and contact the people overseas who manufacture those items, to get product samples, and to negotiate an agreement. In this chapter, I show you how to do exactly that.

Identifying Countries That Have What You Need

When you're looking to be an importer, one of the first things you have to do is identify countries that have the products you want. Depending on what you want to import, you may be limited in your choice of countries. Not every country has every product.

In Chapter 9, I fill you in on some online research sources, including Background Notes (www.state.gov/r/pa/ei/bgn/) and Country Commercial Guides (www.buyusainfo.net/adsearch.cfm?search_type=int&loadnav=no). You may want to scan these resources to see which items countries are primarily importing and exporting. In this context, because you're looking for suppliers for goods to be imported into the United States, also look at what a country is producing and then exporting to other countries (such as the U.S.).

As you narrow down your list of countries that have the product you're importing, consider the following:

- ✔ **Labor costs:** Wage rates in many developing countries are lower, which means you'll be able to source goods at lower costs.

- ✔ **Exchange rates:** Exchange rates fluctuate, but importing is most favorable when your currency is strong.

- ✔ **Transportation costs:** You need to factor in additional costs in moving the cargo from the point of manufacture to the ultimate destination. These costs include shipment of the cargo from the overseas factory to the point of shipment, loading the cargo onto the vessel, overseas shipping, unloading, Customs, and inland freight to the destination. (See Chapter 16 for information on the various terms of sales used in international transactions.)

- ✔ **Whether the U.S. places any restriction on the import from that country:** The number of countries with restrictions is extremely limited. You can determine whether there are any restrictions or constraints from specific countries by dealing with a commodity specialist (see Chapter 3) and by talking to your Customs broker (see Chapter 19).

- ✔ **Whether the country has a preferential trade agreement with the U.S.:** These agreements include the North American Free Trade Agreement (NAFTA), the Dominican Republic–Central America–United States Free Trade Agreement (CAFTA-DR), the Generalized System of Preferences (GSP), and others. See Chapter 2 for a list of countries with which the U.S. has trade agreements.

- ✔ **Your familiarity with the country:** Knowing your target country and having contacts there make doing business easier.

- ✔ **Your understanding of the local language:** If you or your employees don't speak the local language, make sure that English is widely spoken by businesspeople or, if not, that translators and interpreters are available.

- ✔ **Level of economic development:** Trading with developed countries is generally easier than trading with those that aren't yet developed.

Expect a trade-off between prices and levels of regulation and protection. Suppliers in developing countries may be cheaper, but resolving any problems that occur may be more difficult.

- ✔ **Location of the supplier:** The supplier's location affects shipping costs, transit/lead time, and the ease with which you'll be able to visit suppliers if necessary. The farther away a supplier is, the higher the shipping costs will be. Plus, getting the shipment will take longer, and it may be more difficult to meet face to face.

- ✔ **Existing trade with the U.S.:** A high trade volume suggests that other businesses have successfully chosen the route you're considering.

Because the U.S. government is more interested in promoting exports than promoting imports, information on imports isn't as readily available. You have to rely on direct contact with foreign governments or go through U.S. embassies, consulates, foreign chambers of commerce, and foreign trade commission offices.

Finding Overseas Suppliers

After you've identified the countries that can supply the products you want to import, the next step is to find a specific supplier. Choosing a supplier is an important decision — suppliers have the power to make or break you. Ending up with one who isn't reliable or who makes a poor-quality product can be a disaster for your import business.

Before finalizing an agreement to purchase, spend time evaluating the potential supplier. Check the supplier's reputation, reliability, and financial status. Ask for references of other companies that the supplier has done business with in the U.S., and then contact them to confirm quality and reliability.

The International Company Profile is a program of the U.S. Commercial Services of the Department of Commerce. It checks the reputation, reliability, and financial status of prospective trading partners. You can use this program as a primary source of information in finalizing an agreement to purchase with a foreign supplier. See Chapter 11 for information on where to get this report.

In this section, I describe some ways to find overseas suppliers.

Subscribing to trade publications

One of the ways that you can identify potential suppliers is to subscribe to a variety of trade publications. These publications enable prospective overseas manufacturers and agents to advertise their products. They're a great resource that you can use to make initial contact (writing, e-mailing, or faxing a request for additional information, such as a catalog or price list). Some of the publications are both regional and product-specific, so you don't have to wade through a lot of information that doesn't apply to your situation. In this section, I cover some major publications to look into.

Global Sources

If you're interested in finding suppliers from the Far East — Burma, Cambodia, China, Hong Kong, Indonesia, Japan, Laos, Macau, Malaysia, the Philippines, Singapore, South Korea, Taiwan, Thailand, or Vietnam — one of the better trade publications is *Global Sources,* formerly called *Asian Sources.*

You can use this monthly publication to discover an extensive list of products and hundreds of export-ready suppliers in various product categories. Plus it provides an update on all trade shows that feature suppliers from that part of the world.

Here's a list of the available industry-specific publications offered by *Global Sources:*

- ✔ *Auto Parts & Accessories*
- ✔ *Baby & Children's Products*
- ✔ *Computer Products*
- ✔ *Electronic Components*
- ✔ *Electronics*
- ✔ *Fashion Accessories*
- ✔ *Garments & Textiles*
- ✔ *Gifts & Premiums*
- ✔ *Hardware & DIY* (do it yourself)
- ✔ *Home Products*
- ✔ *Machinery & Industrial Supplies*
- ✔ *Medical & Health Products*
- ✔ *Security Products*
- ✔ *Solar & Energy Savings Products*
- ✔ *Sports & Leisure*
- ✔ *Telecom Products*

You can go to www.globalsources.com to view sample pages of the magazine that meets your needs or to register for a free electronic subscription. On the navigation bar of each web page, you see a section called "Sourcing Magazines." Click the "Sourcing Magazines" link and you can select your e-magazine.

AsianProducts

AsianProducts offers catalogs that provide information on where to buy a wide selection of industry-specific products. The catalogs emphasize products produced throughout the Far East, although other regions are also represented. Publications include the following:

- ✔ *Beauty Care Supply Guide:* This resource provides an extensive list of suppliers who provide a wide range of health and beauty care products. The list includes over-the-counter products, salon furnishings, and equipment.

- ✔ *Electronics:* This publication provides an extensive listing of suppliers who specialize in the wireless and mobile communications industry.

- ✔ *Hotel and Catering Supply Guide:* This catalog provides you with an extensive listing of supplies, accessories, and equipment used in the hotel-catering industry.

- ✔ *Industrial Supply Buyer's Guide:* This catalog provides information on suppliers of technical and industrial products, such as tools, equipment, and machinery used by manufacturers.

- ✔ *Made for Export:* This monthly publication presents information on suppliers of consumer goods such as tableware, housewares, jewelry, furniture and interior decoration, leather goods, stationery, promotional items, health and beauty aids, toys, and more. Each issue contains a supplement that focuses on a specific industry.

- ✔ *Medical Equipment Supply Guide:* This is the leading directory in the field of medical equipment and laboratory supply products.

- ✔ *Stationery & Office Products:* This catalog focuses on the stationery and office products industry. It lists suppliers of office furniture, writing instruments, drawing materials, office supplies, and computer accessories.

You can subscribe to print versions of these publications at the publisher's website (www.asianproducts.com/service/printing_media.php) or via Amazon.com. You can also go to www.asianproducts.com/ebook/ to download four free magazines: *Made for Export, Tools, Electronics,* and *Hardware.*

Trade Channel online and Trade Channel — Consumer Products magazine

Trade Channel is a resource that importers can use to source products and find suppliers worldwide. For more than 50 years, *Trade Channel* has been one of the world's favorite import/export journals, providing a complete overview of international trade shows and free sourcing services for volume buyers.

The magazine and website provide information on suppliers of the following consumer products:

- ✔ Food and drinks
- ✔ Health and beauty

✔ Home and household

✔ Luxury goods and gifts

✔ Office supplies, paper, and stationery

✔ Sports, toys, and hobbies

✔ Textiles, leather, and fashion

The website has an easy-to-use product search feature, allowing you to search either by keyword or by its index of products.

You can get a free copy of *Trade Channel — Consumer Products* by going to http://etradechannel.net, clicking the "Publication" link at the top of the page, and clicking the "Please send me free copy" link. You can also download some free issues as PDFs.

Hitting the Internet

The Internet links suppliers and distributors, creating a marketplace where goods are bought and sold. With the click of a mouse, you can have access to suppliers all over the world in a wide variety of industries. The following sites are ones I recommend.

EximData.com

EximData.com (www.eximdata.com) specializes in the field of international trade information and directories. It sells extensive lists of worldwide manufacturers, traders, and suppliers for numerous industries and product categories. Available categories include the following (I've grouped related categories):

✔ **Auto and marine:** Automobiles; tires and tubes; marine equipment

✔ **Chemical and medical:** Chemicals; pharmaceuticals; medical equipment; laboratory instruments

✔ **Cloth and fiber:** Apparel; textiles and fabrics; yarns and threads

✔ **Electrical:** Electricals; electronics

✔ **Food:** Food products; fruits and vegetables

✔ **Gifts and accessories:** Gifts and novelties; gems and jewelry; watches and clocks; handicrafts and decoratives

✔ **Home:** Floor coverings; furniture

✔ **Machinery and building:** Building materials; hardware; hand tools; machinery and spares; agricultural machinery

✔ **Materials:** Iron and steel; leather products; marble and granite; rubber products

✔ **Recreation:** Toys and games; musical instruments

The site provides current and reliable international trade information, market reports, trade directories, and a company directory of import/export businesses all over the world. The directories include the company name, address, city, country, phone, fax, e-mail, and website if available, plus the name of the contact person and the product details.

Kompass: A business-to-business search engine

Kompass (www.kompass.com) is a database of 1.5 million companies in 66 countries, representing 23 million products and services. It includes 2.7 million executives' names and 400,000 trade and brand names.

You can search by company name, product, and/or country. Free search results include the following:

✔ Company name

✔ Company address

✔ Phone and fax numbers

Registered users and subscribers (subscriptions cost $300 to $400) can get additional information, including

✔ Business activities

✔ Business hours

✔ Brief financial information

✔ Executives' names

✔ Export areas

✔ Legal form of business (public corporation, private company, and so on)

✔ Number of employees

✔ Trade names

✔ Year the company was established

Subscribers can search by additional criteria in the database, including Kompass category number, and they can limit their searches to exporters, importers, distributors, producers, subregions of countries, and so on.

Made-in.com

Made-in.com (www.made-in.com) is an international business directory designed for industry, manufacturer, supplier, trade, and service companies. You can search for businesses worldwide free of charge. The website provides a complete, up-to-date directory of business information covering the following areas:

- ✔ **Europe:** Austria, Czechia (Czech Republic), France, Germany, Hungary, the Netherlands, Portugal, Spain, and Switzerland
- ✔ **Asia:** Hong Kong, Russia, Singapore, Taiwan, and Thailand

Alibaba.com

Alibaba.com (www.alibaba.com) is an online marketplace for global and domestic Chinese trade. The site connects small and medium-size buyers and suppliers from around the world.

Recently, I've met more and more participants at my seminars who are using this site with success. One of the more interesting stories involved someone who had an idea for marketing a unique line of very small products. He created the site www.teenieweenieproducts.com, and his initial product idea was a Teenie Weenie Pen. He designed this telescoping pen and went to Alibaba.com to search for suppliers of telescopes. After several communications, he identified a manufacturer who was able to produce the product and placed a purchase order, and a business was born.

HKTDC: Hong Kong Trade Development Council

The Hong Kong Trade Development Council (http://sourcing.tdctrade.com) enables you to buy and sell products from Hong Kong, mainland China, and Taiwan. It also provides information on Hong Kong trade events (exhibitions and conferences) and market intelligence for specific industries (banking and finance, electronics, garments and textiles, gifts and housewares, information and communication technology, timepieces, jewelry, optical products, toys, and sporting goods).

WAND

WAND (www.wand.com) features an advanced directory indexing system that can help match buyers and sellers in every industry and country around the world.

World Chambers Network (WCN): A network of chambers of commerce

The World Chambers Network (WCN; www.worldchambers.com) is an online network of more than 10,000 chambers of commerce and trade promotion organizations throughout the world. WCN includes a database of products and services; national and international company profiles; chamber membership directories; and information on Customs regulations and international and local business, trade, and economic conditions.

Attending a trade show

Trade shows provide all kinds of opportunities for individuals to meet international buyers, distributors, or representatives. Foreign Trade On-Line (`www.foreign-trade.com/exhibit.htm`) provides you with a searchable database (by country, industry, show name, or show date) of international trade shows, conferences, and exhibitions. For more information on attending trade shows, check out Chapter 10.

Contacting foreign governments

Just as the U.S. has offices around the world to promote the sale of American goods, many foreign countries have set up their own offices in the U.S. to promote the sale of their goods in the U.S. These offices can be great resources when you're looking for sources for your products.

My favorite approach for connecting with overseas suppliers is using a country's trade commission offices. These offices are normally separate from the country's consulate, and they provide guidance to U.S. companies looking for suppliers in the selected country. You can request free publications from these trade commission offices, or in many cases you can access the same information on their websites.

Trade with other regions of the world is a vital element of the American economy. International trade is complicated by the numerous restrictions, licensing requirements, trade barriers, and regulations of other countries. Because these regulations can affect trade with these countries, *consular offices* (where representatives of a foreign government represent the legal interests of their nationals) are responsible for providing information on entering the country and on consignment or shipment of goods. Consular offices can even give you suggestions on consumer needs and preferences.

The Office of the Chief of Protocol publishes a complete listing of the foreign consular offices in the U.S. You can get the list at `www.state.gov/s/cpr/rls/fco/`.

Requesting Product Samples and Having Them Inspected

After you've identified potential suppliers and specific products, you may feel like your work is done. But before you buy anything, you need to request product samples. You can use these samples to verify the product's quality, as well as to make presentations to prospective customers. You can also use product samples in identifying the product's designated Harmonized Tariff Classification Code — samples are required in your request for a binding ruling (see Chapter 3).

Also, if you decide to make a purchase and you want to have the product inspected by an independent inspection company (because you can't visit the country and inspect the goods yourself), you need samples to present to the inspection company. The cost of the services of the inspection company varies based on the value of the shipment and which country the goods are coming from.

SGS is the world's leading inspection, verification, testing, and certification company. SGS inspects and verifies the quantity, weight, and quality of traded goods. To have a product inspected, you contact SGS (201 Route 17 North, Rutherford, NJ 07070; phone 201-508-3000; website www.us.sgs.com) and provide it with the following:

- ✔ Information on the product (specifications)
- ✔ The point of shipment
- ✔ The name and address of the supplier
- ✔ The intended ship date

When the goods are ready for shipment, the SGS representative in that country visits and inspects that cargo prior to and during the loading process. After the inspection, and if everything is in order, SGS issues a certified certificate of inspection, confirming that the goods are, in fact, as ordered. If the goods arrive and they aren't what you ordered, you can file a claim. If the cargo is correct but arrives in a damaged condition, you have a claim against the cargo insurance company (see Chapters 19 and 21).

You can contact the world headquarters of SGS at SGS SA, 1 Place des Alpes, P.O. Box 2152, 1211 Geneva, Switzerland; phone +41 22 739 91 11; website www.sgs.com. From the website, you can look up contact information for the entire worldwide network of SGS offices.

Inspection can be costly, so as your relationship grows with a potential supplier, you may be able to eliminate the need for outside inspection. But you should be aware of the inspection option and use it when you have any concerns or want to reduce risk.

Hammering Out an Agreement with Your Overseas Supplier

You've chosen your supplier and you're ready to buy. To make sure that the transaction goes smoothly, you need to come up with a contract that spells out all the pertinent information.

Many potential sources of confusion exist between an importer and an overseas supplier, from language difficulties to differences in business practices. That's why a clear written contract is so important. If disagreements do arise, you'll have an easier time resolving them if you have a written contract than you would if you relied solely on an oral agreement.

Your contract should make all aspects of the trading process — what will happen, when it will happen, and exactly what each party is responsible for at each stage — as clear as possible. Here are the key points of agreement between an overseas supplier and a U.S. importer:

- ✔ **The products:** Specify which goods you're buying, noting the exact specifications with which the products must comply.

- ✔ **Sales targets:** This includes how much you're ordering and the frequency of shipments.

- ✔ **Territory:** Spell out the territory in which the distributor (importer) may sell and whether the distributor (importer) will have exclusivity there.

- ✔ **Price:** How much will you pay? In which currency? At which exchange rate?

- ✔ **Payment terms:** Specify when and how payments will be made. Will the terms be letter of credit, sight draft, open account, 30 days, or consignment? See Chapter 17 for details on payment.

- ✔ **Shipping terms:** Specify exactly who is responsible for shipping costs, duties, and Customs-related formalities. Use internationally accepted incoterms (international commercial terms), such as FOB, FAS, C&F, and CIF (see Chapter 16), so you're on the same page as the supplier.

- ✔ **Level of effort required of the importer:** How hard must you work to sell the products? This entails a minimum order commitment and long-term order commitments. Basically, the supplier wants to make sure you're not going to place one order and then bail on his product if it doesn't work out.

- ✔ **Delivery:** How will the goods be transported to you?

- ✔ **Insurance:** Be clear about who bears what risks (for example, loss or damage) at each stage of the process.

- ✔ **Sales promotion and advertising:** Who will do it? Who will pay for it? How much will be invested in it?

- ✔ **Warranties and service:** How will you handle defective or unsold products?

- ✔ **Order lead time:** Include the procedures that would be implemented if a dispute were to arise — for example, if one party's error causes delays or losses for the other.

- ✔ **Trademarks, copyrights, and patents:** If applicable, who will register, and in whose name will the trademark, copyright, or patent be?

- ✔ **Provision for settlement of disputes:** If there is a dispute, where will legal proceedings be heard?

- ✔ **Provision for termination of the agreement:** If you negotiated an agreement for a particular territory and you aren't happy with the product and want to discontinue that relationship and find a new supplier, you need to know how to get out of the agreement.

The contracts you have with a supplier will evolve as your trading relationship evolves. Early contracts may be on a shipment-by-shipment basis, but longer-term contracts may follow as familiarity and trust develop between the parties.

Chapter 7

Finding U.S. Suppliers for Your Exports

After you decide on a product to export, the next step is to find a U.S. supplier who manufactures or distributes that item. You can locate suppliers by reading trade magazines or newspapers or by using library and online references and specific industry trade directories. After you identify prospective suppliers, you have to contact them, determine their level of involvement in exporting, request specific product information and costs, and eventually negotiate an agreement to purchase and sell their products in other countries.

A key to success in the exporting business is providing your customers with quality products and fast service at competitive prices. Work hard to develop a core group of reliable suppliers in order to make this happen.

Researching Potential Suppliers

A good way to locate suppliers such as manufacturers or distributors is to conduct a search using library or online resources. These resources are readily available and, for the most part, free, though in some cases you may have to complete a registration form.

Thomas Register (ThomasNet online)

The *Thomas Register of American Manufacturers,* a comprehensive directory of American manufacturers and distributors, has been connecting suppliers and buyers for more than 100 years. It lists addresses, locations, telephone numbers, fax numbers, e-mail addresses, websites, and online catalogs. The *Thomas Register* is a publication of the Thomas Publishing Company, 5 Penn Plaza, New York, NY 10017-0266; phone 212-695-0500.

In the past, you had to visit the reference section of your local library to browse through the 30 or so volumes of oversized green books that make up the *Thomas Register.* Today, you can access all this material online through ThomasNet at www.thomasnet.com.

The site also provides other resources:

- ✔ **Solusource:** Here you can search the most complete, up-to-date directory of worldwide industrial information from more than 700,000 suppliers in 11 languages and 28 countries. (You can also use this resource to find suppliers from other countries for goods that can be imported — see Chapter 6.) Website: www.solusource.com

- ✔ **Industry Market Trends:** This is a comprehensive, daily industrial blog with a biweekly newsletter. It publishes the latest industrial developments, best practices, market trends, and opinions of the editors and readers. Website: http://news.thomasnet.com/IMT/

- ✔ *The Industrial Marketer:* This is a free monthly e-newsletter produced by ThomasNet especially for *industrial marketers* (businesses that purchase goods for sale to another business for the purpose of producing another product, reselling it, or using it in the operations of their business). Website: http://promoteyourbusiness.thomasnet.com/industrial-marketer

WAND

WAND (www.wand.com) is an international business-to-business directory featuring one of the Internet's most advanced product category systems for matching buyers and sellers in every industry.

Buyers visiting the website can search for a list of qualified suppliers for specific products. After you identify a supplier, you can send requests for quotations via e-mail or fax to inquire about making a purchase.

The listings for companies on the site may include the following information:

- ✔ Company name
- ✔ Mailing address
- ✔ E-mail address
- ✔ Company website
- ✔ Online product catalog
- ✔ Company information page (info on the history and background of the company)

Lists of suppliers are available in the following product categories:

- ✔ Agriculture and forestry
- ✔ Arts, crafts, and hobbies
- ✔ Automotive
- ✔ Books, music, and video
- ✔ Building and construction
- ✔ Chemicals, inorganic
- ✔ Chemicals, organic
- ✔ Clocks and watches
- ✔ Communications
- ✔ Computer and information technology
- ✔ Consumer electronics
- ✔ Education and training
- ✔ Electrical and electronics
- ✔ Environmental
- ✔ Fashion and apparel
- ✔ Fine art, antiques, and collectibles
- ✔ Food and beverage

- ✔ Gifts and jewelry
- ✔ Home and garden
- ✔ Industrial equipment and supplies
- ✔ Medical
- ✔ Metals
- ✔ Minerals, mining, and drilling
- ✔ Office equipment and supplies
- ✔ Packaging
- ✔ Personal care
- ✔ Photography
- ✔ Plastics and rubber
- ✔ Safety and security
- ✔ Science and technology
- ✔ Services
- ✔ Sports and recreation
- ✔ Textiles and leather
- ✔ Toys and games
- ✔ TransportationIndustry trade directories

Trade associations or independent publishers make available industry trade directories, which provide lists of firms involved in a particular industry. You can use these directories to identify potential suppliers. They're an alternative to the online resources in the preceding two sections.

For example, say you're looking for a manufacturer of food-service equipment and supplies. Using the *Encyclopedia of Business Information Sources,* you look up the food-service industry. Then you look at the listings of available directories for that industry, and you see that Reed Business Information annually publishes the *Foodservice Equipment and Supply Guide,* which lists nearly 1,700 manufacturers of food-service equipment and supplies for $35.

You can use this approach to find a directory for *any* industry in which you've decided to work. I discuss the chief trade directories next.

Encyclopedia of Business Information Sources

The *Encyclopedia of Business Information Sources* (by GALE Research Company) is an industry reference guide that provides listings of available directories, handbooks/manuals, online databases, statistical sources, periodicals, newsletters, and trade/professional associations for an extensive list of industries and topics. It's a valuable resource with many uses related to finding suppliers and customers.

The *Encyclopedia of Business Information Sources,* which costs several hundred dollars, is available in the reference section of most local libraries. Just photocopy the pages for the industries you anticipate working in.

Business Reference Services, U.S. Library of Congress

The Business and Economics Research Advisor (BERA) has made a series of reference and research guides available online for subjects related to business and economics. These resources have been compiled by specialists in the Business Reference Services of the Science, Technology, and Business Division of the Library of Congress.

You can access the site by going to www.loc.gov/rr/business/ and then clicking the Internet Resources link, or you can get there directly by going to www.loc.gov/rr/business/beonline/subjectlist.php. Bookmark this site. It's an excellent resource that provides information on many other areas, not just lists of companies in various industries. The site also provides links to detailed import/export resources, country information, international trade, e-commerce, trade shows, and more.

The Directory of United States Exporters

The *Directory of United States Exporters* (by Commonwealth Business Media, Inc.) provides a geographical and product listing of U.S. exporters. You can locate an exporter by product, company name, or geographic region. The listings provide information about the products and countries with which these exporters are currently doing business.

Why look up other exporters? A company that already does some exporting may be interested in expanding the number of countries it exports to. You can use the directory to identify a company that may have a product that you're interested in but that isn't yet exporting to a country that you have a client in. This kind of a company can be a good resource because the people there are knowledgeable about exporting and may be more interested in working with you than a supplier that does no exporting would be.

The *Directory of United States Exporters* and its sister publication, the *Directory of United States Importers,* are very expensive. Look for them in the reference section of your local library. You can often find used copies for sale at used bookstores (including Amazon.com). In 2007, I bought a 2005 edition for $20.

Note that the current directories are available online only because the company stopped publishing the books in hard copy in 2011. The online version retails for $670 each or $860 for both (see www.piers.com/directories for subscription info). The older editions are okay to work with, but the elimination of the print versions means that eventually you won't be able to get a copy, and libraries won't carry the online version.

Building a Relationship with Your Supplier

After you select a supplier (based on price, availability, product, service, and so on), you have to work at building a solid relationship. Although building a solid relationship with a supplier can take time and planning, doing so makes it more likely that you'll do even more business with the supplier.

Your first orders with a new supplier should be on a shipment-by-shipment basis. As the relationship develops, you may move to longer and possibly exclusive agreements.

Communication is important in developing this relationship. Face-to-face meetings may be difficult, but they can be vital to this trust-building process. Pay attention to your supplier relationships, and look for areas for improvement. Schedule periodic reviews, and if you find any problems, work together to resolve them. On the other hand, if things are going well, look for ways to expand the relationship.

Dealing with Rejection

One of the more frustrating aspects of searching for suppliers is spending a lot of time to find a supplier, only to be rejected.

Gaining access to major branded products is almost impossible because, more than likely, they already have an extensive network of exclusive overseas distributors. For example, you may want to export Johnson & Johnson Band-Aid brand plastic strips, but Johnson & Johnson has factories and exclusive distributors all over the world. If you go through the resources I list earlier in this chapter, however, you'll find names of private-label manufacturers that manufacture comparable products and don't have those agreements — and you'll probably find some that are excited about the prospect of doing business with you.

If you encounter U.S. suppliers who aren't interested in exporting, be sure to explain the benefits of doing business internationally (see Chapter 2 for a list of benefits). You can link doing business with other countries to increasing profits and sales or to protecting the company from losing market share to its competitors. The supplier may talk about the risks and headaches involved in doing business internationally. Assure the supplier that it will be dealing with you and that you'll handle all the paperwork involved with exporting.

Be patient, don't give up, and keep searching. Always keep your eyes and ears open, and if a supplier rejects your overtures, keep looking.

Drafting an International Sales Agreement

When you're figuring out your role in the export business, you have two main options. You can structure your business as one of the following:

✔ **Distributor:** A distributor is an independent company that purchases products from a supplier, takes title to them, and resells them. A distributor purchases products at a negotiated price and is compensated by selling them at a higher price.

✔ **Sales agent:** A sales agent does not purchase goods from the supplier. Instead, the agent finds customers and solicits offers to purchase the product from the supplier. An agent, who does not take title to the goods, earns a commission.

If you're set up as a distributor, the provisions of your international sales agreement should include the following:

✔ **Territory and exclusivity (if possible):** The agreement should specify the countries in which you'll be allowed to sell the goods. The supplier can set limits on where you may be able to sell.

✔ **Pricing:** Include the price the supplier will charge, the terms and conditions of sale, and what the method of payment will be.

✔ **Minimum purchase quantities:** In most distributor agreements, the supplier expects a commitment for a significant quantity to be purchased. Before a distributor provides an exclusive arrangement in a territory, a provision for minimum purchase quantities is included in the distributor agreement.

✔ **Restrictions on handling competing products:** Normally, a supplier in a distributor agreement wants to include a provision that the appointed distributor won't handle competing products. This is especially true if the supplier grants an exclusive right of distribution.

✔ **Effective date:** The agreement should specify the date it will become effective, as well as the expected duration of the agreement and the procedures for modifying, extending, or terminating the agreement.

✔ **Use of trade names, trademarks, and copyrights:** The agreement needs to clarify when and how trade names, trademarks, and copyrights may be used and who will have the responsibility of registering them in the foreign country.

✔ **Warranties and product liability:** The agreement should specify how defective or unsold products will be handled. It should also clarify the responsibilities concerning product liability insurance.

If you're set up as a sales agent, provisions of the sale agreement should include the following:

✔ **Commissions:** A sales agent is paid a commission for her efforts in soliciting orders that are accepted by the supplier. Generally, commissions are paid only when the supplier receives payment from the ultimate customer.

✔ **Prices:** Because there's no sale directly between the supplier and the agent, the supplier usually requires that the agent quote only agreed-upon prices.

Part III

Identifying Your Target Market and Finding Customers

The 5th Wave   By Rich Tennant

"I like the numbers on this company. They show a very impressive acquittal to conviction ratio."

In this part . . .

1 explain the importance of developing a marketing plan and conducting market research. I give you lots of information on online, library, and industry trade resources — all of which you can use to identify customers overseas for the products that you want to export and customers in the United States for goods that you want to import.

Chapter 8

Looking at Marketing

In This Chapter

▶ Knowing what marketing is and why it matters

▶ Selecting your target market and studying buyer behavior

▶ Understanding how to develop a marketing plan

▶ Pricing, promoting, and distributing your product

You've established your business, chosen a product, and identified a supplier. Now you need to find customers for those products. And that's where marketing comes in. In this chapter, I show you how to develop a comprehensive marketing program to get your imports and exports into the hands of the users.

Entire books have been devoted to the topic of marketing, with much more detailed information than I can provide in this chapter. If you want to take your marketing up a notch, check out *Marketing For Dummies,* 3rd Edition, by Alexander Hiam, MBA (Wiley), or *Small Business Marketing For Dummies,* 2nd Edition, by Barbara Findlay Schenck (Wiley).

What Is Marketing?

Most people, when asked to define the term *marketing,* relate it to a number of its functions — functions that are really only a part of marketing. For example, some people say that "marketing is advertising" or "marketing is promotion" or "marketing is selling." Marketing is all these things but none of them exclusively.

A textbook-style definition of *marketing* says that it is

▸ The process of creating and delivering goods to customers

▸ A system designed to plan, price, promote, and distribute products to individuals or businesses in order to satisfy the objectives of an organization (such as profits, sales, or market share)

Marketing starts with an idea — an idea that either a manufacturer or a marketer has initiated. That idea is transformed into a product and is ultimately acquired by the end user. Between the idea and the end user, you need to do the following:

1. **Transform the idea into a product.**

2. **Price the product.**

3. **Promote the product.**

4. **Select where you're going to put the product so it can end up in the hands of the end user.**

 You can know all about the rules and regulations, and you can find the products, but if you don't understand the marketing process, you'll never get the products into the hands of customers.

Understanding Types of Markets

A *market* is a particular group of people who have a need for a product, along with the authority, willingness, and desire to spend money on the product. There are two main types of markets: the consumer market and the business-to-business market. I cover each of these in this section.

The distinction between a consumer product and a business product is not about the product; it has to do with the *reason* the product is purchased.

Considering the consumer market

The *consumer market* is a particular group of people who have the authority, willingness, and desire to take advantage of the products that you're offering for their personal use or for use within their household. For example, if I'm importing crystal giftware items from the Czech Republic and I'm selling them directly to consumers on eBay or through my store, then I'm dealing with the consumer market.

The consumer market is large and dynamic. The challenge in dealing with this market is understanding what the market for your particular product looks like and how it's changing. Anticipating which marketing strategies will work with the consumer market can be difficult because what worked yesterday may not work today.

Market relationships in action

Still not clear on the difference between a consumer relationship and a business-to-business relationship? Here's an example: Paper Stick Company sells white rolled paper sticks to the ABC Lollipop Company. The relationship between Paper Stick Co. and ABC Lollipop Co. is a business-to-business market relationship because ABC is purchasing the sticks to produce another product, lollipops.

ABC Lollipop sells the lollipops to Super Saver Supermarkets. The relationship between ABC and Super Saver is a business-to-business market relationship, because Super Saver is purchasing the lollipops from ABC for the purpose of reselling them to consumers.

Kathleen goes into the local Super Saver Supermarket, purchases a bag of lollipops, and takes it home. The relationship between Super Saver and Kathleen is a consumer market relationship because Kathleen is purchasing the lollipops for her personal use or use within her household.

Boning up on the business-to-business market

The *business-to-business market* consists of businesses that have a need, along with the authority, willingness, and desire, to acquire the products that you're offering for use within their business. Choosing this market involves selling directly to other businesses instead of to individuals.

The business-to-business market consists of businesses that purchase goods for one or more of the following purposes:

- ✔ **To produce other goods:** For example, you may import yarn that you'll sell to sweater manufacturers in the United States. Those manufacturers will use the yarn to produce sweaters.

- ✔ **To resell the goods to other businesses (such as wholesalers or retailers) or individual customers:** For example, maybe you import yarn that you'll sell to yarn stores, which then sell the yarn to their knitting-needle-wielding customers.

- ✔ **To use the goods in the operations of the organization's business:** For example, maybe you import office supplies and sell them to a business that will use those supplies in the day-to-day operations of its business.

If you're exporting, don't forget governments as possible business-to-business markets. Many foreign governments require large quantities of goods, and they issue *government tenders* (requests for quotations), which offer interesting business opportunities. For example, the Ministries of Health from many Middle Eastern countries publish an annual request for bids on a wide variety of supplies — usually requests to purchase significant quantities with very competitive pricing. When I was an exporter, I received a copy of these tenders and submitted a bid. I once received an order for 52,000 bolts of absorbent gauze measuring 36 inches by 100 yards. The selling price for each bolt was about $15, giving me an order for $780,000.

Identifying Your Target Market

The *target market* is the group of consumers whose needs you'll focus your marketing efforts on. This market is a more specific group of customers than those found in the market as a whole. Identifying your target market is the first step in marketing. To identify your target market, you need to do the following:

- ✔ **Research the market.** This involves identifying the market, the needs of the market, and customer expectations as well as finding out what current and potential customers are doing.

- ✔ **Segment the market.** This involves identifying groups within groups. You find groups of customers within a general market who have different wants and needs, identify the characteristics that distinguish one segment from another, and identify how current suppliers are satisfying the needs of these segments.

- ✔ **Explore buyer behavior.** This involves determining which factors influence the way the market behaves when making decisions about what to buy and where, when, from whom, how often, and most important, why to buy the product.

In this section, I cover these three steps to identifying your target market.

Researching the market

Market research consists of all the activities that help you get the information you need when making decisions about your product, its price, and your promotion and distribution strategies for your customers. It involves the collection, analysis, and interpretation of data about your market and competitors. (In Chapters 9 and 10, I cover market research issues pertinent to exporting and importing.)

The primary objective of market research is to help you identify your target market and provide you with competitive product information. You need to know everything you can about the people who have the authority, willingness, and desire to take advantage of the products that you're offering. You also need to know everything you can about your competition.

In market research, data may be primary or secondary.

Primary data

Primary data are facts that you're collecting for yourself through your own research. Here are three methods of gathering primary data:

- ✔ **Observational research:** Observational research is collecting data by watching someone's actions. Internet cookies are one type of observational research. A cookie records a person's activities when visiting a website — it keeps track of the pages a visitor views and the time she spends on those pages.

- ✔ **Survey research:** This involves gathering data by interviewing people. You can interview them in person, by mail, over the phone, or via the Internet.

- ✔ **Experimental research:** In experimental research, you gather data by observing the results of changing one variable while holding other variables constant. For example, maybe I want to measure the impact that a product's location on a shelf has on sales. The variable that I will manipulate is the shelf the product is located on — top, middle, or bottom. Other factors, such as the product's size, packaging, and price, remain unchanged.

  The first week, I put the product on the top shelf and record sales. The next week, I move the product to the middle shelf and again record sales. In week three, I move the product to the bottom shelf and again record the sales. I've conducted experimental research, and the information I've gathered is how the shelf the product is located on affects sales.

Secondary data

Secondary data are available facts that someone else has gathered for some other purpose. Secondary data sources include the following:

- ✔ **Business and marketing publications and directories:** Use these references to gain information about what's going on in an industry or to find a list of firms within an industry or business. You can identify the availability of such publications using the *Encyclopedia of Business Information Sources* (Gale).

- ✔ **Marketing and research company websites:** These include sites such as Gallup (www.gallup.com), ACNielsen Retail Index (www.acnielsen.com), and Fuld & Company Internet Intelligence Index (www.fuld.com/Tools/I3/).

> ✔ **Government agencies and publications:** Check out `www.usa.gov/directory/federal/index.shtml` for a directory of all U.S. government agencies.
>
> ✔ **Professional association sources:** To identify specific industry trade associations, visit your local public library and ask the reference librarian for a copy of the *Encyclopedia of Business Information Sources,* which offers a detailed list of trade and professional associations for a wide variety of industries and subjects.

Segmenting the market

Market segmentation is a process where you divide the total market for a particular product into several smaller groups that have certain similarities. A *market segment* is a set of individuals or businesses that share a common characteristic and have similar needs and desires.

Manufacturers often segment the market. Next time you're in the drugstore or supermarket, check out the toothpaste aisle and pay attention to all the different kinds of toothpaste offered for sale just by Crest alone. Toothpaste isn't just toothpaste anymore. You can get pastes, gels, toothpaste with whitener, toothpaste for tartar control, and more. Crest is using a segmentation strategy — it makes slight variations to the product, enabling each product to appeal to a different target market.

One of the benefits of segmentation is that all businesses, but especially those that are smaller and have limited resources, are able to compete more effectively by directing their resources to specifically selected markets. Segmentation also benefits medium-size firms in that it enables them to develop a strong position in a specialized segment.

An extreme form of segmenting the market is referred to as *niche marketing.* Niche marketing is an approach that divides the market segments into even smaller subgroups. The benefit of this approach is that you can tailor your products and marketing strategies even more precisely to appeal to this smaller segment. Plus, because many of these markets are very small, you face fewer competitors.

The product that you choose to import or export can be targeted to the consumer market, the business-to-business market, or both. But these two markets have distinctively different needs, wants, purchasing procedures, and buying patterns.

In this section, I fill you in on how to segment the consumer market and how to segment the business-to-business market.

Segmenting the consumer market

You can segment the consumer market in four ways:

- ✔ **Demographic:** Demographic segmentation is the process of dividing the market according to variables such as age, gender, family size, income, education, and so on. Demographics are the most common basis for segmenting the consumer market.

  For example, say a company manufactures a line of disposable razors. When the company markets the products to men, the razors have a yellow handle. But the company can take the same disposable razor, change the handle from yellow to pink, and market it to women.

  When you're evaluating different products, keep an open mind. Always look at the product and how, with modifications, you can make it appeal to different markets based on any demographic variables.

- ✔ **Geographic:** Geographic segmentation is the process of dividing the market based on the geographic distribution of the population. Different geographic areas have distinctive characteristics, which may require adjustments to the marketing strategies. For example, are you looking at marketing your goods in rural areas, urban areas, or suburban areas?

- ✔ **Psychographic:** Psychographic segmentation involves identifying attributes to what a person thinks or feels. You look at the entire market and divide it on the basis of personality characteristics, motives, and lifestyle. For example, bottled-water companies package their goods in a variety of bottle types to satisfy different lifestyles and motives. They may produce a bottle with a flip-top lid for athletes or people on the go.

- ✔ **Behavioral:** Behavioral segmentation is the process of dividing the market on the basis of how the consumer behaves toward the product. This usually involves some aspect of product use (light, moderate, or heavy users). A company may make a generic line to target the heavy user, whereas another line targets either the brand loyal customer or the light user, where cost is less of an issue.

Segmenting the business-to-business market

The process of segmenting the business-to-business market is different because there are fewer customers than in the consumer market. A more focused marketing effort designed to meet the specific needs of a group of similar customers is far more efficient for the business-to-business market and will likely be more successful.

Here are the bases that you can use to segment the business-to-business market:

- **Customer location:** Some industries are geographically concentrated. For example, computer companies are concentrated in Silicon Valley.

- **Customer type:** You can market your goods to a variety of industries. For example, if you're importing some form of small electronic motors, your market could be spread over several industries. Types of customers include manufacturers, distributors, and retailers.

- **Size:** Many sellers divide the market into small and large accounts, potentially using different pricing and distribution strategies for different accounts.

- **Buying situation:** The situation surrounding the transaction can be a basis for segmenting a market. You may have to modify your marketing efforts to deal with different buying situations:

  - **New task:** In this case, a company considers purchasing a given item for the first time. This purchase usually involves a significant initial investment, and the company will spend lots of time evaluating alternatives (such as a lollipop company considering the purchase of a new lollipop machine).

  - **Straight rebuy:** A straight rebuy is a routine, low-involvement purchase that involves minimal information needs and no major involvement in evaluating alternatives (such as purchasing cleaning supplies for a manufacturing facility).

  - **Modified rebuy:** This situation is somewhere in between new task and straight rebuy. A buyer needs some information and will spend some time evaluating alternatives (such as a lollipop manufacturer that is evaluating different suppliers of paper sticks).

Exploring buyer behavior

Behavior is the way someone acts. If you're going to develop a marketing plan, you need to identify how the buyers will act when making decisions about what they'll purchase and where, when, how often, from whom, and most important, why they'll purchase the goods that you're offering. In other words, you need to know the factors that will influence the way the buyer behaves.

The factors influencing buying behavior are different for consumer and business-to-business markets. I outline both in this section.

Buyer behavior in the consumer market

Before making a purchase, consumers go through a decision-making process. This process is similar to the process they'd use to solve a problem:

1. **The consumer identifies that something is lacking or that a situation needs to be dealt with.**

2. **The consumer identifies the alternative product or products that will address the problem and then seeks out alternative brands and gathers information about them.**

3. **The consumer identifies the benefits and drawbacks of each of the alternative products.**

   When evaluating each alternative, the consumer considers each of the following questions:

   - Is it feasible? Can I afford it?

   - To what extent is the alternative satisfactory, and does it actually address the problem?

   - What are the possible consequences of the alternative?

4. **The consumer decides to buy or not to buy, and if the consumer decides to buy, he makes other decisions relating to the purchase (including where and when to make the purchase).**

5. **The consumer looks for assurance that he's selected the correct alternative.**

The amount of time the consumer spends on each of these steps depends on the category of the product. If the product is a *convenience good* (an item that has a low unit price, such as a gallon of milk or a loaf of bread), the amount of time spent on each stage is minimal. If the product is a *big-ticket item* (such as a computer, television, or car), the consumer may spend more time evaluating alternatives before making the decision.

So what factors influence the consumer's decision-making process? In the consumer market, behavior is influenced by three kinds of factors:

✔ **Personal factors:** These include

   - **Motivation:** Consumers look for products that will satisfy their needs, whether those needs are *physiological* (food, drink, and shelter) or *psychological* (affection, belonging, self-esteem).

   - **Attitudes:** These are predispositions (either favorable or unfavorable) toward something, someplace, or someone. The consumer has already made up his mind that he either likes or dislikes something, someplace, or someone.

- **Personality:** These are traits such as self-esteem, the extent to which the consumer believes that he can control events affecting him, the rigidity of his beliefs, and so on.

- **Perception:** Consumers gather information before making a choice, and perception is the process of receiving, organizing, and assigning meaning to that information. Perception is how the consumer goes about interpreting and understanding the situation, and it plays a role in the stage where the consumer identifies alternatives (Step 2). Consumers pay attention to and remember things that are important to them; they ignore and forget those things that may be inconsistent with their beliefs and attitudes.

✔ **Interpersonal or social factors:** The way that consumers think, believe, and act is usually determined by their interactions with other individuals. Friends, families, and households can influence consumer attitudes, values, and behavior. If the whole family prefers Coke to Pepsi, the person doing the shopping may be swayed more to Coke than to Pepsi, regardless of what he likes.

✔ **Situational factors:** Situations can play a large part in determining how consumers behave. Things like the surroundings, terms of purchase, and the moods and motives of consumers can influence their behavior. For example, you may not have given much thought to which brand of soda you buy, but as you're walking down the aisle of your grocery store, you see that Pepsi is on sale, and you buy it.

Buyer behavior in the business-to-business market

The business-to-business market consists of individuals and organizations that purchase goods for the purpose of production of other goods, resale, or use in the operations of their business. Buyer behavior in the business-to-business market is more logical than it is in the consumer market; it's not as influenced by the personal or interpersonal factors you find in the consumer market.

To better understand business-to-business buyer behavior, you need to understand the characteristics of demand in the business-to-business market:

✔ **Demand is derived.** The demand for the business product is generated from the demand for the consumer products in which the business product is used. For example, the amount of rolled white paper sticks that I sell to Lolly's Lollipop Company is derived from the consumers' demand for Lolly's Lollipops. If Lolly's sells no lollipops, then I won't be able to sell Lolly's Lollipop Company any rolled white paper sticks.

✔ **Demand is inelastic.** Demand for a business product responds very little to changes in price. For example, any major changes in prices for my sticks to Lolly's Lollipop Company will not influence the amount of sticks it purchases, simply because if Lolly's isn't selling any lollipops to its customers, it doesn't need to purchase the sticks from me.

✔ **Demand is widely fluctuating.** Businesses are worried about being low on inventory when consumer demand increases. On the other hand, they don't want to have too much inventory if consumer demand declines.

✔ **Buyers are well informed.** Business-to-business buyers are knowledgeable and aware of alternative sources of supply and competitive products. Buyers tend to specialize in certain items, and the costs are extremely high if they make a mistake. For example, if they order the wrong goods or pay too high a price, they may have to close their production line and raise prices.

The decision-making process for a buyer in the business-to-business market is pretty much the same as it is in the consumer market (see the preceding section). However, here are some differences in business-to-business buying behavior:

✔ The business buyer is more practical, rational, and unemotional.

✔ The business buyer is primarily concerned with issues such as price, quality, service, and delivery.

✔ The business buyer is under intense quality and time pressure.

In the consumer market, usually one person decides what, were, when, from whom, and why she's going to buy something. On the other hand, in the business-to-business market, the decisions are usually made by a variety of individuals, known as the *buying center.* The buying center includes all individuals who are involved in the purchase decision-making process. The members of this unit may serve in one or more of the following roles:

✔ **Users:** These are individuals who are using the product. For example, when I sell rolled white paper sticks to Lolly's Lollipop Company, the production supervisor and some operators need to be concerned about the product. They want to make sure that the product meets their specifications and that they won't have any problems while they're running the equipment and producing the product.

✔ **Influencers:** Influencers are the individuals in the organization who have expertise or financial positions that they can use to influence product and purchase specifications. These people, using their positions in the organization, develop the specifications and identify acceptable suppliers.

✔ **Deciders:** Deciders are the individuals who actually make the buying decision about the product and supplier. In some cases, the decider may be the purchasing agent.

✔ **Gatekeepers:** These individuals control the flow of purchasing information within and outside the organization. A gatekeeper can be the receptionist or administrative assistant who schedules appointments.

✔ **Buyers:** Buyers are the individuals who interact with the vendors, coordinate the terms of sales, and process the actual purchase orders.

My experience with a buying center

I was selling products to pharmaceutical manufacturers in Puerto Rico, and I had a new source of supply for the goods: a local manufacturing facility on the island. In the past, I'd been supplying them with products from the main factory in Connecticut. But I was able to offer them the locally produced item at a savings of 40 percent to 50 percent, mainly due to reduced shipping costs.

I was confident that when I made the offer to the buyer in the purchasing department, I'd be able to get all the business and eliminate my competitors. But to my surprise, the buyer had a nominal say in changing the source of supply. In addition to getting the buyer's approval, I also had to get the approval of the production supervisor, the marketing department, and the pharmaceutical company's quality-control department.

The facility based in Connecticut had been inspected and approved as a source of supply. As soon as I changed the production facility to Puerto Rico, the company needed to come and inspect the plant, putting it through the complete approval process. Without this approval, I couldn't provide them with products from this facility at the lower cost.

Eventually, I was able to get the business, but there was a delay of six months while we waited for all the parties to visit, inspect, and approve the facility.

Say you import ceramic giftware from Italy and you want to sell the products to a department store such as Target. You need to realize that the final decision to purchase from you may be made by many different individuals within the organization. You need to identify all the individuals who may be part of this buying center.

Developing Product Strategies

Product strategies help create the value the customer sees in the product. This part of the marketing plan focuses on the uniqueness of your product and how the customer will benefit from using the products you're offering.

Benefits can be intangible as well as tangible. For example, if you're selling a nontoxic cleaning product, your customers will benefit by having a cleaner house, but they may also enjoy better health and avoid damaging the environment. Identify as many benefits as possible for the product. Then emphasize the benefits that your targeted customers will most appreciate in your marketing plan.

The key issues involved in developing product strategies include the following:

- ✔ Which products or services should you offer? What should be the breadth and depth of your product mix? How many different product lines will you carry, and what sort of variety will you provide for each product line?
- ✔ How should the products be branded or otherwise identified?
- ✔ How should the products be packaged?
- ✔ What will your guarantee and warranty policies be?

I cover each of these issues in this section.

Product mix

One of the first product strategy decisions that you have to make is identifying the product lines and mix of products that you're going to offer to your customers. A *product mix* is a listing of all products that you'll be offering for sale, and a *product line* is a group of products that are intended for similar uses and have similar characteristics.

For example, say you're importing giftware from the Far East. The product mix is a list of all the items that you're offering for sale. It may be made up of a variety of ceramic, crystal, wood, pewter, and glass giftware items. Ceramic, crystal, wood, pewter, and glass represent the different product lines.

A product mix has both breadth and depth. *Breadth* is the number of product lines you're carrying. In this example, that's five — ceramic, crystal, wood, pewter, and glass. *Depth* is the variety of items offered within each product line. For example, in your pewter product line, you may offer cups, trays, candlesticks, goblets, and more. You need to decide how narrow or wide your product mix will be and whether the product line offerings are going to be shallow or deep.

 Initially, you're probably better off starting with one limited line of products. After your business starts to grow, you may extend the product line or expand the product mix. For example, you may start off selling pewter giftware. After you experience some success, you expand your product mix by adding crystal or ceramic giftware items. Or you extend your product line by going from selling cups, goblets, and trays to selling cups, goblets, trays, and candlesticks.

Pondering the product life cycle

The life cycle of a product includes four stages:

✔ **Introduction:** During the introduction stage, you usually have a low level of sales and profits.

✔ **Growth:** The growth stage entails a rapid increase in sales and profits.

✔ **Maturity:** The maturity stage shows a continued increase in sales but at a declining rate.

✔ **Decline:** The sales volume decreases significantly during the decline stage.

Bottom line: Nothing lasts forever. When a product starts to have a significant decline in sales, it's in the decline stage. When that happens to your product, you have three options for extending the life of the product. You can

✔ Modify or improve the product. This can be something as simple as changing the packaging.

✔ Identify new uses for the product.

✔ Identify new markets for the existing product.

Branding

After the product mix, the next product-related decision is how you want your products to be identified. A *brand* is a name or mark that's used to identify the products of one seller and to differentiate them from competing products.

You can use the brand names and marks of the manufacturer, develop your own brand, or offer a private label (store brand) for your customers.

If you decide to develop your own brand, you may have to make minimum quantity commitments with your suppliers. These minimum purchase quantities may prove to be expensive, so as a startup, selling the products using the manufacturer's brand may initially be more cost-effective.

If you're not willing to assume the responsibilities and costs of developing and promoting a brand, developing a brand may not be for you. Or you may decide not to develop your own brand because your products can't be physically different from the products of other companies.

Packaging and labeling

After you've developed and branded your product, the next step is to address the features of packaging and labeling. Packaging is intended to do the following:

✔ Protect the product as it moves between the producer and final customer

✔ Protect the product from the time it is purchased until the time it is used

✔ Assist the customers in considering the purchase of the product

✔ Promote the product

Here are some packaging factors that are somewhat unique to international marketing:

✔ Changes in climate across countries may require protective packaging against cold or heat.

✔ Because of possible lengthy transportation times, packaging needs to be able to protect the goods against breakage or damage.

✔ Smaller packages may be required in low-income countries.

✔ Smaller packages may be more common in countries where shoppers make frequent trips.

✔ The color of the packaging may have cultural significance. For example, white is the color of mourning in Asia, and green signifies good luck in the Islamic world.

Labeling, in its most basic form, provides information to the customers. You can use a brand label applied to your product to differentiate your products from competitive offerings. A descriptive label provides information about how the product is used or manufactured and/or other relevant features.

If you're exporting products that are ultimately going into the consumer market, be sure to offer bilingual labeling. Canadian products should be labeled in both English and French.

Warranties and guarantees

The purpose of a warranty is to assure the buyer that the product will perform up to reasonable expectations.

Say you decide to import lamps from Italy, and you sell them to retail furniture stores in the United States. When you make the sale to the retailers, you provide them with a guarantee that the product will perform as expected. Mary visits the store, purchases the lamp, and takes it home. When she arrives home, she realizes that the lamp is defective. She returns the lamp to the store for credit. The store contacts you, the importer, and asks for a credit or requests that the product be repaired.

At the time you purchase the lamps from the supplier in Italy, you must have an agreement as to how you'll handle defective products. The agreement with your supplier should state that if the product is defective, credit will be issued to you — and the agreement should explain how. Will you have to return the product to the supplier in Italy? If the product can be repaired, will it be repaired in the United States, or does it have to be returned to Italy for repair? Make sure you have this understanding in place before you place the order and coordinate payment with the exporter.

Pricing Your Products

Price is the amount of money that the customer needs to acquire your product. When you're setting the price for your product, do so with one of three objectives in mind:

- **Profit:** There are two profit-oriented goals: Maximize sales or achieve a target return or desired profit level.

- **Sales:** The pricing objective may be to set the price to increase or maximize sales volume or to maintain or increase your share of the market.

- **Image:** Decide whether you want to convey an image of prestige or discount.

To accomplish your objective, you have two possible strategies:

- **Penetration:** Penetration is the strategy employed when you want to go into the market with a low price and place the emphasis on the sales objective.

- **Skimming:** Skimming occurs when you enter the market with a high price, placing an emphasis on the profitability objective.

Several factors influence the price you set:

- **The nature of the market:** Look at the demographic characteristics of the market (such as age, income, level of education, socioeconomic class, and so on) together with the physical location of the market.

- **The nature of your product:** Would the product be categorized as a *convenience good* (low unit price, purchased with little effort), a *shopping good* (for which customers compare products on the basis of price, quality, style, and so on), or a *specialty product* (one that the consumer makes a special effort to secure)?

- **Your competition:** When you evaluate or set a price, look at what others are charging for similar products. Unless your products are unique, competition plays a role in the setting of the price.

✔ **Your costs:** Charge a price that covers your costs. No business can stay in business if it continues to sell products below cost for any period of time.

✔ **Economic forces:** Consider what's going on with the economy. What's the interest rate? What's the value of the dollar in relation to the currency of another country? Is either country in a period of inflation? Is a recession on the horizon?

✔ **Political forces:** If you're selling goods in a politically risky country, the greater the risk and the higher the price.

Specific issues and questions you need to address include the following:

✔ **What should be the basic price?** This is your standard price, sort of the same as the manufacturer's suggested retail price (MSRP) or list price.

✔ **What discounts (or extras) will you allow?** For example, will you offer *trade discounts* (price reductions given to members of the trade, such as wholesalers and retailers), quantity discounts, *promotional discounts* (price reduction given to the buyer for performing promotional services, such as prominently displaying products), or *seasonal discounts* (discounts offered when customers place orders during a low season)?

✔ **How should the price relate to cost?** Almost everyone agrees that prices should cover costs. However, not every product must be priced to cover its *own* individual costs each time it is sold. You may choose to sacrifice profits on one item to support the sale of other more profitable items.

✔ **When and under what conditions should a price be changed?** Decide when you want to increase or reduce prices. For example, if you note that economic forces are raising interest rates, you may decide to lower prices, or vice versa.

✔ **Should you charge different prices to different customers?** Will you offer one price to a small mom-and-pop store and another price to a retail chain like Wal-Mart?

Laws such as the Robinson-Patman Act prevent price differentials, but not all price differentials are illegal under the act. Price differentials are against the law only if the effect is to reduce competition. ***Note:*** You're still allowed to give quantity discounts.

The correct way to price an import product is to first set its price point in the market and then work back to a free on board (FOB) factory value. Table 8-1 shows the pricing for a hypothetical shipment of wooden toys from San Pedro Sula, Honduras, to New York. The shipment is 108 dozen toys, packed 27 dozen per case. Each case measures 36 inches by 36 inches by 36 inches and weighs 80 pounds. If you're importing these items and selling them in the United States, you'd start by filling out the top line (your retail price point) and work your way down the list, filling in the Cost per Piece column for every step.

Table 8-1	An Import Pricing Example	
Items	*Cost per Piece*	*Explanation*
Retail price point in New York	**$4.00**	
Subtract the retail markup	−$2.00	50 percent off retail
Importer/distributor price	**$2.00**	
Subtract the importer/distributor markup	−$0.80	40 percent off FOB warehouse
Cost FOB warehouse	**$1.20**	
Subtract the forwarding/inland freight for 4 cases	−$0.03	$30 + $0.02/pound (this varies depending on your situation), so $30 + (80 pounds/case × 4 cases × 0.02) = $36.40 for 1,296 pieces (because there are 27 dozen, or 324/case) = $0.028 (which rounds to $0.03)
Cost landed, duty paid	**$1.17**	**This varies depending on your situation.**
Subtract the Customs clearance and bond (**Note:** The clearance and bond vary from one situation to the next. Ask your Customs broker for estimates.)	−$0.08	($60 + $40) ÷ 1,296 pieces = $0.077 (which rounds to $0.08)
Cost, insurance, and freight (CIF) New York	**$1.09**	
Subtract the cost of warehouse-to-warehouse insurance	−$0.01	Approximately 0.75 percent
Cost and freight (C&F) New York	**$1.08**	
Subtract the cost of ocean freight	−$0.31	$400 ($400 ÷ 1,296 pieces = $0.308, which rounds to $0.31)
Free on board (FOB) vessel	**$0.77**	
Subtract forwarding and port charges	−$0.06	$80 ($80 ÷ 1,296 pieces = $0.062, which rounds to $0.06)
Free alongside ship (FAS) vessel	**$0.71**	
Subtract inland freight to port	−$0.02	$0.06/pound (320 pounds × $0.06/pound = $19.20 ÷ 1,296 = $0.02)
Value FOB Factory	**$0.69 per piece**	

Promoting Your Product

Promotion is anything that you do to inform, persuade, influence, and/or remind your target market about the products that you're offering. To accomplish these objectives, you have to identify an element of the promotion mix to use. That is, you have to decide on the blend of advertising, personal selling, sales promotion and publicity that you can use to best accomplish the desired objective. In this section, I cover the promotion mix, promotion strategies, and social media tools you can use to promote your products.

Looking at the promotion mix

Promotion includes all types of marketing activities designed to stimulate demand. The *promotion mix* consists of advertising, personal selling, publicity, and sales promotion:

- ✔ **Advertising:** Advertising is any nonpersonal communication that you pay for in order to inform, persuade, influence, or remind the target market about the products that you're offering. Advertising can consist of the electronic media (radio or TV), print media (magazines or newspapers), or other categories (such as the Internet, direct mail, transit advertising, and so on).

  Trade publications that target businesses in particular industries often have classified ads at the back. These classifieds can be an effective and inexpensive way to let people know about the products you're selling. Find a copy of the *Encyclopedia of Business Information Sources* (check your public library), search for your desired industry catalog, and identify a trade periodical for that industry or product category.

- ✔ **Personal selling:** Personal selling is a personal communication of information between a buyer and seller. A salesperson (you or someone you hire) makes a presentation to inform, persuade, and influence the buyer about your products.

  If you're an exporter, keep in mind that personal selling is often more important in the international market than it is in the domestic market, because mass media (TV, radio, newspapers, and so on) may not be available, and wages are lower in many developing countries.

- ✔ **Publicity:** Publicity is an unpaid-for communication through the media about you and your products. For example, if you're an importer, you can get some publicity by donating a product that you're importing to charity.

- ✔ **Sales promotion:** Sales promotions are devices (such as product samples, coupons, point-of-purchase displays, and so on) that are used to stimulate demand for your product. You can also use sales promotions to support advertising and personal selling.

Integrated marketing communications (IMC) is a process used to plan, develop, execute, and evaluate the communications that a business uses to connect with its target market. IMC coordinates the promotional elements of advertising, personal selling, publicity, and sales promotion.

Choosing a push or pull strategy

A promotion strategy aimed at middlemen is called a *push strategy,* and a promotion strategy directed at end users is called a *pull strategy.*

A typical channel of distribution may look like this:

Importer/exporter → wholesaler → retailer → consumer

In a push strategy, the importer or exporter targets her promotional effort toward the wholesaler or retailer. For example, the importer or exporter offers the wholesaler or retailer free goods. The free goods are an attempt to influence that wholesaler or retailer to purchase more goods for the purpose of pushing them through the channel of distribution.

Push is the primary promotion strategy used by most small to medium-size import/export businesses.

In a pull strategy, the importer or exporter targets her promotional efforts to the consumer in the form of advertising. The intent is for the consumer to see the advertising and be pulled into the store to look for the products.

Coming up with a promotion strategy

When you're coming up with your promotion strategies, consider the following:

- ✔ **Is there a promotional opportunity?** An *opportunity* is anything external to the organization that has a positive impact on the organization. You can identify opportunities by monitoring the environment and trying to identify those factors (a competitor's going out of business, special discounts offered from your suppliers, and so on).

- ✔ **Who should you target with your promotion?** Will you target the consumers or the intermediaries (wholesalers/retailers/industrial distributors)?

✔ **What should your promotional message be?** How are you going to get
the attention of your market and influence them? The message has two
elements — the *appeal* (the benefit that the customer will get for accepting your message) and the *execution* (how you're going to get the attention of that person with your appeal).

✔ **What promotional media should you employ?** Will you use radio, television, magazines, newspapers, direct mail, or the Internet? You need to
select the media that will best reach your target market.

✔ **How much should you spend on promotion?** The best approach for
developing a promotion budget is to figure out the objectives you want to
achieve with the promotion program. Then figure out what that will cost.

Using social media for promotion

The growth of social media (Facebook, Twitter, and other online tools) has
impacted the way organizations communicate with their target markets.
Social media marketing programs can create content that attracts attention
and encourages readers to share it with their social networks. Increased
communication for businesses fosters company and product awareness and
improved customer service.

Here's a list of types of social media options that you can use:

✔ **Social networking services:** These sites allow individuals to interact
with others and build relationships. When a company joins these sites,
individuals can interact with the company about its products. Social
Networking sites include full networks (Facebook, MySpace, and so on),
microblogging networks (such as Twitter), and professional networks
(such as LinkedIn and Plaxo).

✔ **Blogs:** A blog is a website that allows a company to provide detailed
information about its products and services, and readers can post their
opinions or reactions. A blog can include testimonials and links to social
networks such as Facebook, MySpace, and Twitter. Blogs can be regularly updated, and you can use them as a promotional tool to attract and
retain customers.

✔ **Social media sharing services:** Use these sites to post and comment
on videos (as on YouTube, Vimeo, or Ustream), photos (as on Flickr,
Photobucket, or Picasa), and audio podcasts (as on Podcast Alley or
BlogTalk Radio).

✔ **Social bookmarking services:** Users of these services provide links to
web pages that they want to remember or recommend to others. These
services include recommendation services (such as StumbleUpon and
Delicious) and social shopping servicers (such as Kaboodle and ThisNext).

Social media is an inexpensive and easily accessible platform around which a business can develop a marketing campaign. The one negative is that the majority of these services require a major investment of time to initiate and maintain these channels of communication.

For more information on marketing via social media, read *Social Media Marketing All-In-One For Dummies* by Jan Zimmerman and Doug Sahlin (Wiley). It's a collection of eight books, including The Social Media Mix, Cybersocial Tools, Blogs and Podcasts, Twitter, Facebook, LinkedIn, Other Social Media Marketing Sites, and Measuring Results; Building on Your Success.

Distributing Your Product

The final piece in your marketing plan is *distribution* — how you get the product in the hands of the end user. During this stage, you have to identify the *distribution channel,* the people and businesses involved in the transfer of title of a product as the product moves from the producer to the consumer or the business user. You want to use a distribution channel that meets the needs of your customers while providing you with a competitive advantage.

Agents are marketing intermediaries who bring buyers and sellers together but do not take title to the goods. Wholesalers and retailers are marketing intermediaries who bring buyers and sellers together and *do* take title to the goods. (See Chapter 2 for more information on agents and distributors.)

If you're selling to the consumer market, you can select any of the following channels of distribution:

- ✔ You → consumer
- ✔ You → retailer → consumer
- ✔ You → wholesaler → retailer → consumer
- ✔ You → agent → retailer → consumer
- ✔ You → agent → wholesaler → retailer → consumer

If you're selling to the business-to-business market, here are your distribution channel options:

- ✔ You → business user
- ✔ You → industrial distributor → business user
- ✔ You → agent → business user
- ✔ You → agent → industrial distributor → business user

For distribution, consider questions such as the following:

✔ **Should you sell direct or use middlemen?** Will you be using a direct channel of distribution (selling directly to the consumer)? Or will you use wholesalers or retailers as part of the channel? In the business-to-business market, you have to determine whether you want to deal directly with the business user or engage the services of an industrial distributor.

✔ **What types of distribution channel components should you use?** For example, will you sell your product in department stores, discount houses, mail-order establishments, variety stores, or drugstores?

✔ **Should you use multiple channels of distribution or just one?** In some cases, you may want to deal direct. In others, you may want to use a wholesaler or other middleman who will sell to the retailer.

The channel of distribution that's right for you depends on a number of factors, which I show you in Table 8-2.

Table 8-2   Choosing the Length of the Distribution Channel

Factor	*Deal Direct*	*Use Intermediaries*
Number of customers	Fewer customers	More customers
Geographic location of the customers	Concentrated in a geographic area	Spread out
Size of the order	Large	Small
Value of the product	High value	Low unit price
Product perishability	Short shelf life	Long shelf life
Technical nature	Complex product	Nontechnical — you won't need specially trained representatives

Chapter 9

Researching Export Markets

*I*f you want to be a successful exporter, you need to research your potential markets before you get into the game. *Market research* is the process of collecting data and putting that data into a format that you can use to identify opportunities and limitations within those individual foreign markets.

Sure, you can begin exporting without doing any research, but research reduces uncertainty. It gives you the information you need to decide which countries offer the best opportunities for success. In this chapter, I guide you through the process of conducting market research for your export business so you have the best chance to succeed.

Taking a Step-by-Step Approach to Export Market Research

When you're starting to think about exporting a product to other countries, you may have visions of conquering the world: "My product will be on every store shelf in every country in the world!" Just as you need to choose the product that's right for you (see Chapter 5), you need to choose the market or country that's right for your product.

In this section, I walk you through a step-by-step approach that helps you identify the more desirable markets while passing over those that are less than desirable.

Screening your potential markets

When you're screening potential markets, pay attention to the needs of the markets as well as which markets are growing and offer you the greatest potential for success. In this section, I show you how to do that.

Step 1: Focus on needs

A logical first step is to conduct an initial screening based on need. A *need* is a lack of something. If a market doesn't need your product, no amount of effort on your part will allow you to successfully market goods in that country. For example, if your product is air conditioners, you likely wouldn't find much of a market for them in Iceland.

Try locating statistics on current product exports to the countries you're considering. With this information, you can identify which products are being sold where and by whom. If a product is being sold in the market, you'll be able to identify whether a need or demand exists for your product.

To get export statistics, check out the following:

- ✔ **International Trade Administration (ITA):** The ITA promotes trade and investment and ensures fair trade and compliance with trade laws and agreements. On the ITA website (www.ita.doc.gov), you can access information and services on U.S. international trade policy.

- ✔ **U.S. Exports of Domestic and Foreign Merchandise report:** The U.S. Census Bureau publishes the U.S. Exports of Domestic and Foreign Merchandise (EM545) report, which is available at www.census.gov/foreign-trade/reference/products/catalog/ftdproductsa.html. The report is extremely valuable because it allows you to compute the average price of the unit exported.

- ✔ **U.S. International Trade in Goods and Services report:** The U.S. Department of Commerce releases trade statistics in its U.S. International Trade in Goods and Services report (referred to as FT900). To access and download this report, visit www.census.gov/foreign-trade/Press-Release/current_press_release/.

- ✔ **USA Trade Online:** USA Trade Online (www.usatradeonline.gov) provides U.S. import and export statistics from more than 18,000 commodities traded worldwide, as well as the most current merchandise trade statistics. You can subscribe online or by calling 800-549-0595, option 4, or 301-763-2311. The cost is $75 per month or $300 per year.

  You can also access this site at no charge at more than 1,100 federal depository libraries nationwide. To find a federal depository library near you, go to www.gpoaccess.gov/libraries.html. This site is a service of the U.S. Government Printing Office (GPO).

Step 2: Narrow down the list of countries

Narrow down the list of countries by identifying five or so of the fastest growing markets for your product. Determine whether this growth has been consistent over the past few years.

Look at sales over the past two to four years. Try to identify those markets where the growth has been consistent from year to year. Also, try to figure out whether economic conditions (such as inflation or recession) could've impacted these trends.

Step 3: Develop a secondary list

Come up with a secondary list of countries — ones that may not be as large as your top five but that may provide opportunities for future growth. Look for markets that are beginning to grow and that have fewer competitors than those in your top five. If an emerging market is beginning to open, you may find the number of competitors less than you find in established markets. The countries representing these up-and-coming markets should also have higher growth rates, thus offering some exciting potential.

Step 4: Narrow down the list to the most-promising markets

Narrow down the list to what you consider the most-promising markets. Consult with the trade consultant at your local district office of the U.S. Department of Commerce. Also consult with Small Business Development Centers (www.sba.gov/sbdc), freight forwarders, business associates, and others before moving on to the assessment stage.

Assessing your target markets

A *market* is a particular group of people who have the authority, willingness, and desire to take advantage of the products that you're offering. The *target market* is the specific segment to which you direct your marketing strategies.

After going through the initial screening and identifying countries that have a basic need for your product, evaluate each of these options in relation to the environmental forces — financial, economic, political, legal, socio-cultural, competitive, and so on (see Chapter 1 for more on environmental forces). This section covers those forces.

Step 1: Focus on financial and economic forces

Your first step is to look at factors such as trends in inflation rates, exchange rates, balance of payments, and interest rates. Credit availability and the paying habits of customers are other factors to consider.

A country's *balance of payments* (BOP) is a summary of all economic transactions between that country and the rest of the world over a given period of time. It measures the movement of money into and out of a country. If more money is leaving the country (through imports) than is coming into the country (through exports), the country has a deficit. If more money is flowing into a country than leaving it, the country has a surplus.

If a country has a surplus in its BOP, you may see more potential to export goods to that country. On the other hand, if the BOP is running at a deficit, this may not be an attractive market in which to export your goods — but you may find some interesting importing opportunities there.

One financial force to consider is fluctuations in the exchange rates. A strong U.S. dollar makes American goods more expensive in foreign markets, and a weak U.S. dollar makes American products more affordable there. In other words, a strong U.S. dollar hurts U.S. exporters but benefits U.S. importers.

Step 2: Pay attention to political and legal forces

After considering financial and economic forces, look at elements such as entry barriers to the market, exchange rate controls, and other barriers such as political instability, tax laws, safety standards, price controls, and so on.

Entry barriers, such as tariffs and quotas, can hinder your ability to export goods to a country. A *tariff,* or duty, is a tax on goods being imported into a country. A high tariff may make a product too expensive, eliminating a country from your consideration. A *quota* is a limit on the amount of goods from a specific country over a specified period of time, which can restrict your ability to sell as well.

Go to http://export.gov/logistics/eg_main_018142.asp for tariff and tax information for exporting to 110 countries. Or check out CUSTOMS Info (http://export.customsinfo.com). Users of this free service can look up country tariff information for shipments originating in the United States. You're required to register for access to this free service, but a valid e-mail address is all that's required to sign up.

The subscription-based version of this service is helpful if you want to source products from countries such as China and then ship them to some country (other than the U.S.) where you have contacts. Subscribers to CUSTOMS Info can look up tariff information for shipments that originate and ship from any country to any other country in the CUSTOMS Info Global Tariffs database. Subscribers also benefit from additional sources of exporter information, such as the following:

> ✔ **ECCN Finder:** The Export Control Classification Number (ECCN) is a five-character number for every export product that identifies the category, product group, type of control, and country group level of control

as specified in the U.S. Commerce Control List. The ECCN Finder helps exporters match Schedule B numbers with ECCNs to help find items that have been flagged by the U.S. government for export control.

A *Schedule B number* is a U.S. Census Bureau publication based on the Harmonized Commodity Description and Coding System.

 ✔ **GISTnet:** At www.gistnet.com, you can look up guides for 210 countries to get info on export requirements, restrictions, contacts, and reference data.

For information on political and policy stability, check out the following:

 ✔ **Political Risk Services:** Political Risk Services (http://prsgroup.com) publishes 100 country reports that monitor the risks to international business over the next five years. International Country Risk Guides (ICRGs) and related publications monitor 161 countries, rating a wide range of risks to international businesses.

 ✔ **Business Environment Risk Intelligence:** Business Environment Risk Intelligence (BERI; http://beri.com) provides clients with individual country risk reports.

Step 3: Suss out socio-cultural forces

Culture is the sum total of all the beliefs, values, rules, techniques, and institutions that characterize populations. You need to be aware of the components of a culture (see Chapter 1) in order to make sure your product and the country in question are a good match.

Go to www.cyborlink.com for brief descriptions of various countries' populations, cultural heritages, languages, and religions. You can also find information on do's and don'ts of appearance, behavior, and communication for an extensive list of countries.

Another interesting site to explore is www.countryreports.org, which provides country information on a wide range of topics, including cultural information, customs and culture (including eating, recipes, fashion, family, socializing, religion, sports and recreation, and holidays), geography, history, national symbols, economy, population, and government. Costs to gain complete access to the entire site are $4.75 for 5 days, $8.75 for 60 days, or $18 for one year.

Step 4: Consider competitive forces

Considering competitive forces means looking at the following:

 ✔ The number and size of competitors

 ✔ Competitors' marketing strategies relating to promotion, pricing, and distribution

✔ The quality levels of competitors' products

✔ Whether competitors' products are imported or locally produced

✔ The extent to which competitors cover the market

These are just some of the questions that management needs to evaluate pertaining to the presence of competition in a potential market. Understanding the competitor and its operations is critical for success.

You can identify sources of competition, along with domestic production in targeted countries, by using the Industry Sector Analysis Reports prepared by the U.S. Department of Commerce. They're available in the Market Research Library found at www.export.gov.

Making conclusions

After reviewing all the data, you have to decide which markets will allow you to make the most effective and efficient use of your resources. In general, if you're new to exporting, one or two countries may be enough to start with.

Analysis is important, but nothing's better than a personal visit to the market that appears to offer the best potential. Here are two U.S. Department of Commerce programs that can assist you in making your initial visits to a foreign market:

✔ **Matchmaker Trade Delegations:** The U.S. Department of Commerce matches U.S. firms with prospective agents, distributors, and other kinds of business contacts overseas. Trade specialists evaluate the potential of a U.S. firm's product, find and screen contacts, and handle logistics. This is followed by an intensive trip filled with meetings with prospective clients and in-depth briefings on the economic and business climate of the countries visited.

✔ **Gold Key Service:** This is a program of the U.S. Commercial Service, which assists U.S. companies in securing one-on-one appointments with prescreened agents, distributors, sales representatives, and other strategic business partners in targeted export countries. Fees for this service can vary depending on the scope of the work and the country. As an example, the cost for Gold Key Service for Saudi Arabia is $765 for the first day and $385 for subsequent days.

For information on both of these services, contact a trade specialist at your local Department of Commerce Export Assistance Center (www.buyusa. gov/home/us.html).

Doing Research Online

Export.gov (www.export.gov) is the U.S. government's one-stop portal for current and potential U.S. exporters. It consolidates export programs and foreign market intelligence across 19 federal agencies and presents it on one easy-to-use website. This site guides people who are new to exporting through the export process step by step. It also provides detailed foreign market information, industry market intelligence, information on federal export assistance and financing programs, and trade leads (on a subscription basis).

Here's a sample of some of the kinds of useful documents you can get from using the resources available at Export.gov:

- ✔ **Background Notes:** Background Notes (www.state.gov/r/pa/ei/bgn/) provide info on a country's geography, people, government, economy, history, political conditions, foreign relations, and more.

- ✔ **Country Commercial Guides:** Country Commercial Guides (or "Doing Business In" guides) are how-to guides on doing business in more than 120 countries. They include information about market conditions, best export prospects, export financing, distributors, and legal and cultural issues for each country. You can access these guides by going to www.buyusainfo.net, selecting the country you're interested in from the country drop-down list, and selecting "Country Commercial Guides [CCG]" from the report type list. This information is also available on Export.gov.

- ✔ **Industry sector analysis reports:** Industry sector analysis reports are market research reports produced in-country by a Foreign Commercial Services officer. They provide insight into specific industry and service sectors, and they cover market size and outlook, characteristics, competition, and opportunities. The reports include the following industries:

  - Aerospace and defense
  - Agribusiness
  - Apparel and textiles
  - Automotive and ground transportation
  - Chemicals, petrochemicals, and composites
  - Construction, building, and heavy equipment
  - Consumer goods and home furnishings
  - Energy and mining
  - Environmental technologies
  - Food processing and packaging

- Health technologies

- Industrial equipment and supplies

- Information and communication

- Marine industries

- Paper, printing, and graphic arts

- Security and safety

- Services

- Used and reconditioned equipment

This information is also available free of charge in the U.S. Commercial Market Research Library. Just go to www.buyusainfo.net and select the industry you're interested in from the industry drop-down list. You can also go to Export.gov to access this info.

✔ **International market insight reports:** International market insight reports are custom reports prepared on a case-by-case basis by the economic and commercial sections of U.S. embassies and consulates for the U.S. Commercial Service. They assist in identifying unique market situations and opportunities for U.S. businesses, and they're available through the National Technical Information Service (NTIS; www.ntis.gov) or at www.buyusa.gov.

Chapter 10

Researching Import Markets

. . . .

In This Chapter

▶ Researching the market at home

▶ Understanding your competitors and their marketing strategies

▶ Recognizing the research benefits of trade shows and merchandise marts

. . . .

To succeed as an importer, you need to understand the characteristics of the buyers and the strengths and weaknesses of your competitors. You need to compile data on the competition's products and the alternative marketing strategies that they're using to satisfy the needs of their customers. Of course, you can begin the process of importing without research, but research reduces uncertainty, providing information that you can use to make decisions as you get started.

After you've identified the product that you're going to import (see Chapter 5), you need to understand how those products are marketed in the United States. You identify your target market and try to find out which other business are selling similar products to your target market. You use research to determine what the competitors are selling, how they're selling it, the pricing programs they're using, how they're promoting the product, and which distribution channels they're using (see Chapter 8).

The purpose of this chapter is to show you how to take your import product and use available research tools to better understand your customers and the competitive forces in the market. I show you how to identify your target market for your import, how to look for a trade show or merchandise mart in your area, and what sort of data you need to collect.

Identifying the Characteristics of Potential Buyers

Market research starts with identifying the target market (see Chapter 8). The *target market* is a part of the market as a whole — it's the particular group of people you're going to focus your attention on.

A *market* is comprised of individuals or organizations with needs to satisfy, who have the authority, willingness, and desire to take advantage of the product that you're selling. There are two different markets — the consumer market and the business-to-business market. The consumer market consists of individuals who buy goods for personal or household use; the business-to-business market consists of organizations that buy goods for the purpose of producing another product, to resell the items to other businesses or to consumers, or to use the goods in the operations of their own business.

All customers in the consumer and business-to-business markets have these three essential characteristics:

✔ **They have a particular need.** People have all kinds of needs, including basic survival needs (food, shelter), rational needs (dependability, durability), and emotional needs (security, friendship, acceptance).

✔ **They have enough money to buy what you're selling.** Just because someone *wants* something doesn't mean she has enough money to buy it.

✔ **They have decision-making power or the authority to make the purchase.** Take your time and find the person who has the actual authority to make the choice of buying your product.

Based on these characteristics, your job as an importer is to answer the following questions:

✔ What need does my product or service satisfy?

✔ Who needs and can afford what I'm offering?

✔ Who has the authority to say "yes" to the product or service I'm offering?

Your answers to these questions form the foundation of what you need to find out from your marketing research efforts. When you know who your target market is, you can find out more about the specific characteristics of the customers you're targeting by looking at their interests, age, heritage, income level, education, sex, family status, and occupation.

Researching Your Competitors

A critical part of market research is finding out who your competitors are. Being aware of the strengths and weaknesses of specific competitors can help you identify problems and opportunities that you want to address in your own business. Knowing what the competition does right (and wrong), what competitors charge for their products or services, and where they seem to be headed can give your business a significant boost. In this section, I note the type of information you need, direct you to some publications, and tell you how to do a little detective work at trade shows and merchandise markets.

Knowing what kind of info to look for

You need to examine the markets on the basis of a variety of elements of competition, such as the following:

✔ **The number of competitors:** If you find a market that includes a lot of competitors, you may decide to change focus or look for another product.

✔ **The competitors'** *market share* **(the proportion of total sales of a product during a particular period of time in a particular market controlled by a particular company):** The market share tells you whether the market is dominated by key players. If a few companies have a bulk of the market share, you may decide to direct your efforts to other products or markets. Or you may discover that customers are looking for another choice because they're unhappy with the firms that are currently controlling the market.

If you find the market dominated by many firms or a few large firms, consider focusing on a particular niche, a market segment that isn't as large but may be more profitable. For example, you may decide to import a sari, the traditional female garment in India, Pakistan, Bangladesh, Nepal, and Sri Lanka, instead of focusing on women's clothing, a much broader category.

✔ **The competitors' marketing strategies:** Identify their product, pricing, promotion, and distribution strategies.

✔ **The effectiveness of your competitors' promotional programs:** Promotion is anything that the firm uses to inform, persuade, influence, or remind the target market about the product the firm is offering.

✔ **The quality of your competitors' products:** How does your product compare? Is quality a factor, and if so, can you charge a higher price for a higher-quality product? If the quality of your products is lower, will you have lower prices?

✔ **Your competitors' pricing policies:** Are they using a skimming or penetration strategies? *Skimming* involves entering the market with high prices, placing an emphasis on profits. *Penetration* involves selling the goods at low prices, focusing on sales volume.

✔ **Your competitors' distribution policies:** What channels of distribution are your competitors using? Are they dealing direct with consumers or business buyers, or are they using intermediaries (wholesalers, retailers, or industrial distributors)? Are your competitors offering any trade discounts, offering consignment merchandise, absorbing freight expenses, or extending payment terms?

✔ **The extent to which your competitors cover the market:** This review may show you that they're missing something that can, in turn, be an opportunity to you.

Finding and organizing your information

When researching the competition, follow these steps:

1. **List your key competitors.**

2. **Rank the competitors according to overall strength.**

3. **Identify which of the companies from Step 1 is your most vulnerable competitor.**

4. **List the competitive changes you anticipate in the future.**

5. **For each competitor in Step 1, identify the following:**

   - Its principal competitive strength

   - Its overall marketing strategies

   - The products it offers and the strengths and weaknesses of those products

   - How it's selling its products (is it using its own sales force, or is it employing the services of manufacturers' agents?)

   - The market segments it's selling to

   - The form type and amount of advertising or sales promotion it uses

   - Its pricing approach

   - Any reason for customer preferences of products from a specific company

   - Whether the competitor poses any specific opportunities or threats

Here are some secondary research sources that can assist you in performing this competitive analysis:

- ✔ **Trade associations and business directories:** You can locate a trade association and business directories for any industry by using the *Encyclopedia of Business Information Sources* or the *Encyclopedia of Associations,* both published by Gale Research. Also, *The American Wholesalers and Distributors Directory* includes details on more than 18,000 wholesalers and distributors.

- ✔ **Direct-mail lists:** You can purchase mailing lists for practically any type of business. The Standard Rates and Data Service (SRDS) Directory of Mailing Lists is a good place to start looking. The SRDS directory is a catalog and directory of every commercially available mailing list, including source details and references to the list broker and/or manager, by category.

Most major public libraries have a current or year-old set of SRDS directories, and some libraries have the directory on computer. You can also access the directory at www.srds.com and, for an annual subscription fee, use all the SRDS directories and updates on an unlimited basis.

✔ **Market research:** Someone may have already compiled the research you need. MarketResearch.com (www.marketresearch.com) is a provider of market intelligence products and services. Their collection gives you access to research from a wide variety of sources, providing business information on industries, demographics, regions, companies, products, and trends. Other directories of business research include *Simmons Study of Media and Markets* (Simmons Market Research Bureau, Inc.) and the *ACNielsen Retail Index* (ACNielsen Co.).

Going undercover: Researching at trade shows and merchandise marts

Whether you're an existing company looking for ways to expand your operations or you're an entrepreneur looking to start your own import business, your company is in a precarious position. The marketplace is constantly changing. Companies are always introducing new products or implementing new marketing strategies. To succeed, you need to know what's going on within your chosen industry segment.

As an importer, you can accomplish a lot by attending trade shows, visiting local merchandise marts, and talking to prospective customers. At these events and locations, companies are trying to sell products similar to the ones that you're interested in importing. There's no better place to access the kind of competitive data you need. This kind of research is not time-consuming, complex, or expensive.

A *trade show* is an exhibition organized so that companies in a specific industry can showcase and demonstrate their products and services. A *merchandise mart* is a permanent trading center or marketplace housing manufacturers or regional wholesale showrooms; their main goal is to join legitimate buyers with manufacturers and wholesalers.

I'm not suggesting that you make an investment by renting space, setting up a booth, and attempting to sell your products at these shows. I'm saying that *visiting* a trade show as a guest and becoming a sort of detective is the best approach. There's nothing illegal, immoral, or unethical about visiting the booth of a company that's selling a product you're thinking about importing.

A case study: Researching markets for Bolivian pewter giftware

I was once approached by a firm in Bolivia that manufactured pewter giftware items. The manufacturer presented me with information about the product line and preliminary pricing levels.

Before I could decide whether I was interested in handling the products, I had to determine how this category of products was marketed in the United States, as well as whether this manufacturer's products were competitive and would fit into the marketplace. My starting point with this project was to identify my target market. I decided that I would target either gift wholesalers or some of the larger retail stores selling giftware products.

My next step was to research which other firms were acting as suppliers of pewter giftware items to my selected target market (gift wholesalers and larger gift retailers). I needed the names of these companies, the mix of products that they were offering (such as cups, goblets, candlesticks, and so on), and their wholesale and suggested retail prices.

I identified a merchandise mart in New York that specialized in giftware items being sold to the trade. I identified myself as the owner of a firm involved in the giftware business and was given a listing of exhibitors at the merchandise mart. In the index of the listing, I identified all the firms in the building that were offering pewter giftware items in their showrooms. Then I visited each of these showrooms. During my visit to a showroom, I looked at the different types of pewter the exhibitor was selling. I tried to identify whether the items were imported (and if so, which country they came from) or manufactured domestically. During the visit, I collected brochures and noted the wholesale prices and suggested retail prices.

After making the rounds, I returned to my office with a far better understanding of how the giftware market worked, what sort of pewter items were being sold, and how they were being sold. With this data, I was able to go back to my contact in Bolivia and develop an import program, narrowing his product offerings and deciding to focus on those items where research showed me that he could be competitive with the comparable items currently in the market.

Where to find a trade show or merchandise mart

You can find trade shows all over the world. Two good resources are available at most local libraries. Ask the reference librarian whether your library has either of these books:

- ✔ *Trade Shows Worldwide: An International Directory of Events, Facilities, and Suppliers* (The Gale Group) provides detailed information from more than 75 countries on more than 10,800 trade shows and exhibitions.

- ✔ *The Directory of Business Information Resources: Association, Newsletters, Magazines, and Trade Shows* (Grey House Publishing) provides concise information on associations, newsletters, magazines, and trade shows for each of 90 major industry groups.

If your library doesn't carry these books, don't run out and buy them. They're very expensive, and odds are, your library has another trade show directory that you can use instead.

In addition to checking at your local library, you can find all kinds of information online:

- ✔ **Global Sources Trade Show Center** (`tradeshow.globalsources.com`)**:** This is a free website that provides current, detailed information on more than 1,000 major trade shows worldwide, including events within the United States, with an emphasis on "Asia and Greater China." You can search for a trade show by product, supplier, country, and month of the year.

- ✔ **The Javits Center** (`www.javitscenter.com/events.aspx?mid=244`)**:** Located in New York City, the Javits Center is home to many trade shows. This website lists upcoming shows at the center.

- ✔ **BizTradeShows** (`www.biztradeshows.com`)**:** This online directory of trade fairs and business events brings you a detailed list of exhibitions, trade shows, expositions, conferences, and seminars for various industries worldwide. You can search for trade shows by industry, country, city, and date and get information on individual trade events, along with their event profile, organizer, exhibitor and visitor profile, venues, and dates.

- ✔ **Trade Show News Network/TSNN** (`www.tsnn.com`)**:** This online database allows you to search for trade show events by the event name, industry, city, state, country, and date.

Merchandise marts are kind of like permanent trade shows. A particular trade show is usually held once or twice a year, whereas the merchandise marts are open year-round, possibly on a specific schedule program. If you miss a trade show because of scheduling conflicts, a merchandise mart is a great alternative.

You can find a directory of merchandise marts by state at `resources.com`. Here are some specific merchandise marts you may want to check out:

- ✔ **AmericasMart Atlanta,** 240 Peachtree St. NW, Suite 2200, Atlanta, GA 30303-1327; phone 404-220-3000; website `www.americasmart.com`

- ✔ **California Market Center,** 110 E. 9th St., Suite A727, Los Angeles, CA 90079; phone 213-630-3600; website `www.californiamarketcenter.com`

- ✔ **The Park Expo and Conference Center** (formerly the Charlotte Merchandise Mart), 2500 E. Independence Blvd., Charlotte, NC 28205; phone 704-333-7709; website `www.ppm-nc.com`

- ✔ **Columbus MarketPlace,** 7001 Discovery Blvd., Dublin, OH; phone 888-332-8979 or 614-339-5100; website `www.thecolumbusmarketplace.com`

✔ **Dallas Market Center,** 2100 Stemmons Freeway, Dallas, TX 75207; phone 800-325-6587 or 214-655-6100; website www.dallasmarketcenter.com

✔ **Denver Merchandise Mart,** 451 E. 58th Ave., Suite 4270, Denver, CO 80216-8470; phone 303-292-6278; website www.denvermart.com

✔ **Gift Mart of Kansas City,** 9517 B Metcalf Ave., Overland Park, KS 66212; phone 913-687-8059; website www.giftmartofkansascity.com

✔ **L.A. Mart,** 1933 S. Broadway, Los Angeles, CA 90007; phone 800-526-2784; website www.lamart.com

✔ **The Merchandise Mart,** 222 Merchandise Mart Plaza, Chicago, IL 60654; phone 312-527-4141; website www.merchandisemart.com

✔ **Miami International Merchandise Mart,** 777 NW 72nd Ave., Miami, FL 33126; phone 305-269-4811; website www.miamimerchandisemart.com

✔ **Minneapolis Mart,** 10301 Bren Rd. W., Minnetonka, MN 55343; phone 800-626-1298 or 952-932-7200; website www.mplsgiftmart.com

The New Mart, 127 E. Ninth St., Los Angeles, CA 90015; phone 213-627-0671; website www.newmart.net

✔ **New York MarketCenter,** 230 Fifth Ave., New York, NY 10001; phone 800-698-5617; website www.230fifthave.com

✔ **The New York Merchandise Mart,** 41 Madison Ave., 39th Floor, New York, NY 10010; phone 212-686-1203; website www.41madison.com

✔ **Northeast Market Center,** 1000 Technology Park Dr., Billerica, MA 01821 phone 978-670-6363 or 800-435-2775; website www.northeast marketcenter.com

✔ **Pacific Design Center,** 8687 Melrose Ave., West Hollywood, CA 90069; phone 310-657-0800; website www.pacificdesigncenter.com

✔ **Pacific Market Center,** 6100 4th Ave. S., Seattle, WA 98108; phone 800-433-1014 or 206-767-6800; website www.pacificmarketcenter.com

✔ **San Francisco Giftcenter & Jewelrymart,** 888 Brannan St., Suite 609, San Francisco, CA 94103; phone 415-861-7733; website www.sfgcjm.com

✔ **7 W New York,** 7 W. 34th St., New York, NY 10001; phone 212-279-6063; website www.7wnewyork.com

What to do when you get there

When you visit a trade show or merchandise mart, gather as much data as possible about the items you're considering importing. Remember, you aren't attending the trade show to exhibit products — you're there to learn about the items you want to import and how they're being marketed and distributed in the United States.

Identify exhibitors that are selling products similar to yours and do the following during your visit:

- ✔ **Identify their marketing strategies.** What is their product mix? How are they pricing the items? What are some of their promotional programs? How are the products being distributed?

- ✔ **Determine the quality level of competitive products.** How do the products being presented at the show or in the mart compare? Is quality a factor when the customer is deciding to purchase?

Make note of any differences between the products you want to import and those that are already in the marketplace. You may be able to identify opportunities in the marketplace that you can take advantage of (for example, lower prices, improved quality, unique product features, and so on).

When you're talking to people at trade shows and merchandise marts, be subtle. You don't want to come right out and say, "Hey, I'm thinking of importing a product like this." You need to be a detective of sorts. In some cases, you may get the most information by saying that you're interested in purchasing the exhibitor's products. Here are some questions you may want to ask:

- ✔ What are the features and/or specifications of this product?

- ✔ Where was this product made?

- ✔ What are your most recent product introductions?

- ✔ Where are your goods distributed from?

- ✔ What are your pricing policies? Do you offer credit terms, discount policies, promotional incentives?

Ask for brochures, catalogs, and price lists.

After your initial conversation, if you feel comfortable with the people you've been talking to — and if *they* seem comfortable with you — you *may* want to take a risk and ask a more intrusive question, such as one of the following:

- ✔ Who are your suppliers, and are you satisfied with them?

- ✔ Would you consider switching vendors? (You may even say, "I have a similar product that could be imported from *<country name>*. I'd like to make a sales presentation to you at your office sometime if that's possible.")

- ✔ What factors do you consider when making a decision to purchase an item?

Don't overstay your welcome or take up too much of a person's time. Be a keen observer of her body language and tone of voice. The goal is to get information, not to annoy people.

Chapter 11

Making Export Contacts and Finding Customers

*I*n this chapter, I explain how to make contacts and find customers in other countries for the goods that you've decided to export. After you've identified the most promising markets and the strategies to enter them, the next step is to locate actual customers. If a customer is the end user of your product, the result may be a simple transaction. Otherwise, you may need a representative or distributor in that country to reach the eventual user.

You may be able to identify customers by attending trade shows, participating in trade missions, or engaging in alternative promotional programs such as direct mail. When you're identifying contacts and developing sales leads, you need to know who the potential buyers are, which trade shows will be most effective, and which marketing techniques will work the best.

This chapter guides you through the various sources that you can use to locate customers and evaluate trade shows and missions. Your job is to take advantage of these sources and match them with your selected products and markets.

U.S. Department of Commerce Business Contact Programs

The U.S. Department of Commerce (DOC) assists exporters in identifying and qualifying leads for potential customers, distributors, agents, joint venture partners, and licensees, using both private and public sources. The DOC has an extensive network of foreign *commercial service officers* who are product, country, and program experts in countries that represent more than 95 percent of the markets for U.S. goods.

The officers provide these services at U.S. embassies and consulates around the world. If these offices aren't staffed, the economic officer from the U.S. State Department in the embassy or consulate can provide these services.

In this section, I cover the various DOC business contact programs you can take advantage of. These programs can provide critical information about international markets and targeted marketing services to help you evaluate your export potential and assist you in making contacts and finding prequalified buyers overseas.

If you have any questions, contact a trade specialist at the nearest DOC Export Assistance Center — go to `export.gov/eac/` and enter your zip code to find the center nearest you. Or you can call the Trade Information Center at 800-872-8723. Information on DOC programs is also available at `export.gov`.

International Partner Search

The *International Partner Search* is a customized search for qualified agents, distributors, and representatives on behalf of a U.S. exporter — a search that doesn't require the exporter to travel overseas. Commercial officers based in consulates and embassies around the world prepare a report and deliver detailed information on up to five prescreened international companies that have reviewed your product literature and expressed an interest in representing you. You receive contact information as well as some general comments about the reputation of the agent/distributor, her reliability, and so on.

You can get an International Partner Search application form by contacting the trade specialist at your local Export Assistance Center (`export.gov/eac/`). The fees depend on the scope of the work involved, but expect to pay around $700 or $800 (possibly more, possibly less).

Commercial News USA

Commercial News USA is the official export promotion magazine for the DOC. It provides worldwide exposure for U.S. products and services through an illustrated magazine and website (`www.thinkglobal.us`). The magazine, which is published in both English and Spanish editions, serves as a showcase for American-made products and services. Each issue reaches an estimated 400,000 readers in 178 countries. You can download a PDF of the latest issue from the website.

Trade leads generated by *Commercial News USA* can help you identify export markets and contacts that can lead to direct sales, representation, or distributorship agreements. If you're interested in advertising in *Commercial News USA,* call 800-581-8533. Listings in *Commercial News USA* describe the features of your export product or service together with your name, address, phone number, and e-mail address.

Commercial News USA also covers a variety of industry categories, including the following:

- Agriculture
- Automotive/aviation and marine products
- Business services
- Consumer goods
- Electrical/electronics
- Environmental
- Franchising
- Health and beauty/fashion
- Hotel and restaurant services and suppliers
- Information technology/telecommunications
- Materials
- Medical/scientific
- Safety and security
- Sports and recreation

Commercial News USA excludes pharmaceuticals, medicines, agricultural commodities, sexually oriented products, alcoholic beverages, and arms and ammunitions. Any items listed in the publication must be at least 51 percent U.S. content.

Customized Market Research

The Customized Market Research program is generated by the U.S. Commercial Service, which is the trade promotion unit of the International Trade Administration. In 107 U.S. cities and in more than 80 countries, the U.S. Commercial Service has trade specialists who will work with your company to help you get started in exporting or to increase your sales to new global markets.

The *Customized Market Research Report* is an individualized response to issues related to your specific product or services. Trade specialists conduct interviews and surveys before providing you with info on the overall market-ability of your product, main competitors, competitive pricing, distribution and promotion practices, trade restrictions, and potential business partners. Fees for such research are subject to the scope of the work but can range from $1,000 to $5,000 per report per country.

The Video Market Briefing service also provides market research for specific products together with an evaluation of alternative market-entry strategies and a formal written report. Additionally, you'll participate in a videoconference with local industry professionals so you can get immediate answers to any questions you may have.

For information on the Customized Market Research program and the Video Market Briefing service, contact the trade counselor at your local Export Assistance Center (export.gov/eac/).

International Company Profile

The International Company Profile is a program of the U.S. Commercial Services that checks the reputation, reliability, and financial status of a prospective trading partner. It provides information on the type of organization, the year it was established, the size of the business, the business's general reputation, and the territory covered by the business, as well as the business's product lines, principal owners, preferred language, and financial/trade references. The profile also provides the commercial officer's comments on the suitability of the company as a trading partner.

Many businesses use the International Company Profile program as their main source of information in the final process of qualifying potential foreign clients. It can also be beneficial in evaluating the creditworthiness of companies in the international marketplace.

For example, suppose you're a U.S. exporter and you receive a significant order from a German importer that you know nothing about. Or suppose you need information on a potential overseas sales agent, or you need to know the current product lines of a prospective foreign distributor. Because of the long distances and unfamiliar business practices, you need as much information about a potential partner as possible. Before accepting this order, appointing an agent, or working with a distributor, sound business practices require you to minimize your risks — which you can do by acquiring an International Company Profile.

Fees for the International Company Profile depend on the scope of the work. Contact the trade counselor at your local Export Assistance Center for an application (export.gov/eac/).

Trade Leads Database

The Trade Leads Database provides you with potential customer contacts and info on foreign government tenders gathered through international U.S. Commercial Service offices. The objective of the program is to expand U.S. exports by providing U.S. suppliers with credible, complete, and timely trade leads from reputable firms around the world. *Trade leads* may be requests for manufactured goods, services, representation, investment, joint ventures, licensing, or foreign government procurement bids. The database is designed to provide U.S. exporters with

- ✔ Specific market opportunities from overseas buyers with serious intent
- ✔ The information necessary to follow up on the leads

All U.S. firms capable of exporting, trade associations, banks, state trade and development agencies, chambers of commerce, export trading/management companies, information vendors, newsletters, and other trade information distributors are current clients of this program.

Here's how it works: U.S. and Foreign Commercial Services (US&FCS) personnel in overseas posts gather private and public trade leads through routine activities such as trade shows, seminars, market research studies, International Partner Searches (covered earlier in this chapter), and personal contacts. The leads may be for a one-time sale or for a continuing source of supply.

All trade leads are free of charge and available through `export.gov/tradeleads/index.asp`. To access the database, you're required to register, which simply involves providing your name, address, and other contact information.

If you're interested in exploring a posted trade opportunity, you can reply directly to the requester/buyer cited as the contact in each lead. The trade specialists at the local Export Assistance Center (`export.gov/eac/`) will advise you of any leads that may be of interest and provide assistance in responding to them. The specialists can also help you in following up to facilitate sales.

Gold Key Service

Gold Key Service is a program that helps U.S. businesses secure one-on-one appointments with potential prescreened business partners. The services also include market research, onsite briefings, interpreter services for meetings, and assistance in developing follow-up services.

The Gold Key Service is especially beneficial to firms that have an interest in expanding the operations of their existing organization. The service is costly (fees depend on the scope of the work), but the DOC will do all the preliminary work, making sure that the time and funds spent during the visit will be used effectively and efficiently.

Video Gold Key Service is an alternative approach to Gold Key Service. It likewise includes scheduled meetings with potential business partners and an industry briefing with trade professionals; however, all meetings take place through videoconference.

You can get more information on both services by contacting the trade specialist at your local Export Assistance Center (export.gov/eac/).

Platinum Key Service

Platinum Key Service is a level above Gold Key Service (see the preceding section). This customized service provides support on a much wider range of issues for which you may need a more sustained level of assistance. The services provided can include (but are not limited to) identifying markets, introducing new products, and identifying major project opportunities.

Platinum Key Service also provides some unique options:

- **Government tender support:** Many foreign governments announce requests for quotations on a wide variety of goods. Often, these requests come from government agencies (such as the Ministry of Health) and are awarded through a competitive bidding process. These requests for quotations are a major source of business, and one of the benefits of Platinum Key Service is that it identifies areas in which your company may be able to participate in the bidding process.

- **Assistance in the reduction of market access barriers:** Many countries decide to impose barriers to trade to protect their domestic industries or to improve their balance of trade and/or payment positions. These barriers take the form of *tariffs* (taxes on goods being imported into a country), *quotas* (limits on the amount of a specific good that a country allows to be imported), and *subsidies* (government assistance programs for domestic goods). Platinum Key Service works with the authorities to reduce these barriers and create sales opportunities.

- **Assistance on regulatory and/or technical standards matters:** When you're doing business with other countries, you soon find out that all countries have almost as many regulatory agencies to deal with as you find in the United States. Platinum Key Service guides you through this process, making you aware of all the detailed requirements that you need to comply with in your attempt to do business internationally.

Platinum Key Service is best suited for existing businesses that are looking to expand their operations abroad. The fees for this program are subject to the scope of the work and the desired length of assistance (six months, one year, and so on).

U.S. Department of Commerce Trade Event Programs

Depending on the nature of your product, you may have trouble selling it to a buyer just by writing and presenting sales literature. Many buyers want to examine the product in person — in many cases, there's just no substitute for an actual presentation. You can make such a presentation by participating in trade shows, trade missions, matchmaker delegations, and catalog exhibitions.

Exhibiting at trade shows is a very expensive option, one you should consider only if you're looking to expand the operations of an existing business. If you're an entrepreneur, you can use these shows to do some product and market research, as opposed to exhibiting. I discuss research at trade shows in Chapter 10.

Many private and government-sponsored trade shows exist. Because of the expense involved, you may want to consider participating in a Department of Commerce–U.S. Pavilion if you're new to exporting. Go to export.gov and click on the "Trade Events" link to find information on all future DOC-sponsored trade events or shows.

Trade Fair Certification program

The U.S. Commercial Service's Trade Fair Certification program is a cooperative arrangement between private-sector trade-show organizers and the U.S. government to encourage U.S. businesses to promote products through participation in overseas trade shows.

Trade-show organizers may apply for Trade Fair Certification in order to offer U.S. exhibitors the export assistance services provided by the U.S. Commercial Service. Certified organizers are permitted to manage a U.S. Pavilion at the trade show. These organizers focus their efforts on attracting new-to-export small and medium-size firms, and they can provide assistance on issues like freight forwarding, Customs clearance, exhibit design, and onsite services.

Trade associations, trade-fair authorities, U.S. show organizers, U.S. chambers of commerce, U.S. agents of overseas fair organizers, and other private-sector entities that organize and manage international fairs overseas are eligible to seek certification to organize a U.S. Pavilion.

Trade Fair Certification tells you the following about a trade show:

✔ The show is an excellent opportunity for U.S. firms to market their goods and services abroad.

✔ The U.S. show organizer/agent is a reliable firm capable of effectively recruiting, managing, and building a U.S. Pavilion or organizing a group of U.S. firms at a particular fair.

✔ The U.S. government is supportive of the event to potential exhibitors and visitors, to the host country government and business community leaders, and to foreign buyers/attendees.

You can get a description of the program, benefits, guidelines, and an application by going to export.gov/tradeevents/eg_main_018558.asp.

International Buyer Program

The International Buyer Program (IBP) provides support to major U.S.-based trade shows that feature products with export potential. The U.S. Commercial Services based in foreign consulates recruits foreign buyers to attend selected trade shows in the U.S. These trade shows are publicized through newsletters, magazines, chambers of commerce, government agencies, and so on. The potential of connecting with a buyer for your exports is greatly enhanced when you participate in a trade show that's part of the IBP.

You can get more information on this program, including a link to a complete listing of U.S.-based trade shows that Commercial Service officers are recruiting foreign buyers to attend, by going to export.gov/ibp/eg_main_018009.asp.

Certified trade missions

A *trade mission* is a group of individuals who meet with prospective overseas customers. These missions are scheduled in specific countries to assist participants in finding local agents, representatives, or distributors in the country. The DOC certifies these trade missions, which are organized by state or private trade promotion agencies. The missions can include market briefings, appointments with prospective buyers, and opportunities to meet with high-level government or industry officials.

You can access a current list of trade missions by product category and country by going to export.gov/eac/trade_events.asp, selecting "Trade Mission" from the Search by Event Type drop-down list, and clicking on the "View Events" button.

The Virtual Trade Mission service provides meetings with prescreened international firms via videoconferencing. It allows you to meet with partners without the expense of traveling overseas. This program enables companies to get answers to their market questions in an interactive, two-hour video-conference. The program offers the following benefits to exporters:

✓ Opportunities to explore international markets without leaving the United States

✓ Independent evaluations of your product or service

✓ Face-to-face meetings via videoconferencing with prescreened business partners

To set up a Virtual Trade Mission, contact the Export Assistance Center near you (export.gov/eac/).

Multi-State Catalog Exhibition program

The Multi-State Catalog Exhibition program is uniquely suited to individuals and small businesses because it requires a much smaller investment than a trade mission or personal visit. It presents product literature to invited interested business prospects. If someone expresses interest in a product, the trade lead is forwarded directly to the U.S. exhibitor/participant.

The fees for participating in the program are nominal and include the cost of the literature and the appropriate shipping expenses. You can get information about the program by contacting the trade specialist at your local Export Assistance Center (export.gov/eac/).

Additional Resources for Exporters

In addition to events and programs supported by the U.S. Department of Commerce, you can find contacts and customers in other resources.

The Export Yellow Pages

The Export Yellow Pages is a reference tool that foreign buyers use to locate U.S. goods and services. It's basically an electronic matchmaking or trade contact program. The program is a public-private partnership between the DOC's Manufacturing and Services Unit and Global Publishers of Milwaukee, Wisconsin.

The Export Yellow Pages lets you present your products to foreign buyers at no cost. If you're a manufacturer, you can register your business profile for free at www.exportyellowpages.com. Nonmanufacturers, such as freight forwarders, sales agents, and other service firms, can register their business profiles for free in the U.S. Trade Assistance Directory at ustradeassistance.com, which is available as a supplement to the Export Yellow Pages.

To receive a free copy of the Export Yellow Pages, contact your local Export Assistance Center (export.gov/eac/).

The Small Business Administration's Trade Mission Online

Trade Mission Online is a database of U.S. small businesses that want to export their products for use by foreign firms and for businesses seeking U.S. suppliers for trade-related activities. You can find information on these services at www.sba.gov/about-offices-content/1/2889/resources/13179 or by contacting the U.S. Small Business Administration Office of International Trade at 202-205-6720 or www.sba.gov/about-offices-content/1/2889.

State and local government assistance

Each state provides services to local firms that produce products and are interested in exporting. Services can range from supporting trade missions to providing counseling services. You can go to www.sidoamerica.org/State-Trade-Directory.aspx to locate state-sponsored trade agencies.

Chapter 12

Locating Customers for Your Imports

In This Chapter

▶ Getting a research game plan

▶ Finding trade directories and associations

▶ Locating manufacturers' agents to help you identify prospects and sell products

*I*n this chapter, I outline an approach you can use to identify prospective customers in the local marketplace for the goods you're importing. After you've identified the most promising markets and identified the strategies to enter them, the next step is to locate actual customers. If the customer is the end user of your product, you can have a simple transaction. If not, you may have to reach the eventual user through an agent or distributor.

Using Industry Distributor Directories

After you've identified your target market (see Chapter 8), you need to find lists of prospective customers for the items you're importing. One of the quickest and easiest ways to do this is through industry trade directories. They're usually compiled and published by various industry trade organizations and are available for a small fee.

So how do these directories work? Here's an example: I had a client in Canada who manufactured white rolled paper sticks. He manufactured and marketed these sticks to health and beauty aid firms that manufactured cotton swabs. My client was looking for ways to expand his business and generate increased sales because the cotton swab market was very stable and the potential for growth was almost nonexistent.

My approach was to look at the product and see whether I could identify a new and different market for his product. After giving it some thought, I realized that those rolled white paper sticks are also used in the manufacture of lollipops. The task at hand was to identify lists of lollipop manufacturers and contact those manufacturers.

Using the *Candy Buyers' Directory,* I was able to identify all the lollipop manufacturers in North America. This annual directory, a publication of the Manufacturing Confectioner Publishing Company (www.gomc.com), is a comprehensive reference source of candy, chocolate, confectionery, and cough drops companies in North America. It lists manufacturers, sellers, and importers of these items, including brand names and products.

Almost every industry or product category has a directory. In this section, I steer you toward distributor directories you can use no matter what product you're importing.

Encyclopedia of Business Information Sources

When you're looking for customers for your imports, one of the best resources available in the reference section of most public libraries is the *Encyclopedia of Business Information Sources,* published by Gale. This publication identifies print and electronic sources of information. The listings are arranged by subject and then by type of resource — directories, online databases, periodicals, newsletters, and trade and professional associations.

Using my candy manufacturer example from earlier in the chapter, I went to the library, asked the reference librarian for the *Encyclopedia of Business Information Sources,* opened it up to the candy industry section, went to the listing of directories, and noted the following:

> *Candy Buyers' Directory.* Manufacturing Confectioner Publishing Company. Annual. Lists confectionary and snack manufacturers by category and brand name.

You can do this for any industry. The encyclopedia includes more than 1,100 business, financial, and industry topics, so you shouldn't have any difficulty finding a directory for the products you've chosen to deal in.

The Directory of United States Importers

The Directory of United States Importers is a publication of UBM Global Trade. It provides a geographical and product listing of U.S. importers, allowing you to locate an importer by product, company name, or geographic region. You can use the directory to identify potential customers for any product that you want to import. The listings provide information on the products as well as the countries with which these importers are currently doing business.

You can use *The Directory of United States Importers* to identify companies that are currently importing products that you're interested in but that aren't importing them from a country where you've identified a supplier. You'll find that many times, people who are importing are always actively seeking alternative sources of supply.

Here's an example. I was contacted by a firm in Bolivia that was able to supply me with alpaca fiber, which is used to make knitted and woven blankets, sweaters, hats, gloves, scarves, textiles, coats, and bedding. My next task was to find customers for this product. Using the product index of *The Directory of United States Importers,* I identified firms in the United States that were importing alpaca and other wool products. I crossed off the firms that were listed as doing business with Bolivia. All the remaining firms on the list were potential customers that I could contact with my offering.

You can find the directory of importers and its sister publication — *The Directory of United States Exporters* — in the reference section of many public libraries. And you can often find used copies for sale at a deep discount. However, editions from 2011 and after are available online only, and the price is steep — a yearly subscription costs $670.

Encyclopedia of Associations

Companies that manufacture similar products or offer similar services often belong to industry associations. These associations help resolve problems between their member companies and consumers. Most industry associations also provide consumer information and education materials through publications and on their websites.

If you've selected a product to import and you've identified the type of company to target, you can contact the industry association and try to get your hands on the membership roster, which can serve as your list of prospective customers.

You can identify the industry association simply by using the *Encyclopedia of Business Information Sources* (which I discuss earlier in this chapter) or you can visit the local library and ask the reference librarian for the *Encyclopedia of Associations,* published by Gale.

This encyclopedia can help you identify trade associations for any industry that deals with a product you've decided to import. For example, I had to source information about photovoltaic systems, a solar energy product. I didn't have much information on the product or the industry, so I used the

Encyclopedia of Associations, went to the solar energy listing, and looked at the trade/professional associations. I identified several organizations, including the Solar Energy Industry Association in Washington, DC. When I contacted that association, I found a wealth of valuable information.

Finding Customers with Salesman's and Chain Store Guides

If you're an importer, you can also find buyers through the Salesman's Guides and Chain Store Guides. These directories are available either in a print or CD version through Forum Publishing Company, 383 E. Main St., Centerport, NY 11721 (phone 800-635-7654; website: `www.forum123.com`). These guides are detailed lists of customers for a wide variety of products that you can import.

Salesman's Guides

Salesman's Guides enable you to do the following:

- Identify prospects who are likely to buy.
- Discover price ranges of the products your prospects carry.
- Customize your product offerings and presentations to potential customers based on geographic location, product specialty sales volume, size, or price range.
- Coordinate a successful product mix (see Chapter 8) by conferring with your target buyers; this type of customer feedback then lets you build a catalog of items that the market prefers.

Each special market directory provides data on sales volume, store type, and descriptions of lines, as well as complete contact information on thousands of industry executives and buyers, including complete address, phone, and fax numbers.

Here's a list of available Salesman's Guides and types of available information:

- **Men's & Boys' Wear Buyers:** This is a listing of 6,000 top-rated retailers indexed by state, city, and store name, enabling you to pinpoint new prospects with the buyer contact information.
- **Women's & Children's Wear Buyers:** This is a listing of women's, misses', and juniors' sportswear buyers; ready-to-wear buyers; women's, misses', and juniors' accessories and intimate apparel buyers; and

infant- to teen-wear buyers. The lists provide store names, addresses, and telephone numbers in addition to individual contact information so you can target your sales and prospecting efforts.

✔ *Mass Merchandisers & Off-Price Apparel Buyers:* This guide provides you with all buyer contacts, sales volume, lines carried, and branch locations of more than 2,000 mass merchandisers, indexed by state, city, and name.

✔ *Gift, Housewares, & Home Textile Buyers:* This guide lists more than 15,000 executives and buyers for more than 7,500 stores and mail-order catalog companies that sell gift, housewares, and home textile products throughout the U.S.

✔ *Corporate Gift Buyers:* This directory profiles more than 14,900 companies. The listings contain the contact information for more than 14,900 executives and buyers who are responsible for the selection and purchasing of corporate gifts.

✔ *Premium, Incentive, & Travel Buyers:* This directory provides a list of more than 20,000 decision-makers who plan or purchase ad specialties, corporate gifts and awards, sales incentives, and safety incentives from more than 12,000 firms. The listings include contact names and titles, street addresses, phone and fax numbers, and website and e-mail addresses.

Chain Store Guides

Chain Store Guides are a primary source of information that business professionals rely on for timely and accurate data on the retail and food-service industries. The information is available in print, on CD-ROM, and online. Here are the Chain Store Guides available:

✔ *Directory of Apparel Specialty Stores:* This guide provides information on more than 5,100 retailers operating more than 70,700 stores involved in the sale of women's, men's, family, and children's wear.

✔ *Directory of Department Stores:* This directory provides detailed information on more than 2,000 headquarters listings, including 1,583 shoe retailers and more than 100 product lines. It gives you access to more than 7,500 buyer and key personnel names.

✔ *Directory of Home Furnishings Retailers:* This guide features detailed information on more than 2,900 headquarters in the U.S. and Canada with contact information for more than 8,600 key executives and buyers.

- ✔ ***Directory of Discount Stores & Specialty Retailers:*** This guide provides an in-depth look at the mass-merchandising segment, bringing you access to nearly 7,000 company listings and more than 24,500 key personnel.

- ✔ ***Directory of Dollar Stores:*** This guide includes comprehensive coverage of the dollar store industry, one of today's fastest-growing retail market segments. It provides 1,100 qualified company listings.

- ✔ ***Directory of Drug Store & HBC Chains:*** This guide provides profiles on nearly 1,700 U.S. and Canadian headquarters operating two or more retail drug stores, deep discount stores, health and beauty care (HBC) stores, or vitamin stores that have annual industry sales of at least $250,000.

- ✔ ***Directory of Home Center Operators & Hardware Chains:*** This guide lists more than 4,900 company headquarters and subsidiaries operating almost 23,500 units in the large and fast-growing home improvement and building materials industry. The guide includes 19 major buying/marketing groups and co-ops.

- ✔ ***Directory of Supermarket, Grocery, & Convenience Store Chains:*** The companies in this database operate more than 41,000 individual supermarkets, superstores, club stores, gourmet supermarkets, and combo-store units. A special convenience store section profiles the headquarters of 1,700 convenience store chains operating more than 85,000 stores.

- ✔ ***Directory of Single Unit Supermarket Operators:*** This guide provides information on 19,000 key executives and buyers in the supermarket industry, plus information on their primary wholesalers.

- ✔ ***Directory of Wholesale Grocers:*** This targeted database allows you to reach food wholesalers, cooperatives and voluntary group wholesalers, nonsponsoring wholesalers, and cash-and-carry operators who serve grocery, convenience, discount, and drug stores. Info includes company headquarters, divisions, branches, and more than 13,000 key executives and buyers.

- ✔ ***Directory of Chain Restaurant Operators:*** This guide offers information on more than 5,900 listings within the restaurant chain, food-service management, and hotel/motel operator markets in the U.S. and Canada.

- ✔ ***Directory of High Volume Independent Restaurants:*** This guide gives you information on over 5,100 independent restaurants featuring casual, fine dining, and family restaurants in the U.S. and Canada.

- ✔ ***Directory of Food Service Distributors:*** This guide provides information on 5,400 food-service distributors operating in the U.S. and Canada. Contact information for 25,700 key executives is included, along with each company's distribution centers, restaurant/institution sales, product lines, and trading areas.

Contacting the Manufacturers' Agents National Association

A *manufacturer's agent* or *manufacturer's representative* is an independent agent wholesaling organization that's responsible for selling all or part of a company's products in an assigned geographical territory. The firms are independent and not employees of the manufacturer. Agents are used extensively in the distribution of products and usually have contractual arrangements with the companies they represent. An agent usually represents several noncompeting manufacturers of related products.

Many new firms have limited financial resources and don't have the ability to hire their own sales force. Using these representatives can be a cost-effective alternative because they're paid a commission for what they actually sell. Even if you're an importer, not a manufacturer, these individuals still can represent you if you have products that are comparable to their current representations.

With a little bit of research, you can locate agents or representatives who can work with you. You can use the *Encyclopedia of Business Information Sources,* go to your chosen industry classification, and look at directories or periodicals — in many instances, agents are listed in directories or trade periodicals.

Another resource is the membership-based Manufacturers' Agents National Association (MANA). You can find out about their services at `www.mana online.org`. MANA is an online source of information for companies that want to outsource their sales effort. The organization requires you to complete an application for associate membership. The annual dues are $399 and include access to the member area of the website, where you find the online directory, the contracts package, commission survey results, and an archive of *Agency Sales* magazine articles sorted by subject. Membership also includes counseling and discounts on the seminars, ads, and printed publications. The online directory is a searchable database that allows you to identify agents by territory, product, or customers served.

Putting It All Together to Find Customers

In this section, I walk you through an example that uses resources listed in this chapter, ultimately coming up with a listing of customers and sales representatives. You can adapt this process to find customers and sales reps in any industry.

Say you're interested in importing food-service supplies from Korea, and you've identified a Korean supplier that can provide a quality line of products. After developing a list of the products that you'll be importing, you have to figure out how — and from whom — the restaurants, supermarkets, convenience stores, and other members of the food-service industry purchase such goods.

Your first visit is to the library, where you look at the *Encyclopedia of Business Information Sources* for food-service industry listings. You find an entry for the *Directory of Food Service Distributors,* published by Chain Store Guides. The publication, which is available in both print and electronic formats, includes an exhaustive list of distributors of food and equipment to restaurants and other food-service establishments. You acquire this directory, select a region, and do a direct-mail campaign offering your products. (Direct mail is one option. Having a sales representative contact your target market and make formal presentations is even better.)

Wanting to know more about the industry, you go back to the *Encyclopedia of Business Information Sources,* now looking under periodicals. You see a listing for *Foodservice Equipment & Supplies* magazine. You're thinking about subscribing, so you call the publisher and ask for a sample copy.

When reviewing the magazine's classifieds section, you identify an organization referred to as Manufacturers' Agents Association for the Foodservice Industry (MAFSI; www.mafsi.org). MAFSI is a not-for-profit association for independent manufacturers' representative agencies and the manufacturers they represent.

You contact MAFSI and purchase a copy of its membership directory. You review this membership roster and identify agents who are already representing noncompeting manufacturers of your products.

After developing a list of prospective agents, you contact them by phone or mail and try to determine each one's interest in acting as a representative for you. As part of your proposal, you design an introductory, commission-based incentive package that they should find appealing.

Part IV
Negotiating around the World

The 5th Wave   By Rich Tennant

"I've heard that in China, it's good to have some Guanxi when you go into a business negotiation. Let's stop at a market and pick some up before tomorrow's meeting."

In this part . . .

I focus on what you need to know to better understand the process of negotiating around the world. This information will assist you in avoiding mistakes and pitfalls in international negotiating. Anyone involved in importing or exporting needs to negotiate the best possible deal with people from different countries and backgrounds. Negotiating in another country, with different customs and approaches to doing business, can be quite difficult. With the information in this part and some hard work, you'll have the skills to negotiate with anyone from anywhere around the world.

Chapter 13

How Negotiations Work

After you've decided on a product and have identified a supplier, you need to negotiate the terms of purchase. Some people consider negotiation unpleasant because it involves conflict. But understanding more about the process enables you to manage the negotiations with confidence, increasing the odds that the outcome will benefit both parties.

This chapter helps you understand the process of negotiations, protects you from making a deal that you may regret, and enables you to make the most of your resources. I define the negotiations process and identify the issues to include in your discussions. I take you through the stages of negotiations and end with what it may take to close the deal.

This chapter simply explores the key aspects of the negotiations process. Chapter 14 identifies what makes global negotiations different. And in Chapter 15, I take you to seven regions around the world, exploring specific skills that you may need for effective business negotiations.

Negotiations Defined

Negotiating is the process you follow in attempting to get someone to do what you want her to do. It entails communicating back and forth for the purpose of reaching an agreement that's acceptable to both parties. In import/export, that agreement may be on the price that you want to pay a supplier for a product or what you want someone to pay for a product that you're selling.

Negotiating has to do with persuading while making sure that the other side feels good about the outcome. A win-win negotiation is important. Both parties have to feel that the outcome is positive. The problem with win-lose negotiations is that the loser later tries to get even. He may not get you today or tomorrow, but he'll get even at some point.

What You Can Negotiate About

Although deals can be complex, there are only a few main issues you can negotiate about:

- ✔ **Territory:** You can negotiate about whether you'll have any limits on where and to whom you may sell the products. For example, say I'm a U.S. manufacturer of disposable medical supplies. I manufacture a line of products that may be sold over the counter (adhesive bandages, cotton balls, and so on) as well as a similar line of products that may be targeted to hospitals. I can appoint a distributor in Saudi Arabia and specify that this distributor in Saudi Arabia will be my distributor for sales to hospitals. Then I can appoint a different company to be my distributor in Saudi Arabia for sales to supermarkets, drugstores, and so on.

- ✔ **Exclusive or nonexclusive:** If you're an importer, you may negotiate over whether you have exclusive or nonexclusive distribution rights. If you're an exporter, sort out which rights you're providing to the individual you're selling the products to.

- ✔ **Performance:** Discuss minimum performance requirements. For example, if I'm a U.S. distributor appointed by a Bolivian pewter manufacturer, will I be required to meet certain sales targets during the term of the agreement? And what happens if I don't meet these sales targets?

- ✔ **Products:** Discuss the products covered by the agreement, including their specifications. Talk about quality, service, and training.

- ✔ **Price and payment terms:** Set down a detailed price schedule and payment terms. See Chapter 17 for details on methods of payment.

- ✔ **Shipping terms, risk of loss:** Shipping terms (see Chapter 16) provide information on which expenses are the responsibilities of each party in the transaction. They also indicate where title will pass from the exporter to the importer.

- ✔ **Restrictions on carrying competitive products:** In this part of the negotiations, you clearly explain what kinds of products are considered competitive products. You also reach an understanding on whether the agent or distributor may handle a competitive line of products during the term of the agreement or for a period of time after the termination of the agreement.

✔ **Governing law and language:** Different countries have different laws about contracts. Negotiate which country's law governs the agreement or whether both parties will adhere to some international standard. Also note which language is the language of the official version of the contract. Although the contract may be bilingual, one language should take legal precedence in case of a language dispute.

✔ **Provision for settlement of disputes:** Most disputes between parties arise out of different expectations about their obligations to each other. The negotiations need to detail each party's expectations to reduce the possibility of surprises. Make sure you negotiate how you'll resolve disagreements. For example, you want to establish an alternative dispute-resolution procedure prior to submitting the dispute to arbitration or commencing court proceedings.

✔ **Length and termination of the agreement:** Discuss the length of the agreement and under what conditions it can be canceled or renewed.

Agreements that are a result of negotiations can be written, spoken, or implied by the actions of the parties involved. Always get agreements in writing. A written agreement clarifies the terms, conditions, and duties of the parties involved and provides strong legal protection if a misunderstanding arises.

The Stages in Negotiations

Both domestic and international negotiations proceed through six stages: preparation, building the relationship, exchanging information/first offer, persuasion, concession, and agreement. I discuss these stages next.

When contacting suppliers (see Chapter 7), negotiate with several firms, and don't stop negotiating after you get an initial offer from your first contact. You'll always find more than one company that can manufacture your product, and some manufacturers will take a more competitive approach in negotiating with you.

Step 1: Research

Fact-finding is a critical stage for what's to come in the negotiations. *Information* is made up of facts presented in a form to assist someone in making a decision. Information is power, which is critical in the early stages of negotiations. The better prepared you are, the more confident you'll be and the more likely that the negotiations will conclude successfully. In this section, I discuss some of the areas you need to research before entering negotiations.

Exploring business culture and etiquette

When you negotiate with individuals from other countries, you'll likely notice a lot of differences in their business culture and etiquette. For example, when I first started doing business with clients from other countries, I always used the approach that "this is the price." But the people in these other cultures were used to haggling. When I kept on losing business, I realized that I had to be a bit more flexible, even if that meant starting at a higher price than I wanted to allow me wiggle room.

Chapter 14 identifies cultural differences, and Chapter 15 provides detailed examples from several regions of the world.

Researching the other party

Finding out as much as possible about the other company is critical. Make sure you consider the following questions:

- Does the organization have a good reputation?
- Are these people generally easy to do business with?
- How much power does the individual you'll be negotiating with have?
- How important will it be to have any agreement in writing?

I discuss some good sources of company information, such as the U.S. Department of Commerce's International Company Profile and the International Partner Search, in Chapter 11.

Knowing yourself

When preparing for the negotiations, you have to know exactly what you want and what's important. Write down your goals and priorities. Your wish list may include concerns besides price. For example, you may choose to negotiate aspects such as exclusivity, delivery times, quality of the goods, payment terms, and so on. (See the earlier section "What You Can Negotiate About" for details.)

Consider preparing a list of concessions — things you're willing to give up — especially if the other culture is into haggling.

Assess what you have to offer. Why might the other party be interested in doing business with an American company? What are your strengths, and how might they benefit your partner?

Also think about your own cultural biases so you can strive for cultural awareness and sensitivity. Knowledge of cultural differences is the key to success when negotiating internationally.

Step 2: Build a relationship

Building a lasting and trusting relationship with the other party can be crucial for the success of your business. This takes time and effort. The partners in negotiations need to get to know each other.

The duration and importance of relationship-building can vary by culture. In most parts of the world, relationship-building is regarded with much more significance than it is in the United States. Establishing productive business cooperation often requires a long-term perspective and commitment. Chapter 15 takes you around the world and highlights the level of importance put on relationships and respect in different countries.

Let your cultural research guide you as you interact with the other party, but be careful not to stereotype. Your business partners are individuals, and they may not adhere to everything you've heard or read about.

Always stay on good terms with your suppliers or customers so you don't adversely affect your opportunities for future negotiations.

Step 3: Exchange information and make the first offer

This stage involves the exchange of task-related information. Each side typically makes a presentation and states its position. A question and answer session usually follows, and the parties discuss alternatives. Be prepared to deal with resistance, bargaining, decision-making, and agreements.

When you make your first offer, always have in mind a settlement range, the areas in which agreement is possible. The range refers to the agreement you ideally want as compared to your bottom line.

Where the information exchange takes place depends on the situation, although most initial dealing is done via correspondence, usually e-mail. As a relationship builds, you may start visiting or meeting individuals for face-to-face negotiations.

When importing, if a supplier offers you a price structure that seems too low, don't be afraid to ask why. You need to make sure the merchandise isn't of low quality or damaged.

Step 4: Persuade

Persuasion is the heart of the negotiations process. For the most part, this occurs over more than one negotiating session, and you can use a variety of tactics — whether or not to make the first offer, how much to offer, when to make concessions, and so on.

The process of bargaining and making concessions is often hampered in an international environment because of differences in verbal and nonverbal communication. Although these behaviors influence every stage of the negotiation process, they play a particularly powerful role in the persuasion stage. See Chapter 15 for details on international communication.

Steps 5 and 6: Make concessions and come to an agreement

During the concessions and agreement stages, you work out the details of the agreement and ensure understanding. Each side may relax some of its demands. The negotiators confirm the agreement with their respective superiors and attorneys if necessary. In the end, all parties agree to and sign the final agreement.

The key to successfully closing a deal is to make sure that your counterpart's needs have been satisfied, that you're at your bottom line, and that this is as far as you're willing to go.

Closing a deal isn't always in your best interest. If you have to go below your least-acceptable position, it might be better not to make the deal. As they say, sometimes the best deal is no deal!

Planning the Negotiations

Planning is the process of setting an objective and then identifying the courses of action that are necessary to accomplish it. Planning is important because it provides you with direction and a standard you can measure performance against.

All parties of a negotiation use the planning stage to prepare their side of the discussion in the hopes of gaining an advantage by the time the negotiation is concluded. Planning negotiations is a simple four-step process:

1. **Identify the issues.**

   In every negotiation, somebody wants something. I mention price, shipping terms, and other negotiable issues in the earlier section "What You Can Negotiate About."

2. **Establish priorities.**

   Individuals involved in the field of exporting or importing are always looking at ways to minimize risk, whether with a fluctuating exchange rate, getting paid, or protecting themselves against loss or damage while the goods are in transit. You need to decide what's most important to you.

   Use research to attempt to understand what the other side wants. You may not be able to find out exactly what the other side wants, but you can estimate. Take stock of what you have to offer that may fit with the other party's priorities.

3. **Identify an acceptable settlement range — that is, an area in which agreement is possible.**

   Describe an ideal situation for yourself. This is your starting point. For example, if you're negotiating the price of a product that you're interested in importing, do research on what a fair or reasonable price would be.

   You also need to decide on an absolute highest price you'll pay. Don't try to get the other side to give you an unrealistically low price, but choose a fair price that allows you to make a profit. Be prepared to walk away from negotiations if the other side isn't willing to compromise on your numbers.

4. **Develop strategies and approaches for reaching an agreement on each of the elements being negotiated, focusing on the priorities you've chosen.**

Chapter 14

What Makes Global Negotiating Different

In This Chapter

▶ Understanding the importance of culture

▶ Identifying differences in the communications process

▶ Finding out how negotiations differ from region to region

*C*ulture is the total of all beliefs, values, rules, techniques, and institutions that characterize a population. In other words, it's what makes individual groups different. The aspects of culture that are especially important to international businesspeople are aesthetics, attitudes and beliefs, religion, material culture, and language. The process of global negotiations differs from culture to culture in language, negotiating style, approaches to problem-solving, gestures and facial expressions, and more.

This chapter identifies what's different about global negotiations and how to deal with those differences as you begin your journey into the world of importing and exporting. I discuss some of the more difficult negotiating problems that you may encounter and offer solutions to them.

Developing Cultural Awareness before Negotiating

All cultures have a set of attitudes and beliefs that influence nearly all aspects of human behavior. These attitudes and beliefs help bring order to a society and its individuals. The more you understand these attitudes and beliefs, the better you're equipped to work with people from other countries.

Be concerned with the way culture influences how individuals from other countries behave. Lack of cultural knowledge can do much to injure your relationship with others. To create opportunities for negotiations, you must not only know the customs and business protocols of your counterparts from other countries but also understand the character of the country, management philosophies, demeanor, and disposition. I provide specific regional information on cultures in Chapter 15.

The following questions may help you develop the necessary cultural awareness prior to the start of negotiations:

- ✔ What must I know about the social and business customs of the country?
- ✔ What skills do I need to possess to be an effective negotiator in the country?
- ✔ Do I have any prejudices and stereotypes about the people in the country? How will these affect my interactions with them and ultimately the negotiations?

Breaking Down the Communications Process

Communication is the process of transmitting information. In effective communication, the message is understood in the same manner as the sender intended it to be sent. The communications process consists of the following:

1. **The *sender* has an idea that needs to be transmitted to a receiver.**

2. **The idea is translated into a message that is then *encoded* into the exact mix of words, phrases, sentences, pictures, or other symbols that best reflect the content of the message.**

3. **The message is then transmitted through one or more *channels* of communication (a face-to-face meeting, a letter, a telephone call, or any combination of these methods).**

4. **The message is received and retranslated by the process of *decoding.***

5. **With two-way communication, the receiver may respond to the original message with a message of her own (*feedback*).**

Anything that disrupts the communications process is called *noise*. Noise consists of distractions that usually have nothing to do with the substance of the message. Factors such as gestures, personal physical distance, and physical surroundings may unintentionally interfere with the transmission of a message.

Negotiating electronically

Today, more and more businesspeople are conducting their negotiations electronically — by telephone, fax, e-mail, or videoconferencing. The Internet is one of the most powerful tools because it offers quick and easy negotiating opportunities with manufacturers, suppliers, and customers. However, it requires more openness, accuracy, and trust in business communication.

When sending e-mails across cultures, avoid ambiguous messages, be specific, and provide background and context for the message to avoid any misunderstandings. It's also a good idea to summarize the message in different words to clarify.

The potential advantages of information technologies are obvious — people can communicate with each other more easily, quickly, and less expensively. The potential disadvantage is that such technologies aren't effective for building relationships where face-to-face dialogue is important.

Such noise is common in international negotiating and requires awareness and an effort from both the sender and receiver to guarantee clear communication. This noise can come from either verbal or nonverbal communication, which I discuss next.

Before initiating negotiations in another country, try to identify and engage a local intermediary. This person can assist you in bridging the cultural and communications gap, enabling you to conduct business with a greater degree of effectiveness.

Communication is not reversible. After you've said something, you can't take it back, although you may be able to explain, clarify, or restate a message. However, after a message has been transmitted, it influences present and future meanings.

Verbal communication: Having a way with words

In spoken and written communication, using the wrong words or incorrect grammar isn't your only concern. The meaning of the message often depends on the *context* — the set of circumstances surrounding those words. To interpret a message correctly, you need to understand the cultural context.

You can understand communication patterns in terms of high-context or low-context cultures. The difference depends on whether the bulk of the information is present in the words of the message or in the context of the conversation. In this section, I discuss both high-context and low-context cultures.

High-context cultures

In a *high-context* culture, information is included in the context of the message, with little communicated in the explicit words of the message. The context in which the conversation occurs is just as important as the words that are actually spoken, and cultural clues are critical in understanding what's being communicated.

Individuals from high-context cultures place a greater responsibility on the receiver than on the sender. The receiver's responsibility is to understand the intent of the message from the context in which the message was sent.

High-context cultures emphasize interpersonal relations in deciding whether to enter into a business relationship. In these countries, meetings are often held to determine whether the individuals can trust and work comfortably with each other.

Here are some examples of higher-context cultures:

- African
- Arab
- Brazilian
- Chinese
- Filipino
- Finnish
- French
- French-Canadian
- Greek
- Hungarian
- Indian
- Italian
- Japanese
- Korean
- Latin American

- ✔ Russian
- ✔ Spanish
- ✔ Thai
- ✔ Turkish

Having an attorney present, particularly at the initial meeting of the participants, in a high-context culture such as Saudi Arabia, Japan, or Egypt, may be viewed as a sign of distrust. Because these cultures value long-term relationships, a partner's assumption that one can't be trusted may be grounds to end the negotiations.

Low-context cultures

In a low-context culture, the words the sender uses explicitly convey the message to the receiver. Such cultures emphasize the specific terms of the transaction. In these countries, lawyers are often present at negotiations to guarantee the rights of their clients.

Here are some lower-context cultures:

- ✔ American
- ✔ Australian
- ✔ English
- ✔ English-Canadian
- ✔ German
- ✔ Irish
- ✔ New Zealand
- ✔ Scandinavian

In low-context communication, it's assumed that the listener knows little and must be told everything. But in a high-context culture, the listener is knowledgeable and doesn't require background information. Communication between high- and low-context people is characterized by a lot of impatience, because the low-context individual may provide more information than is necessary, whereas the high-context individual may not provide enough.

For low-context individuals to understand high-context messages, it's important to listen and observe. Pay attention to the person and the message, and create a rapport to build trust and loyalty. Finally, share your understanding of the message so that the other party can verify its accuracy.

Nonverbal communication: Looking at visual cues

Unspoken language is often just as important as the spoken or written language. Nonverbal communication can tell businesspeople something that the spoken language does not — if they understand it.

A basic knowledge of nonverbal communication in different cultures can help you avoid misunderstandings. Read on for info on gestures, touch, body language, and other forms of unspoken and unwritten communication.

Gestures

Gestures can vary from culture to culture. For example, Americans and most Europeans understand the thumbs-up gesture to mean "all right," but in southern Italy and Greece, it transmits the message for which we reserve the middle finger. Making a circle with the thumb and forefinger is friendly in the United States, but it means "you're worth nothing" in France and Belgium and is a vulgar sexual invitation in Greece and Turkey.

Conversational distances

The distance you stand from someone else frequently conveys a nonverbal message. In some cultures, it's a sign of attraction. In others, it may reflect status or the intensity of the exchange.

General appearance and dress

All cultures are concerned with how they look and make judgments based on looks and dress. Consider differing cultural standards on what is attractive in dress and what constitutes modesty.

Posture

Cultures interpret body posture in different ways. For example, bowing is an indicator of rank in Japan. Slouching is considered extremely rude in most Northern European countries. Having your hands in your pockets is disrespectful in Turkey. Sitting with legs crossed is considered offensive in Ghana and Turkey. And showing the soles of your feet is offensive in Thailand and Saudi Arabia.

Facial expressions

Different cultures can attach different meanings to facial expressions. In most cultures, smiling, crying, or showing anger or disgust is similar everywhere; however, the intensity of the expression varies from culture to culture. For example, many Asian cultures suppress facial expression as much as possible. Many Mediterranean cultures exaggerate grief or sadness, whereas most American men hide grief or sorrow. And some cultures see too much smiling as a sign of shallowness.

Touch

Each culture has a clear concept of which parts of the body one may or may not touch. The basic meaning of touch is to control, protect, support, or disapprove. Consider the following:

- ✔ Islamic and Hindu cultures don't touch with the left hand. To do so is a social insult. The left hand is for toilet functions.

- ✔ Islamic cultures generally don't approve of any touching between genders, even handshakes. However, these cultures consider such touching between people of the same sex, including hand-holding and hugs, to be appropriate.

- ✔ Many Asians don't touch the head. The head is considered to house the soul, and a touch puts that individual in jeopardy.

- ✔ In general, people from China, England, Germany, Japan, and Scandinavia are emotionally restrained and have little public touch. Countries that encourage emotion (Jewish, Latino, and Middle Eastern) accept frequent touches.

Eye contact

In the U.S., eye contact indicates attention or interest, influences persuasion, communicates emotion, and defines power and status. It's important in managing others' impression of you. But as a sign of respect, African, Caribbean, Japanese, and Latin American cultures tend to avoid eye contact.

In Arabic cultures, prolonged eye contact shows interest and helps people understand the truthfulness of the other person. An individual who doesn't reciprocate can be seen as untrustworthy.

How Negotiations Differ Among Cultures

Five basic factors affect negotiations among cultures: attitudes toward time, individualism versus collectivism, role orderliness and conformity, uncertainty orientation, and patterns of communication. I discuss all these factors next.

Considering time influences and the pace of negotiations

Attitudes toward time can create friction for many Americans overseas. How many times have you heard an American say, "Time is money"? But in many countries around the world, time is not of the essence. In Latin America, how many times have you heard "mañana" — tomorrow, later, not today?

Cultures differ in their use of time. Americans, Australians, Germans, and the Swiss are usually fast-paced and extremely punctual. A negotiating session that is to start at 11 a.m. on Monday will start at 11 a.m. on Monday. On the other hand, in Latin America, starting a negotiating meeting an hour late may be considered normal and in some cases expected.

Even though some meetings always start late, you as a foreign visitor should still be punctual.

The pace of negotiations in the U.S. is shorter than in most other cultures. Americans tend to spend little time in orientation and fact-finding as compared to some of their international counterparts. But other cultures take the time to build relationships. If you do your cultural homework, you'll expect that relationship-building phase, and you'll know that the other party won't rush into a decision. The American preoccupation with deadlines can be a liability when you're negotiating with individuals from other countries.

Looking at individualism and collectivism

In a society that favors individualism, people are supposed to take care only of themselves and their families. Americans tend to want the individual to succeed. So in the U.S., you usually negotiate for the top person who represents the company. You try to talk directly to the decision-maker because you don't want to waste time on anyone who isn't.

But in societies that emphasize collectivism, the good of the entire group is put ahead of one's individual needs. In Japan, the emphasis on the group helps explain why the Japanese are slow at making decisions. In a collectivist or group-oriented culture, the group must be convinced.

Countries with generally individualistic cultures include Australia, Canada, England, France, Germany, Holland, Ireland, New Zealand, and the U.S. Places with generally collectivist cultures include Argentina, Brazil, China, Egypt, Greece, Hong Kong, Italy, Japan, Korea, Lebanon, Mexico, Portugal, Scandinavia, Singapore, and Taiwan.

Understanding role orderliness and conformity

Some cultures are characterized by a high need for order and conformity. These countries place a great deal of importance on how things are done. Formalities help establish friendly relations, which many cultures consider necessary for business negotiations.

For example, the Japanese pay a great deal of attention to the presentation of business cards. The Japanese emphasize the relationship, and getting to know the other person brings order and predictability to the negotiation process. On the other hand, negotiators from Canada, Germany, Switzerland, and the U.S. place a greater emphasis on the content of the negotiations than on the procedures. People from these countries are more comfortable with ambiguity.

Looking at uncertainty orientation

Uncertainty orientation refers to the degree to which members of a society feel threatened by ambiguity and are reluctant to take risks. People in cultures with high uncertainty avoidance, such as Argentina, Belgium, Japan, and Spain, tend to minimize the occurrence of unknown and unusual circumstances and to proceed cautiously and follow rules, laws, and regulations.

On the other hand, in a low uncertainty-avoidance culture, such as the U.S., one tends to accept and feel comfortable in unstructured situations or changeable environments and may try to have as few rules as possible.

Paying attention to patterns of communication

Differences in communication patterns influence the international negotiation process. Elements of directness and drive are essential for success in the U.S.; however, many people from other cultures see those behaviors as brash and rude. Individuals from high-context cultures may perceive this approach as aggressive and insensitive. For more information on communication, see the earlier section "Breaking Down the Communications Process."

Chapter 15

Doing Business around the World

- -

In This Chapter

▶ Understanding the business environment of the world's major marketplaces

▶ Knowing the do's and don'ts throughout the world

- -

*T*he growth of international business has been clear and dramatic. We are living in a period of improved technologies and communication, bringing you greater opportunities for interacting with people around the world. Unfortunately, it also increases the chances for misunderstanding. So for now, put away your slick marketing presentations, and take some time to understand your business counterparts abroad. To be successful, you'll likely need to build relationships, pay special attention to courtesy, and get ready for a change of pace.

In this chapter, I provide an overview of some of the skills you need to be an effective negotiator in the seven main business regions (or marketplaces) of the world — Western Europe; Eastern Europe and Central Asia; Latin America and the Caribbean; North America; the Middle East and North Africa; Asia and the Pacific Rim; and sub-Saharan Africa. You can find information on the business environment and some practical do's and don'ts. This chapter also covers cultural factors, because importers and exporters need to appreciate and understand cultural differences.

When doing business internationally, communication takes place between individuals, not cultures. However, cultural awareness will assist you in predicting how people in a certain culture will act, negotiate, and make decisions. Understanding how someone addresses an issue or even simply how that person goes about making decisions will give you an edge.

The Marketplaces of Western Europe

The countries of Western Europe are among the most prosperous nations in the world, attracting the attention of businesses trying to market their products.

Twenty-seven countries belong to the European Union (EU), whose goal is to create a single free market. The members have agreed to reduce trade barriers among themselves in an attempt to become more prosperous. Additional benefits of the Union are common standards, deregulation, and taxation reforms. In 2002, 12 of the EU nations eliminated their national currencies, replacing them with the euro. Germany, the third-largest economy in the world, is the most economically powerful nation in the EU.

The newest EU members used to be part of the Soviet Union (Estonia, Latvia, and Lithuania) or were allied with the Soviet Union politically and economically (Bulgaria, Czech Republic, Hungary, Poland, Slovakia, and Romania). Other countries in Western Europe that are not a part of the EU include Iceland, Switzerland, Norway, Andorra, Monaco, and Liechtenstein. These countries are likewise prosperous and follow free-market policies.

How negotiations work in Western Europe

Building lasting and trusting relationships is important to most cultures within Western Europe. It isn't necessarily required for your initial meetings; however, you'll move forward with serious discussions only after the individual you're negotiating with becomes comfortable in dealing with you.

When communicating in English in a non-English-speaking country, speak slowly using short and simple sentences; avoid using jargon or slang, and regularly summarize key points.

Gestures and body language differ from country to country. For example, people gesture frequently in France, Italy, and Spain, but the Dutch, Swedes, and British use gestures sparingly. In Switzerland, the amount of gesturing even varies within the country — the German Swiss use it sparingly, while the French and Italian Swiss use it more extensively.

Throughout Western Europe, people primarily view negotiations as a joint problem-solving process. Even though the buyer is in a more advantageous position, both buyer and seller are responsible for reaching an agreement. The focus of the negotiations is on both short- and long-term benefits, and the negotiating style is cooperative, stressing compromises. Even if individuals are unwilling to compromise, avoid any confrontation — remain patient, calm, and persistent.

Nations of Western Europe

The Western European countries I cover in this section include Austria, Belgium, Denmark, Finland, France, Germany, Greece, Ireland, Italy, the Netherlands, Norway, Portugal, Spain, Sweden, Switzerland, and the United Kingdom.

Austria

In Austria, business practice and etiquette are similar to American customs; however, you see some important differences. For example, people generally conduct business in Austria in a relatively formal environment. When making appointments with prospective clients, it's customary to make initial contact well in advance, either in writing or by phone. You should address Austrians by title or surname. Austrians are very punctual and expect all meetings to begin as scheduled.

Austrians shake hands with everyone in the group, whenever they're greeting or leaving acquaintances. A woman offers her hand first to the man, and the older person offers his hand to the younger. Handshakes are firm and accompanied by direct eye contact.

Having your hands in your pockets while being introduced or while talking to someone is considered rude in Austria.

Americans inexperienced in discussions with Austrians may at first find some Austrians overly direct in initial meetings; however, keep in mind that directness is seen in the same light as honesty in Austria.

Belgium

Business appointments are necessary in Belgium. The person you're meeting will generally decide the time. Belgians are punctual, and you'll be expected to arrive on time to your appointment. Arriving late may create the impression of unreliability.

Although meetings are formal, first appointments are more social than business-oriented, because Belgians prefer to do business with people they know.

Don't remove your suit jacket during a meeting, and never talk while having your hands in your pockets; Belgians find this to be rude.

If traveling to Belgium, avoid scheduling meetings during July and August, the week before Easter, and the week between Christmas and New Year's. Those are prime vacation times.

Denmark

Danish businesspeople may appear somewhat formal at first but are likely to quickly show a more relaxed side of themselves. The dress code, especially for younger people, may seem a little too relaxed to an American businessperson.

Danes are likely to get down to business right away and are generally conservative and efficient in their approach to business meetings. Handshakes with men and women are the accepted form of greeting. Danes shake hands for greetings upon arrival and departure from a meeting.

Danes tend to be slow and independent when making decisions, so a hard-sell approach may not be a good idea.

Finland

Finland is a modern, commercially mature country that enjoys close relations with its Nordic neighbors. Social and business protocol is similar to that of the United States.

Relationships are important within the social and business world, because Finns prefer to deal with people they know and trust. They're among the most punctual people in the world, so don't be late.

When conversing with a Finn, don't fold your arms, which signifies arrogance and that you're a closed-minded individual. Finns are not comfortable with physical contact, so no back-slapping. Eye contact while conversing is extremely important.

France

The most important characteristic of French business behavior is its emphasis on courtesy and a certain formality. Respect appointment schedules and hierarchical titles, and promptly acknowledge correspondence, whether by mail or by fax. A handshake is customary upon initiating and closing a business meeting, accompanied by a verbal appropriate greeting. If you are meeting with a woman, you should wait for the woman to offer her hand first. Handshakes in France don't usually involve s strong grip. Professional attire is expected.

Germany

Germans do not like the unexpected, and changes — even if they'll improve the outcome — may be not welcome. Nowhere in the world is punctuality more important than in Germany. Arriving even five or ten minutes after the appointed time is a poor start to any business negotiations. Giving compliments is not part of German business protocol and can cause embarrassment.

Germans shake hands both at the beginning and end of a meeting. Handshakes may be accompanied by a nod of the head, which conveys the message that the meeting has gone well.

Greece

When doing business with Greeks, business-related customs, etiquette, and dress are basically the same as in the United States and other Western European countries. A handshake is the customary business greeting for both men and women, and business cards are usually exchanged at the initial meeting. Greek people tend to be physically demonstrative, so your greeting can take many forms, such as an embrace in addition to a handshake.

Greek people in older generations may indicate a "no" response with an upward nod of the head. This gesture is not common with the younger generation.

Ireland

In general, Irish business executives are less formal than their European counterparts, and the use of first names at an early stage of a business relationship is acceptable. Friendship and mutual trust are highly valued. After you've earned this trust, you can usually expect a productive working relationship.

Nonetheless, principles of customary business courtesy — especially replying promptly to sales orders and requests for price quotations — are a prerequisite for success. Business appointments are also required, and visitors are expected to be punctual.

Wear conservative business attire for business meetings and functions. Suits, rather than blazers and slacks, are the norm.

The Irish are comfortable with eye contact. You should never look around when speaking with someone. Winking is not appropriate.

Italy

In general, what is considered good business practice in the United States also applies when doing business with Italians. Italians appreciate prompt replies to their inquiries and expect all correspondence to be acknowledged. Conservative business attire is recommended at all times. Business appointments are required, and visitors are expected to be punctual. The golden keys of customary business courtesy — especially replying promptly to requests for price quotations and orders — are a prerequisite for success.

Italian business executives tend to use titles indicating their positions in the firm. During the first stages of conducting business, let the prospective buyer take the lead, because the American approach of getting down to business may be considered too abrupt.

Avoid commenting on political events or making negative comments about Italy. Some positive and sincere observations about the Italian culture, style, art, history, cuisine, or music are always appropriate. Friendship and mutual trust are highly valued, and after you've established this relationship, you can usually count on a productive business association.

The Netherlands

Punctuality is important in Dutch business culture. If you know that you'll be late for an appointment, be sure to phone ahead and give a plausible excuse. The Dutch value the efficient use of time, and spontaneity is not desirable. Reply promptly to requests for price quotations and to orders.

In general, European business executives are more conservative than their U.S. counterparts; therefore, refrain from using first names until after you've formed a firm relationship. Friendship and mutual trust are important.

Don't be surprised if a meeting begins with little to no socializing. Dutch people value time and don't like to waste time on small talk. However, even though the Dutch are very effective and efficient in business dealings, decision-making is slower than what you may be accustomed to in the United States.

Norway

Norwegians are often direct and do not focus on rituals and social environments for negotiations. In the initial meeting, Norwegians are ready to talk business after only a few minutes of small talk. Norwegians are straightforward in business meetings, so make your presentations precise and concrete. There's no need to be embarrassed talking about price and payment.

Don't make any promises that you can't keep. Norwegians will respect your honesty.

Portugal

The Portuguese business community is very formal, and the use of titles is expected. The Portuguese are also very punctual, and they expect that from others. When greeting a businessperson, a handshake is proper.

In Portugal, legal contracts don't have the strength in business associations that personal confidence built over years of experience offers. Aggressiveness in marketing may be interpreted as socially offensive.

Spain

Spaniards tend to be more formal in business relations than Americans but not as rigid as they've been in the past. A handshake, accompanied by an appropriate greeting, is customary upon initiating and closing a business meeting. Professional attire is expected. Business dress is suit and tie, and business cards are required.

There's no substitute for face-to-face meetings with Spanish business representatives when establishing business relations. Spaniards expect a personal relationship with clients and tend to be conservative in their buying habits.

Don't assume doing business with Spaniards is just like doing business with Mexicans and Latin Americans; Italian or French people would be a better comparison.

Sweden

Swedish businesspeople appear to be willing to spend more time discussing a situation than Americans do. During a business meeting, there's always time to get to know each other and to discuss the program in sufficient detail so that all feel comfortable with the other's position. Promptness for meetings and functions is very important. The handshake, accompanied by direct eye contact, is the standard greeting. Swedes tend to be reserved, so avoid talking with your hands.

Switzerland

Although some American business representatives may find their Swiss counterparts somewhat conservative and formal, business customs with the Swiss correspond generally to those of the United States. Punctuality is very important. What else would you expect from a nation known for its precision watches?

United Kingdom

When doing business with the British, punctuality is important. Arriving few minutes early for safety is acceptable.

Decision-making is slower than an American may be accustomed to, so don't rush the English into making a decision.

For a business occasions, a simple handshake is the standard greeting for both men and women. Privacy is very important to the English, so avoid asking personal questions or intensely staring at another person. Eye contact is seldom kept during British conversations. To signal that something is to be kept confidential or secret, tap your nose.

Personal space is important to the British, so maintain a wide physical space when conversing. Touching others in public is considered inappropriate.

The Marketplaces of Central Europe

The Czech Republic, Hungary, and Poland are considered part of Central Europe and have faced some common problems as they've moved from communism to capitalism. However, they're further along in their economic development than some of the other former Eastern European countries. Most people classify the nations of Central Europe as middle-income countries that are attractive to international businesses.

Economic development has been slower in Albania, Bulgaria, and Romania because of internal political disagreements. The situation is far worse in the former Yugoslavia: Slovenia, Croatia, and Macedonia have partially avoided the economic ravages of war over control of Bosnia in the late 1990s, but Serbia, Montenegro, and Bosnia are still struggling to recover. These countries are not very attractive to individuals engaging in international business.

In this section, I cover the Czech Republic, Hungary, and Poland.

Czech Republic

Czechs are more reserved than Americans, and you should start slowly by building a few good relationships. Czechs prefer to get to know you, to hear about your background and your company. Then, if they're comfortable with you, you can get down to deal-making at the end of a dinner meeting or even at a follow-up meeting. Most Czechs want to build long-term, two-way business relationships and are put off by too much emphasis on an immediate sale.

Czechs may be offended if their foreign visitors address them by their first names without first being invited to do so. Establishing a sense of rapport and a more relaxed attitude may take several meetings.

Hungary

Hungarian business customs are similar to those in the United States and Western Europe. Hungarians consider a personal relationship the basis of business connections. Business entertaining such as lunches, receptions, and dinners are common.

Hungarians are often more formal than Americans. Hungarians usually introduce themselves using family names rather than first names. Hungarians also address each other with their family name, followed by their first name — for example, Nugent Robert. Business cards follow this convention unless printed in English. Hungarian business partners will appreciate even a small effort to learn basic greetings in Hungarian.

Poland

In general, conducting business in Poland is highly compatible with doing business in the U.S. In general, Poles are hard-working and trustworthy.

It's customary to greet Poles by shaking hands. A businesswoman should not be surprised if a Polish man kisses her hand upon introduction, at subsequent meetings, or when saying goodbye. American men are not expected to kiss a Polish woman's hand but may simply shake hands.

The Marketplaces of Eastern Europe and Central Asia

Eastern Europe (the former Soviet Union) continues to undergo vast political and economic changes. This region is a truly difficult place to do business in, primarily because of these political and economic changes.

The various countries that were once part of the Soviet Union, of which Russia is the largest, are now part of the Newly Independent States (NIS). The five Central Asian republics of the former Soviet Union — Kazakhstan, Uzbekistan, Tajikistan, Turkmenistan, and Kyrgyzstan — declared their independence when the Soviet Union dissolved in 1991. They're primarily poor Muslim countries, with little purchasing power.

How negotiations work in Eastern Europe and Central Asia

Because of the strong influence of the communist system, Eastern Europe tends to be a collectivistic culture. People from these countries belong to groups that are supposed to look after them in exchange for loyalty. The benefits to the group are the most important element in many business discussions.

Building lasting and trusting relationships is critical for the success of your business. This relationship-building and the pace of negotiations tend to be slow, so be patient.

In general, Eastern Europeans are direct in their verbal communications, making firm requests and demands. At times, these discussions can come across as abrupt and aggressive to people of other cultures. Physical contact is infrequent, and personal space is generally closer than you may find in the United States. Handshakes are firm and brief, and hand and arm gestures can be expressive.

Nations of Eastern Europe

The countries I cover in this region include Kazakhstan, Romania, Russia, Turkey, and Ukraine.

Kazakhstan

Kazakhs draw on a combination of Russian and Central Asian cultural influences, and customs may depend on the ethnicity of the person you're meeting. At business meetings, it's customary to shake hands and call people by their first name and *patronymic* (an adaptation of the father's first name) — for example, Christopher [son of John] — though the use of just the first name is also acceptable.

Kazakhstani businessmen are generally less direct than American businessmen. What can be accomplished in a few meetings in the U.S. may take more time and effort when dealing with Kazakhs, requiring patience and discipline on your part.

Romania

Special customs are not significant in business dealings in Romanians; Western business standards apply, and Romanians generally have positive attitudes toward people from the United States. Romanians are friendly, and shaking hands is the normal form of greeting. Sometimes a man, usually from an older generation, may kiss the hand of a woman in greeting.

Business cards are important and should be given to each individual present at a meeting.

Romanians use the formal addresses of *domnul* (sir) and *doamna* (madam) when addressing one another, although first names are used among younger people and in business with English-speaking partners. At a dinner meeting, it's customary to say *pofta buna* (bon appétit) before eating and *noroc* (cheers) before drinking.

Russia

The Russian market is extremely competitive. Salesmanship is a key factor, and U.S. firms should be prepared to describe the competitive advantages and factors that would distinguish the U.S. firm in the marketplace.

Establishing a personal relationship with business partners is a critical factor in the successful negotiation of major projects, in government procurement, or in developing long-term business relationships. Scheduling meetings with potential Russian business partners can be frustrating, as punctuality isn't a high priority. Business cards are important and are exchanged freely. Cards should have regular contact information and an e-mail address and website if available. Russians are very formal, so unless invited to do so, do not use first names.

Russians are known as great "sitters" during negotiations, which demonstrates their tremendous patience. Some Russians still view compromise as a sign of weakness and often refuse to back down. To these individuals, compromising is bad business. As a foreigner, you should realize that "final offers" are often not actually the end of negotiations and that oftentimes the outcome will be more attractive if you can hold out.

Turkey

Turks are hospitable people, and you'll do well to offer normal courtesies and respect and to take the time to know your Turkish counterparts. In general, a personal relationship is an important basis for a successful business relationship in Turkey. Allowing time for friendly conversation before commencing with a business agenda is usually important. Business cards are almost always exchanged.

The North American gesture for "no" (shaking the head from side to side) is a Turkish gesture for "I do not understand." Here are the two ways Turkish people indicate "no":

- ✔ Raising the eyebrows in a subtle way, sometimes accompanied by the sound "tsk"

- ✔ Accompany the eyebrows' arching with a backward tilting of the head and lowering of the eyelids

Ukraine

The legacy of a centralized authority, bureaucracy, and an unwillingness to take initiative has been imprinted on the character of Ukrainian business. Ukrainian businesses are often difficult to deal with, and until you have a signed agreement, don't get excited about the deal.

In Ukraine, never accept the first "no" as an answer. "No" is a quick and automatic response. Simply remain pleasant and try to establish a personal relationship. Ask again in a different way, and be prepared to wait — final offers are almost never final offers.

The Marketplaces of Asia and the Pacific Rim

Asia, which represents over half the world's population, is a source of both high- and low-quality products. Much of the vast potential of this region comes from China and Japan. China is becoming a major economic power, and the Japanese economy is second only to that of the United States. This is due primarily to the cooperation between the government and industry in China and Japan. In China, this close cooperation can at times make negotiating difficult, because for the most part, you'll be dealing with the government and its policies.

The Four Tigers — which include South Korea, Taiwan, Singapore, and Hong Kong — make up another part of the area's economic powers. These four regions are among the fastest-growing in the world, and they offer exciting opportunities for individuals involved in importing and exporting.

The Pacific Rim includes Australia and New Zealand, which traditionally have had close ties to the United States.

India is also a story of growth and opportunity. It offers many wide and diverse business prospects for importers and exporters.

Other countries in Asia that are affecting international business include Thailand, Malaysia, Vietnam, and Indonesia.

How negotiations work in Asia and the Pacific Rim

Diversity abounds in Asia, which is a collection of races, languages, religions, and different cultures.

Asians tend to place a great deal of importance on relationships. The building of long-lasting relationships is a key for business success. In negotiations, decision-making tends to be slow, and it requires approval of the group.

The concept of "saving face" is critical. Asians will go to great lengths to avoid embarrassment. Causing the other party to lose face is not easily forgotten, nor is it easily forgiven.

When dealing with Asians, meetings are often held to determine whether the individuals can trust and work comfortably with each other. Body language, gestures, and other forms of nonverbal communication, with the exception of personal space, are different from the North American perspective. Brief handshakes and bows are commonplace.

Individuals from this region are punctual, so make and keep appointments. They're also of the less-is-more school, so keep presentations short, get to the point, and don't go into too much detail. The people of Asia and the Pacific Rim tend to be open-minded and trusting until given a reason not to be. They're very formal, and rules and regulations take precedence over emotions and feelings.

Nations of Asia and the Pacific Rim

Significant regions in Asia and the Pacific Rim include Australia, China, Hong Kong, India, Indonesia, Japan, Malaysia, New Zealand, Pakistan, Philippines, Singapore, South Korea, Sri Lanka, Taiwan, Thailand and Vietnam.

Australia

Conducting business with Australians is relatively easy for American companies because the language, cultural environment, business practices, and customer expectations are similar. Australians are friendly and open, and directness and brevity are valued. Your opinions will be respected; however, be an active listener, and ask if you don't understand something in a negotiation.

China, including Hong Kong

Business/name cards are important in Chinese business and will almost always be exchanged upon meeting a stranger in such a context. Hold the card in both hands when offering it to the other person; offering it with one hand is considered ill mannered. When receiving a card, use two hands and study the card. Acknowledge it with thanks and initiate conversation when feasible. Carry a small card case — you should never write on a business card or put it in your wallet or pocket.

Do not use large hand movements. The Chinese do not speak with their hands, and your movements may be distracting to your host. Bowing or nodding is the common greeting; however, you may be offered a handshake. Wait for the Chinese to offer their hand first.

Americans encounter few if any cultural problems when conducting business with Hong Kong, a Special Administrative Region (SAR) of China. Business meetings tend to be formal in Hong Kong, and business acquaintances are usually addressed as Mr. or Ms., unless they state that their first name should be used.

Americans should be aware that personal names in Chinese culture follow a number of rules different from those of personal names in Western cultures. Most noticeably, married Chinese women in Hong Kong usually retain their maiden names as their family name rather than adopting the name of the husband. This is also the case in mainland China. In some exceptional cases in Hong Kong, married women, especially civil servants, do put their husband's name, hyphenated, in front of their maiden name.

It's common in China to show one's surprise or dismay by sucking air in quickly and loudly through the lips and teeth. If you see this gesture, consider modifying your request. Your host is obviously displeased.

The handshake is more common in Hong Kong than in the rest of China; however, a slight bow is still a sign of respect.

For more details on Chinese business culture, check out *Doing Business in China For Dummies,* by Robert Collins and Carson Block (Wiley).

India

Indians appreciate punctuality; however, they don't always practice it.

Business with Indians is highly personal, and a great amount of hospitality is associated with doing business, so be prepared for a lot a small talk before you get down to serious discussions.

During negotiations, you should note that the word "no" has harsh implications in India. It's more common for your business associate to be evasive, which is considered more polite. For example, you should never directly refuse an invitation. An "I'll try" response is an acceptable refusal.

Indians feel that the head is considered the seat of the soul, so never touch someone else's head, not even to pat the hair of a child. Also note that the use of leather products, including belts or handbags, may be considered offensive, especially in temples, because Hindus revere cows.

You can find out more about business in India in *Doing Business in India For Dummies,* by Ranjini Manian (Wiley).

Indonesia

Many Indonesians do not conduct business transactions or make decisions in the direct fashion Americans do, so be prepared to spend a good deal of time with clients before getting down to the business transaction. Because Indonesians do business with "friends," people who they know, developing a rapport is crucial. Although quality and price are important, those elements are often secondary to the personal interaction of the business partners.

Indonesians rarely say "no." This subtlety is lost in English, as Westerners sometimes interpret this as deceit, but Indonesians are simply being polite by their own cultural standards. Here are some guidelines:

- ✔ Any time an Indonesian says "yes, but," it means "no."

- ✔ When there are any qualifications attached, such as "It might be difficult," it means "no."

- ✔ A clear way for an Indonesian to indicate "no" is to suck in air through the teeth. This sound always indicates a problem.

- ✔ Evasion is indicative of a "no," even if the person has said neither "yes" nor "no." He or she may even pretend that the question was never asked.

Japan

In Japan, the customary greeting is the bow. However, some Japanese may greet you with a handshake, albeit a weak one. Do not misinterpret a weak handshake as an indication of character. If you are greeted with a bow, return with a bow as low as the one you received. How low you bow determines the status of the relationship between you and the other individual. When you bow, keep your eyes low and your palms flat next to your thighs.

The business card, which the Japanese refer to as *meishi,* should be given with both hands after the bow. Take special care in handling cards that are given to you. Do not write on the card, and do not put the card in your pocket or wallet — these actions are viewed as defacing or disrespecting the business card. Upon receipt of the card, make a photocopy in your mind of the name and title of the individual. Examine the card carefully as a show of respect.

Understand that the Japanese prefer not to use the word "no." If you ask a question, they may simply respond with a "yes" but clearly mean "no." Understanding this is critical in the negotiation process. When a Japanese businessperson's response is "I'll consider it," the actual meaning may actually be "no."

Malaysia

Malaysia has three major ethnic groups, each with its own traditions: Malay, Chinese, and Indian. In general, Malaysians are direct, open, and punctual, which are valued traits in business dealings. Personal contact is important. However, you should be aware of religious and cultural traditions, which differ for each ethnic group. For example, Malay Muslims may feel uncomfortable in business or social functions where alcohol or pork is served, and you should take note that items (such as business cards) should always be presented or received using the right hand.

New Zealand

New Zealand business customs are similar to those practiced in the United States. It's common and courteous practice to make and keep appointments in a timely manner.

When meeting someone and when leaving, use a firm handshake with good eye contact. Good eye contact means looking into the other person's eyes when shaking hands, not looking down at your hand. Maintain eye contact during the handshake. You're not staring but showing genuine interest in meeting or seeing the person.

Pakistan

Pakistani businessmen are formal, reserved, and deliberate. Business dealings move at a much slower pace than you may be comfortable with. Business meetings usually start off with a handshake. Men shake hands with other men; however, strict Muslim men avoid touching women. Pakistani women have few legal rights, and only a small minority have achieved success in business.

Philippines

The Philippine business environment is highly personalized. Business matters are always best dealt with on a face-to-face basis in a warm, polite, and pleasant atmosphere. Filipinos often prefer an atmosphere of calm and restraint, avoid direct confrontation, and typically offer a polite reply coupled with a smile rather than an outright "no" to the other party's ideas.

A "yes" can mean anything from "I agree" to "maybe" or even an outright "no." To guarantee that the Filipino means yes, get it in writing.

It's common for business associates to make personal inquiries about family, marital status, ethnicity, hobbies, after-hours activities, and other topics that Americans typically consider rather personal. Be prepared to discuss generalities of family hobbies, sports, and American customs, because Filipinos see this as a way to become better acquainted.

Singapore

The people of Singapore must like and be comfortable with you as a precondition of doing business.

In Singapore, business discussions are usually conducted in a very straightforward manner. Singaporeans are punctual and rarely disagree openly. Commenting that a question was not even asked usually indicates a "no."

Business cards are a must. They're immediately exchanged during business and social meetings. The East Asian practice of presenting a business card with both hands is observed.

South Korea

South Koreans have a great respect for age and hierarchy, which means that they generally prefer to meet to discuss business with persons of the same or parallel rank. The exchange of business cards is a means by which South Koreans discover the name, position, and status of the other person. Businesspeople should always have their business cards ready and should treat the exchange of a South Korean counterpart's card with respect, always pausing to read the card. Receive and present cards and other items with both hands as a sign of respect.

South Koreans may ask direct questions about your age, marital status, and other personal information to help them determine how they should interact with you. A strong grasp of the English language is uncommon among South Koreans.

South Koreans can prove to be subtle and effective negotiators, and a commitment to a rigid negotiating stance early on may work against you. A South Korean customer who doesn't like your style may turn down your offer even if it includes the best price, technology, and profit potential. South Koreans prefer to do business with people with whom they've formed a personal connection or with people they've met through a trusted intermediary.

South Koreans may not place the same importance on the written letter of agreement as people in the United States do. South Koreans see the letter as a start of a process, with Koreans interpreting a contract as a loosely structured consensus statement broadly defining what has been negotiated but leaving sufficient room to permit flexibility and adjustment. Simply put, you should be aware that a written contract is subject to change and renegotiation.

Sri Lanka

In Sri Lanka, the language of business is English. Business cards are a necessity. Courtesy is highly valued in Sri Lanka, and personal graciousness may play a role in securing deals.

Taiwan

Business relationships with the Taiwanese are based on respect and trust. You should never criticize a competitor or avoid admitting that you don't know the answer to a question.

Business is competitive, so be prepared to discuss all elements of your planned dealings in detail. Bargaining is a way of life, so also be prepared to compromise.

Handshakes are for casual meetings and introductions. Bowing slightly with your hands to your sides and your feet together is a good way to show respect.

Thailand

Business relationships with Thais are not as formal as those found in Japan, China, Korea, or the Middle East, but neither are they as relaxed and impersonal as is common in the United States. If possible, get a prior introduction or personal reference before approaching potential business contacts.

The Thai cultural values of patience, respect for status (age, authority, and so on), and not losing face are significant factors in business relationships.

Vietnam

The business practices of the Vietnamese are often more similar to those of China, Japan, and Korea than to those of its Southeast Asian neighbors.

The pace of negotiations is extremely slow, and at times you may find that a Vietnamese person wants to renegotiate a deal that has already been agreed to. At times, American businesspeople become frustrated with a Vietnamese person's apparent inability to make a decision or with the fact that decisions are reversed. This is indicative not of the person's ability or willingness to work with foreign businesspeople but of complexities behind the scenes. The apparent decision-maker doesn't always have the only say in negotiations.

Relationships are also very important in Vietnam, as they are in general throughout the region. Your counterpart will want to know who they're dealing with before getting in too deep. American businesspeople need to understand this aspect and be patient if their Vietnamese counterparts seem reluctant to move on a transaction immediately.

Before initiating contact with a Vietnamese company, try to find a third party or intermediary to introduce you.

The Marketplaces of the Middle East and North Africa

The region of the Middle East and North Africa — the Arabic world — includes countries such as Saudi Arabia, Israel, Egypt, the United Arab Emirates, Syria, Iran, Iraq, Jordan, Lebanon, Oman, Algeria, and Morocco.

How negotiations work in the Middle East and North Africa

Individuals coming from this region are not as punctual as their American counterparts. People of the Middle East and North Africa tend to arrive late for meetings — don't take it personally if they don't even show up.

Names in the Middle East are often confusing to Americans, so try to get the names (in English) of those you'll be meeting, speaking to, or corresponding with ahead of time. That way, you can find out both their full names and how to address them in person.

In all nations of this region, religion plays a very important role in both the history and current business environment. The predominant religion is Islam.

Bargaining is part of the everyday life in the Middle East and North Africa, and solid personal relationships are keys to success.

In verbal communication, Arabs tend to be indirect and vague by American standards. For example, when you make a proposal, Arabs seldom say "no," even if they disagree with you.

If you ask someone whether your proposal is good and your Arab counterpart hesitates and then agrees, the hesitation is a strong indication that he actually disagrees.

Gestures tend to be expressive, and eye contact is important. Arabs maintain a closer physical distance than is common in the United States. Touching or embracing upon meeting is common. A traditional Arab greeting between men involves each grasping the other's right hand, placing the left hand on the other's right shoulder, and exchanging kisses on each cheek.

Nations of the Middle East and North Africa

The countries I cover in this region include Egypt, Israel, Kuwait, Morocco, Saudi Arabia, and the United Arab Emirates.

Egypt

The Egyptian market is complex and highly competitive, so study the market well before engaging in business. A good Egyptian agent can help you a great deal. Get acquainted with the local culture, and take time to develop an appreciation for the Islamic faith. To please your business counterpart from Egypt, attempt to learn as many Arabic phrases as possible.

Be patient. Business with Egyptians is conducted somewhat slowly. When you visit a businessperson, don't just walk in, shake hands, and get down to business. If you've previously met with the person, chat about common friends and ask after his family.

Israel

Israel's business environment has no particular business protocols; it mainly follows Western conventions, which makes most U.S. businesspeople feel very comfortable in doing business in Israel.

Israelis arrive well-prepared for meetings and are very direct. Provide your hosts with an agenda outlining your objectives in advance. Exchanging business cards is common, although some Israelis may be less aware of this practice. Provide your business card early on and, if receiving a card in return is important, politely request one if the other party doesn't offer one.

In Israel, the Sabbath begins at sunset on Friday and ends at sunset on Saturday. When in Israel, no business is conducted on the Sabbath. The work week runs from Sunday through Thursday.

Kuwait

English is widely spoken in Kuwait, and many Kuwaiti business professionals were educated overseas, so you'll have minimal language difficulties in Kuwait.

A personal relationship provides an important basis for successful business ties in Kuwait. Allowing time for friendly conversation before commencing with a business agenda is essential. The pace of business is slower than it is in the United States. Meetings always start slowly and consist of a lot of small talk before you get down to serious discussion. The Kuwaitis will let you know when they're ready to talk business.

Morocco

Moroccan business representatives are increasingly interested in exploring business ventures with U.S. companies. Implementation of a free trade agreement has opened new sectors and attracted a large number of U.S. firms to explore the local market.

Many of Morocco's businesspeople were educated in Europe. Morocco is a former French protectorate, and many of its business practices are based on the French system. The main language used in business discussions is French.

Many aspects of Morocco's rich culture and heritage are absorbed in its business etiquette, so make every effort to understand the subtleties of this aspect of doing business. Build trust and friendship in order to build the business.

Saudi Arabia

The pace of business with Saudis is much slower than in the United States, so be patient. Decision-making can be a long, drawn-out process. Saudis speak at a much closer distance than North Americans do, so try not to back up if someone steps into your personal space.

At the initial meeting, let the Saudi party initiate the greeting. Westernized men shake hands with other men. A more traditional Saudi greeting between men involves each grasping the other's right hand, placing the left hand on the other's right shoulder, and kissing each cheek.

Use the right hand in preference to the left. As in other Islamic counties, the left hand, which is reserved for hygiene, is considered unclean. Do not discuss women, not even to inquire about the health of a wife or daughter. Also avoid the topic of Israel. Sports is an appropriate topic.

Communications occur at a slow pace. Do not feel obligated to speak during periods of silence. "Yes" usually means "possibly." At a meeting, the person who asks the most questions is likely to be the least important. The decision-maker is often a silent observer.

United Arab Emirates

The approach to doing business in the United Arab Emirates is similar to that of Saudi Arabia and Kuwait. On the other hand, the culture in the Emirates is essentially conservative Muslim, but it's tolerant up to a point. In the Emirates, you find men and women working together in offices, and you see women in positions of responsibility.

In a business meeting, it's considered impolite to begin addressing business topics without taking several minutes for small talk. Courtesy is more emphasized in the Emirates than in typical U.S. business meetings.

Never ask about a man's wife. Business cards and gifts should be offered with the right, not left, hand. Never sit with the sole of your foot facing someone.

The Marketplaces of Sub-Saharan Africa

Sub-Saharan Africa includes countries such as Nigeria, South Africa, Zimbabwe, Zaire, Angola, Zambia, Tanzania, and Kenya. Nigeria and South Africa are the major players in business.

How negotiations work in sub-Saharan Africa

When negotiating business in sub-Saharan Africa, realize that people may expect things to be done their way. However, some among younger generations may have greater international experience and can be quite open-minded. Building lasting and trusting relationships is important to most people in this region. Your counterparts may expect to get to know you better as you do business together.

When doing business in sub-Saharan Africa, frequently emphasize the long-term benefits and your commitment to the business relationship you're seeking to build. Business relationships in this region exist both at the individual and at the company level. Most individuals from sub-Saharan Africa only want to do business with people they like and trust.

Interrupting others is considered rude. Periods of silence do not necessarily convey a negative message. Although most Africans avoid confrontation, they're often direct and may be very blunt. They don't find it difficult to say "no" if they dislike a request or proposal.

Body language, gestures, and physical contact can be frequent. At an initial meeting, frequent eye contact conveys sincerity. However, a subordinate makes eye contact less often when dealing with a superior, and it's important not to stare at people.

Negotiations tend to be slow and drawn out. Building a relationship, gathering information, and getting a decision take a great deal of time. Sub-Saharan Africans like to bargain and haggle, and they get upset when you fail to play along.

Should a dispute arise at any stage of the negotiations, you may be able to reach a resolution by relying on a personal relationship and showing willingness to compromise.

Nations of sub-Saharan Africa

In this section, I focus on doing business in Nigeria and South Africa.

Nigeria and other West African nations

Nigeria is Africa's most populous country, accounting for approximately one-sixth of its people. As a gateway to 15 smaller West African countries, Nigeria can be a very rewarding market for U.S. exporters who take the time and effort to understand its market conditions and opportunities, find the right partners and clients, and take a long-term approach to market development. With Nigeria's growing and increasingly sophisticated consumer base, coupled with a strong like for U.S. products and American culture, opportunities are impressive.

Nigeria can also pose challenges, including inadequate energy and transportation infrastructure and the threat of crime and corruption. Nevertheless, U.S. companies that take a careful and informed approach to the market can do well and develop longstanding and profitable business relationships and operations in Nigeria for the West African markets.

During a business meeting in Nigeria, address people by their titles, particularly the honorific titles of traditional leaders. Your company representatives should be flexible in business dealings and able to make decisions on contractual matters without lengthy referral to another associate.

Conduct important business with Nigerians face to face. No worthwhile transactions can be completed quickly or impersonally.

South Africa

South Africa, a country of about 50 million people, is rich in diverse cultures. It has enjoyed economic stability and has a pro-business environment. South Africa is a logical and attractive choice for U.S. companies looking to enter markets in sub-Saharan Africa.

Business customs in South Africa are generally similar to those in the United States and Western Europe. Business cards are usually simple, including only the basics such as company logo, name, business title, address, telephone number, fax number, e-mail, and web address.

South Africans are also very punctual. South African businesspeople make every effort to be on time for appointments.

Afrikaners, who are of European descent, seldom show their emotions openly. Black South Africans may be less restrained.

The Marketplaces of North America: Focusing on Canada

Although Mexico and countries in Central American technically are part of North America, I discuss those countries in the next section. Here, I focus on Canada.

North America is designed to promote free enterprise and competition. The United States is a dominant market for Canadian products, receiving more than three-quarters of Canada's output in a typical year. The trading relationship between the United States and Canada is one of the largest in the world. Canada's strong infrastructure and proximity to the U.S. market make it an attractive location for doing business.

But although Canada has close political and economic ties with the United States, Canada strives to retain a separate cultural identity.

Familiarize yourself with the culture, history, and geography of the province you're dealing with when developing personal contacts in business dealings. Business culture varies somewhat throughout Canada, depending on the region. Most Canadians identify very strongly with their province. French Canadians especially tend to have a strong sense of cultural identity and are very nationalistic.

Historically, there has been long-standing conflict between French-speaking Canada and English-speaking Canada. Note that although English and French are both official languages of business, all international business is conducted in English. Firms exporting products to Canada must be aware of the country's labeling laws.

Canadians are well informed and comfortable with reasonable discussions. The pace of negotiations in Canada is similar to the pace in the United States; however, don't be surprised if a final decision gets hung up on details. Verbal communication is direct and open. If your Canadian counterpart doesn't like your proposal, your offer will be promptly declined. Little to no touching takes place, and handshakes are firm and brief.

When doing business in Canada, make a good first impression in any sales communication. Sell the reliability and honesty of yourself and your company before trying to sell your product or service.

Business customs when dealing with Canadians are very similar to those in the United States. For example, an exchange of business cards is expected at business meetings.

The Marketplaces of Latin America

Latin America generally refers to Mexico, Central and South America, and parts of the Caribbean. This large market is characterized by significant differences in wealth, and economic and political power remains concentrated in the hands of a few, although you do see a growing middle class in countries such as Brazil and Mexico.

How negotiations work in Latin America

With the exception of Brazil, where the national language is Portuguese, nations in Latin America speak Spanish. The attitude toward time is less rigid than among North Americans, and a 30-minute delay is often considered prompt.

Latinos usually stand closer together during conversations, so be prepared for that plus casual touching and, of course, the *abrazo,* or embrace, among good friends. You may even be surprised when a Latin businessman holds your elbow while conversing or walks down the street arm-in-arm with you.

Latin Americans are very warm and friendly people and enjoy social conversation before getting down to business. This is a calculated process aimed at getting to know you personally. Latin Americans tend to be more interested in you, the person, than you as a representative of some business. Do not be surprised if you're asked for a favor, which is part of their tradition of starting a personal relationship.

The main meal of the day is usually taken at midday. However, feel free to host your business guests over dinner in the evening. Most Latin American businesspeople know about U.S. dining customs and in their own country will entertain in the evening at a restaurant for special occasions. When toasting, the host is customarily expected to make the first toast, with the guest then responding.

One cultural note when doing business in Latin America: Don't say that you're from "America." In Latin America, the term "America" denotes both North and South America. Therefore, call yourself a North American (*norteamericano*).

Nations of Latin America

The countries I cover in this section include Argentina, Brazil, Chile, Colombia, Costa Rica, Ecuador, Guatemala, and Mexico.

Argentina

Argentine business and customs are generally more formal than those in the United States. Business dress, appearance, and general demeanor are more conservative. Courtesy is very important, and efforts to rush a business deal are unlikely to meet with success.

Shake hands with everyone in the room upon arriving and leaving. Among Argentines, it's customary for men to give women they meet for the first time a kiss on the right cheek. However, businesspeople from the United States should shake hands with Argentine women until a friendly relationship has been established.

Be sure to have an ample supply of business cards printed in Spanish as well as English.

Argentines are tough negotiators. Concessions don't come quickly or easily. Good relationships with counterparts shorten negotiations. Contracts are lengthy and detailed. A contract is not final until all of its elements are signed. Any portion can be renegotiated. Get everything in writing.

Brazil

The pace of negotiations with Brazilians is slower than in the U.S. and is heavily based on personal contact. It's rare for important business deals to be concluded after only one visit. Many Brazilian executives do not react favorably to being rushed. They prefer a more continuous working relationship.

Be prepared to commit long-term resources (both in time and money) toward establishing strong relationships in Brazil. Brazilian importers tend to be most concerned with after-sales service provided by the U.S. exporter.

Personal space standards of Brazilians are different from those in the United States. A Brazilian may stand very close while speaking, pat a business contact on the shoulder, or even hug that person. Despite the difference in personal space, you should act formal during an initial meeting.

Communication in Brazil tends to include people interrupting each other constantly. This is a sign of interest in the subject, not of disrespect.

Chile

U.S. business representatives find that business practices in Chile and the United States are very similar. Many Chilean businesspeople are well-educated professionals who travel internationally and speak English. However, not all speak English, and visitors often find the ability to speak Spanish very useful, if not a must. Product marketing or company promotional literature should be in Spanish.

Male Chileans may greet each other with hearty hugs, with women customarily kissing each other on the cheek. Most people from Chile have two surnames: one from their father, which is listed first, followed by one from their mother. Only the father's surname is used when addressing someone.

Have business cards printed in English on one side and Spanish on the other. Generally, cards are presented to everyone in a meeting. Titles are important and should be included on business cards. Address a person directly by using his or her title only.

Colombia

Colombians are used to doing business with the United States. Many of them have traveled or studied in the United States and have family members or friends there. Colombian executives and technicians, as well as government officials, travel frequently to the United States for meetings, conferences, trade fairs, training, and tourism.

Handshakes are the customary greeting in business. Colombians take a long time in greetings, so don't rush things. Colombians feel that taking this time conveys respect for the other person. Among friends, expect the *abrazo,* or embrace.

Costa Rica

Costa Rican business executives place great importance on personal contact with their foreign suppliers. During meetings, handshakes are a common greeting. The U.S. company representative should have business cards, proposals, and other material printed in both English and Spanish. Titles are important and should be included on business cards. At least initially, address a person directly by using his or her title only.

For persons who do not have professional titles, show respect by calling a gentleman *Señor* (plus his first name) and a lady *Señora* (plus her first name). Children and subordinates refer to adults in this manner, and referring to the other party this way — unless the person you're addressing has requested otherwise — is a sign of courtesy.

Business negotiations proceed more slowly than in North American culture, and a direct approach may not be viewed as favorably as an indirect one. Impatience is widely viewed as a weakness and can lower your credibility.

Ecuador

Business customs in Ecuador are similar to those in other Latin American countries. Ecuadorians are polite and well-mannered. On business cards and during meetings, the use of a title is common. Business is conducted in Spanish, and your efforts to speak Spanish will be appreciated.

Guatemala

Guatemala has the largest economy of Central America and is one of the most important U.S. trading partners. Guatemalan business executives and government officials place great importance on personal contacts with suppliers.

U.S. suppliers should be prepared to have a local representative or distributor and to travel to Guatemala personally. Visitors are often surprised at the accessibility to key decision-makers and by the openness and frankness of local buyers.

U.S. executives interested in pursuing business in Guatemala should approach local businesspeople in the same manner in which they'd approach good clients in the United States. Individuals interested in selling products in Guatemala should be prepared to explain how their products and services can complement existing products and systems.

Mexico

Patience is key to doing business in Mexico. Business meetings can be lengthy. Etiquette often includes small talk before business.

Mexican social etiquette makes it difficult to say "no." Therefore, "yes" does not always mean "yes." In conversation, Mexicans emphasize tactful and indirect phrasing and may be more effusive than Americans with praise and emotional expressions. Being overly aggressive during a meeting is often considered rude.

Men shake hands upon meeting and leaving and will wait for a woman to be the first to offer her hand. Women may shake hands with men and other women. Many times, a woman may pat another woman's shoulder or forearm or kiss on the cheek.

Mexican men are warm and friendly and make a lot of physical contact. They often touch shoulders or hold another's arm. To withdraw from this touch is considered insulting.

During an initial meeting with Mexicans, refrain from using first names until you've been invited to do so. As with other Latin American countries, titles are important and should be included on business cards. You may directly speak to someone by using his or her title only, without including the last name.

Address a person who doesn't have a professional title by using *Señor* (Mr.), *Señora* (Mrs.), or *Señorita* (Miss) and his or her surname. Mexicans generally use two surnames. The first surname listed is from the father, and the second surname is from the mother. When speaking to someone, use his or her father's surname.

Part V
Completing the Transaction: International Trade Procedures and Regulations

The 5th Wave   By Rich Tennant

" Or, we could just agree to disagree."

In this part . . .

1 focus on a variety of international trade procedures
and introduce you to the terms of sales that are
common in all international transactions. This information
will help you make sense of the costs and expenses that
are included in the quoted price. I also compare and contrast
the alternative methods of payment in international
transactions. Finally, I explain U.S. Customs requirements,
so you can get your goods through Customs.

Chapter 16

Making the Sale: Pricing, Quotes, and Shipping Terms

In This Chapter

▶ Considering pricing and the environmental forces that influence it

▶ Defining the terms of sales commonly used in international transactions

▶ Submitting an export quotation with a pro forma invoice

*A*fter you've decided what to sell and where to sell it, you have to set a price for your product. The price of your product must be high enough to generate an acceptable profit (after all, that's why you're in business) but low enough to be competitive (otherwise, no one will buy what you're selling). Pricing your product properly is key — and so is submitting the quotation to your client in the correct format. Submitting a haphazardly completed quotation may lead to an immediate rejection — and a loss not just to the current sale but also future ones.

When you're preparing an export quotation, you need to select the term of sale and the appropriate method of payment. Plus, you need to understand international shipping terms. I cover pricing, terms of sale, and *pro forma invoices* (the invoices used to quote your price to the prospective seller) in this chapter. For more on methods of payment, turn to Chapter 17.

Pricing Your Exports

When you're trying to determine the price for your product in other countries, answer the following questions:

✔ **Are you trying to penetrate a market for long-term growth, or are you looking for an outlet for excess inventory or outdated products?** Do you want to develop the market for the long term, or are you just looking to make a one-time sale? If you're in it for the long run, you may want to follow a more aggressive pricing approach. If you have some excess or outdated inventory, you may consider selling items at reduced costs, just to move the goods and reduce warehousing expenses.

✔ **At what price should you sell your product in the foreign market?** If you're also selling the products locally, what relation will the export price have in relation to the domestic price? You have to decide whether the price will be higher, lower, or the same as the domestic price. If you're in it for the short term, you may want to focus on a higher price; if you're in it for the long run, attempting to develop the market, you may want to pursue a more aggressive or lower-pricing approach.

✔ **What type of image do you want to convey to your customer in relation to competitive products and other products that you may be offering?** You need to decide what image you want your product to have relative to your competitors. You can decide to present a high-quality image (reflected in a higher price), or you may want to be seen as a lower-cost alternative (reflected in a lower price).

✔ **What price accurately reflects the level of the product's quality?** If you're selling a higher-quality product than your competitors are, that should be reflected in the price.

✔ **Is the price competitive?** You need to be realistic with your price. Remember, when you're exporting, competition will come from

- Local manufacturers in the country you're exporting to.

- Other U.S. manufacturers also exporting products to that country.

- Exporters from countries other than the United States.

✔ **Will you place a greater emphasis on the profit or the sales volume?** You have to decide what's the more important objective — profits or sales. If you're more interested in profit, you'll pursue a skimming strategy; on the other hand, if you want to place an emphasis on sales, a penetration strategy is in order (see Chapter 8 for details on skimming and penetration strategies).

✔ **Should you include any discounts or allowances to the customer?** Will you consider offering cash, quantity, seasonal, or trade discounts?

✔ **To what extent will changes in prices affect the demand for the product?** The consumer market demand is affected by changes in prices — the lower the price, the more the consumer will buy. In the business market, changes in price rarely impact the level of demand.

The *consumer market* is that particular group of people who have the authority, willingness, and desire to take advantage of the product that you're offering for their own personal use. The *business market* is one business selling goods to another business; the business is purchasing those goods to produce another product, to resell it, or to use it in the operations of their business. (See Chapter 8 for more on the consumer and business-to-business markets.)

Consider any additional costs that are the responsibility of the importer, such as duties, Customs fees, and possible currency fluctuation costs. The keys to a successful quotation are understanding the relationship of the domestic price to the export price and understanding the corresponding terms of sale that are used in international transactions (see "Setting the Terms of Sale," later in this chapter).

If your price is too high, your product won't sell. On the other hand, if your price is too low, it'll create a loss. The key elements of selecting the proper price are costs, market demand, and competition, all of which I cover in the following sections.

Considering costs

If you're a manufacturer, an accurate computation of your costs of goods is a key element in determining whether exporting is a viable option. However, when many manufacturing firms that are new to exporting add on the additional administrative costs, freight forwarding, shipping and Customs charges, and so on, they realize that their price is no longer competitive.

The key for many manufacturers is *not* to use this cost-plus approach but to look at exporting as an opportunity to open up new markets for additional sales, generating revenues and spreading the fixed costs over a larger base of sales.

On the other hand, if you aren't a manufacturer and you're operating as an export management company (see Chapter 1), your costs will be based on negotiations with a manufacturer. When you're negotiating a price with the manufacturer, you must stress the importance of being competitive. Tell the manufacturer that this will be an opportunity for the manufacturer to generate new sales in areas it may have previously ignored. In other words, keeping the costs down benefits not just you but the manufacturer as well; if the manufacturer buys into this idea, you have a better chance of getting your products for a competitive price.

When contacting suppliers (see Chapter 7), negotiate with several firms, and don't stop negotiating after you get an initial offer from your first contact. You'll always find more than one company that can manufacture your product, and some manufacturers will take a more competitive approach in negotiating with you.

The price you negotiate ultimately reflects your quotation to your client.

Factoring in market demand

Demand for your product is a function of the following:

- The number of consumers
- The consumers' tastes, attitudes, and ability to pay
- Whether competitive products exist

These factors won't be identical in any two markets — each market is unique. For this reason, you'll likely need to charge different prices in each market in which you sell.

When dealing in consumer goods, per capita income is a gauge of what the customer can pay.

Some popular items (for example, major branded items) may create a stronger demand than anticipated by the characteristics of the market and may not have an effect on prices (in other words, even low-income markets won't affect the selling price). However, keeping products simple (offering alternatives to name-brand items) to reduce your selling price may be an answer to selling in some of these lower-per-capita-income markets.

The affordability of your products is also a function of the fluctuations in the exchange rates. As the value of a currency increases in relation to the currency of another country, the price of the exported product will increase. A decrease in the value of the currency will reduce the price to the foreign customer.

Gauging the competition

In setting prices, take note of competitors' prices. The number of competitors and the way they compete will differ from country to country, so you need to evaluate each market separately. In addition to competing with other firms from your own country, you're likely also competing with local companies (that is, companies that are located in the market where you want to do business) as well as other multinationals from places like Europe and Asia.

If you have multiple competitors in a foreign market, you may have no alternative but to reduce your export price to match the price of your competition. However, if your product is new to the market, you may be able to charge a higher price.

Setting the Terms of Sale

In any sales agreement, you need to provide not only the price but also a corresponding term of sale. *Terms of sale* are the conditions of sale that clarify who is responsible for which expenses as the goods move from the seller to the buyer. Terms of sale are an area of concern for many businesses that are just beginning to export, because international terms of sale can differ from those used in domestic sales.

As an exporter, you need to become familiar with *Incoterms,* the universal trade terminology developed by the International Chamber of Commerce (ICC). The ICC created these terms to describe the responsibilities of the exporter and importer in international trade. Understanding and using these terms correctly is important, because any misunderstanding may prevent you from living up to your contractual obligations and make you accountable for shipping expenses that you initially intended to avoid.

A complete list of important terms and their definitions is provided in *ICC Guide to Incoterms 2010.* You can order the print version online for $90 at www.iccbooksusa.com or by calling 212-703-5066 (an e-book version is also available at a cost of $70).

WARNING!

The terms in international business transactions often sound similar to those used in domestic business, but they can have very different meanings. Confusion over terms of sale often results in either a loss *of* a sale or a loss *on* a sale, so make sure you know the meaning of the terms you're using.

In the following list, I cover shipping terms that are common in all international transactions. You use these terms when making quotations as an exporter or receiving quotations as an importer. The terms identify which specific expenses are the responsibility of the buyer and seller. (See Figure 16-1 for a graphical representation of terms of sale.) For example, if the shipping term is Ex-works (EXW), the exporter is responsible to place the goods on the edge of their loading dock, and all expenses are paid for by the importer, either as a freight collect scenario or an additional charge added to the invoice. When the term of sale if FAS (Free Alongside the ship), the exporter is responsible for all expenses to get the goods to the edge of the ship's loading dock, and all expenses beyond that are the responsibility of the importer.

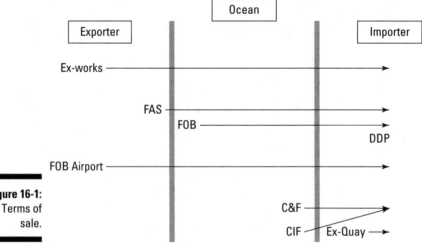

Figure 16-1:
Terms of sale.

✔ **Cost and freight (C&F):** *Cost and freight* means that the exporter is responsible for all costs and freight expenses necessary to bring the cargo to the destination named in the shipping term. The importer is then simply responsible for any unloading charges, Customs clearance fees, and inland freight expenses as the cargo moves from the pier to the importer's warehouse. Title (risk of loss or damage) is transferred from the exporter to the importer as the goods pass the ship's rail in the port of shipment.

✔ **Cost, insurance, and freight (CIF):** *Cost, insurance, and freight* is similar to C&F (see the preceding bullet) with the exception that the exporter is responsible for procuring marine cargo insurance against loss or damage as the goods are transported from the point of origin to the point of destination.

✔ **Delivered duty paid (DDP):** *Delivered duty paid,* followed by the words naming the importer's premises, means that the price includes all expenses as the cargo moves from the seller's factory to the buyer's warehouse. With this term, the exporter bears the full cost and risk involved in moving the cargo from the factory to the destination. DDP represents the maximum obligation for the exporter.

✔ **Ex-quay:** *Ex-quay* means that the exporter is required to make the goods available to the importer on the *quay* (wharf or pier) at the destination named in the sales contract. At that point, title transfers from the exporter to the importer.

✔ **Ex-works (EXW):** The term *ex-works* means that the exporter's only responsibility is to make the goods available at the edge of the loading dock of its facility. For a price quoted using this term, the exporter is not responsible for the loading of the goods onto a truck provided by the importer unless doing so is otherwise agreed to. The importer bears the full cost and risk involved in moving the cargo from the factory to the destination. EXW represents the minimum obligation for the exporter.

Whenever you provide the EXW term of sales, all expenses in moving the cargo from the point of origin to the destination are the responsibility of the importer. The additional costs could include transportation of the cargo to the point of shipment, loading charges, ocean or air freight charges, unloading at the destination, Customs fees, and inland transportation expenses to the destination. These charges will go forward and be collected by the carrier at the destination, or they can be additional charges added to the invoice.

✔ **Free alongside ship (FAS):** *Free alongside ship* indicates that the exporter is responsible for all expenses as the goods are transported from the factory to edge of the ship's loading dock. Any expenses beyond that point are the responsibility of the importer.

✔ **Free on board (FOB):** *Free on board* indicates that the exporter is responsible for all expenses as the cargo is transported to the pier and then loaded onto the vessel at the point of shipment named in the sales contract. Any expenses beyond that point are the responsibility of the importer.

> ✔ **Free on board airport (FOB airport):** Under *free on board airport,* the exporter is responsible for all expenses in transporting the cargo from the factory to the carrier at the airport of departure, and risk of loss or damage is transferred from the exporter to the importer when the goods have been delivered to the carrier. Any additional expenses from the airport to the destination are the responsibility of the importer.

When quoting a price, make the term meaningful to the importer. For example, don't quote your price on a product as "Ex-works Smithtown, New York," which may be meaningless to a prospective foreign buyer. The prospective buyer would probably find it difficult to compute the total costs and then may hesitate in placing an order. Whenever possible, quote C&F, because it shows the buyer the cost of getting the product near the destination. To compute the C&F price, you need to know the specific quantities that will be purchased. If that information isn't available, then quote using the term FAS or FOB.

A freight forwarder can provide assistance in computing freight expenses.

Filling Out the Paperwork: Quotations and Pro Forma Invoices

Many international inquiries begin with a request for quotation, and the preferred form that an exporter uses to submit a quotation is referred to as a *pro forma invoice,* which is a quotation in invoice format. (You can see a sample of this invoice at www.unzco.com/basicguide/figure11.html.) Exporters use pro forma invoices when applying for an import license, arranging for financing, or applying for a letter of credit.

The quotation on the pro forma invoice form should include the following:

- ✔ Names and addresses of the exporter (seller) and importer (buyer)
- ✔ Any reference numbers
- ✔ Listing and description of products
- ✔ Itemized list of prices for each individual item being sold
- ✔ Net and gross shipping weights (using metric units when appropriate)
- ✔ Dimensions for all packages (total cubic volume, again using metric units when appropriate)
- ✔ Any potential discounts

- ✔ Destination delivery point

- ✔ Terms of sale

- ✔ Terms of payment

- ✔ Shipping and insurance costs (if required)

- ✔ Expiration date for the quotation

- ✔ Total to be paid by the importer

- ✔ Estimated shipping date

- ✔ Currency of sale

- ✔ Statement certifying that the information found on this pro forma invoice is true and correct

- ✔ Statement that provides the country of origin of the goods

The pro forma invoice must be clearly marked *pro forma invoice*. If a specific price is being guaranteed, the period during which the offer remains valid must be clearly stated. Also, the quotation should clearly state that prices are subject to change without notice. For example, increases in fuel costs may cause unanticipated increases in freight rates on the part of the carriers.

Chapter 17

Methods of Payment

*I*f you're an exporter and you want to be successful in today's global marketplace, you have to offer your customers attractive sales terms (see Chapter 16) and appropriate methods of payment to secure their business. You want to make sure that you'll get paid while minimizing your own risk and accommodating the needs of your buyer.

If you're an importer, you need to negotiate a payment term that minimizes your risk, with assurances that the goods received are exactly as ordered, on time, and in good condition.

The exporter wants payment as soon as possible, ideally as soon as the order is placed and *before* the goods are shipped to the importer. The importer wants to receive the goods as soon as possible, while delaying payment as long as possible, ideally until *after* he's sold the goods.

In this chapter, I fill you in on the various methods of payment and let you know which options are best for you if you're an exporter and which are best for you if you're an importer.

Looking at the Main Forms of Payment and Analyzing Their Risks

Any international transaction involves risk. You need to understand what those risks are and which actions you can take to minimize them. Here are the primary payments used in international transactions:

✔ **Cash in advance:** This means that the exporter receives his money before making the shipment.

✔ **Letter of credit drawn at sight:** This document, which is issued by the importer's bank, guarantees that the exporter will get paid as long as he presents required documents to the bank before an expiration date.

✔ **Time letter of credit:** This document is the same as the letter of credit drawn at sight except that the exporter gets the money a certain number of days after the documents have been presented and accepted.

✔ **Bill of exchange (documentary collections):** Bill of exchange is like buying something using cash on delivery (COD), except the importer makes the payment when the bank presents the required documents, not when the importer receives the goods. Here are the two types of bills of exchange:

- **Sight draft documents against payment:** The importer pays when the documents are presented.

- **Sight draft documents against acceptance:** The importer makes the payment a certain number of days after he has accepted the documents.

✔ **Open account:** With this method, no bank is involved in the transaction. The exporter sends the documents to the importer and trusts that the importer will send him the money.

✔ **Consignment:** The exporter ships the goods, and the importer has to remit payment for them only after the goods have been sold and the customer pays the importer.

Figure 17-1 illustrates the relationship of these payment methods to the amount of risk for buyers (importers) and sellers (exporters). For the exporter, cash in advance is the most favorable, and consignment is the least favorable. On the other hand, for the importer, consignment is most favorable, and cash in advance is the least favorable.

In the following sections, I cover each of the main methods of payment in detail.

Cash in advance

Cash in advance is the most desirable method of payment from the point of view of the exporter, because he has immediate use of the money and no problems coordinating collection with the banks or shipping companies. This is particularly true if the payment is made by wire transfer; if the payment is made by check, delays may occur as the check clears.

Risk Diagram

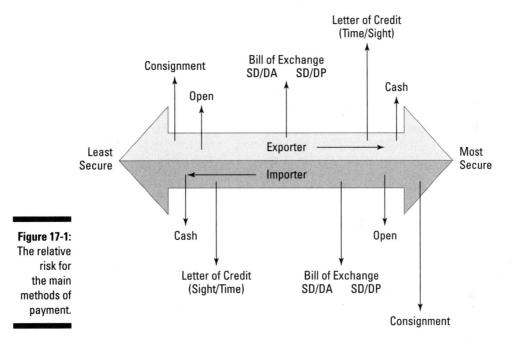

Figure 17-1:
The relative
risk for
the main
methods of
payment.

If you're an importer, you may hear the exporter from another country request terms of *TT*. This stands for *telex transfer,* and it's the same thing as a bank-to-bank wire transfer (or cash in advance).

Cash in advance creates cash-flow problems and increased risk for the importer. So although cash in advance looks great from where the exporter is standing, it's probably not going to be competitive — the importer will likely refuse to make a payment until after receiving and inspecting the merchandise.

Letter of credit

Importers may be concerned that if they make a payment in advance, the goods may not be shipped or the quality of the goods may be inferior, and they'll be left holding the bag. Letters of credit are often used to protect the interests of both parties.

Before you start talking with overseas suppliers or customers, you need to be aware of some of the terminology related to letters of credit:

✔ **Confirmed letter of credit:** A confirmed letter of credit is one whose validity has been confirmed by a bank in the exporter's country. After confirmation, the exporter is guaranteed payment even if the foreign buyer or bank defaults. From the exporter's point of view, foreign political risk is also eliminated, because the seller receives the payment as soon as the documents are presented.

✔ **Irrevocable letter of credit:** An irrevocable letter of credit cannot be amended or canceled without the agreement of all parties — the beneficiary (exporter), the applicant (importer), the issuing bank, and the confirming bank, if the letter of credit is confirmed. A letter of credit should clearly indicate whether it is revocable or irrevocable; however, in the absence of such indication, the credit is deemed to be *irrevocable*.

If you're an exporter, always start negotiations by asking that payment be made by a confirmed and irrevocable letter of credit. Doing so protects you from all commercial and political risks. If you're an importer, keep in mind that unless the supplier has a long-term relationship with you, almost all initial transactions will require that you make payment by a confirmed and irrevocable letter of credit.

✔ **Revocable letter of credit:** As an importer or exporter, you almost always encounter the term *irrevocable* when someone mentions letter of credit payment terms. Still, a *revocable* letter of credit does exist. A revocable letter of credit may be amended or canceled by the issuing bank at any time without prior notice to the beneficiary, up to the moment of payment. It's generally used when the applicant and the beneficiary are affiliated parties or subsidiary companies.

If you're an exporter, do *not* accept a revocable letter of credit as a method of payment. If you do, the importer has the option of canceling the transaction at any time.

✔ **Transferable letter of credit:** A transferable letter of credit allows the beneficiary to request that the issuing bank (or another bank authorized by the issuing bank) make the funds from the credit available in whole or in part to one or mort other parties. Funds can be transferred only when the bank issuing the letter of credit designates it as a transferable letter of credit.

✔ **Back-to-back letter of credit:** A back-to-back letter of credit is a method of financing used when an exporter is not supplying the goods directly. In other words, the exporter is not a manufacturer but is acting as an export management company (see Chapter 1) or as an export agent (see

Chapter 2). The exporter, upon receipt of an irrevocable letter of credit drawn in his favor, arranges to have the advising bank issue a *second* irrevocable letter of credit in favor of the supplier from whom the goods are being purchased. In other words, the exporter uses a portion of the proceeds due from the letter of credit as collateral for the second letter of credit.

Say you're selling (to a client in Saudi Arabia) $20,000 of disposable medical supplies, which you'll be purchasing from Medical Products Manufacturer in Boston for $15,000. The client in Saudi Arabia has agreed to open up a $20,000 letter of credit in your favor for the purchase of these supplies. The manufacturer in Boston won't extend personal credit to you — it wants guarantees that it'll get paid. So you can instruct the advising bank in New York, using the initial credit as collateral, to open up a second letter of credit in the amount of $15,000 in favor of the manufacturer in Boston. You ship the goods, and all required shipping documents are presented to the advising/confirming bank. Upon the bank's acceptance of these documents, the bank remits $15,000 to the manufacturer in Boston and the balance of $5,000 to you.

An exporter can only open a back-to-back letter of credit if the advisee (the importer) has initially designated the letter of credit as transferable.

There are two main types of letters of credit: the *letter of credit drawn at sight* and the *time letter of credit*. I cover each of these in the following sections.

Letter of credit drawn at sight

A *letter of credit drawn at sight* is a document that the importer's bank issues; the bank promises to pay the exporter a specified amount after receiving certain documents stipulated in the letter of credit before a listed expiration date. Figure 17-2 illustrates the process of a letter of credit drawn at sight.

Here's the situation I use in the example: The importer in New York, called ABC Importing, is interested in purchasing 300 dozen sweaters from a supplier in Japan, as detailed on purchase orders 1234 and 1235. The supplier (exporter) in Japan is XYZ International, based in Tokyo. The value of this purchase is $30,000. The terms of payment are going to be FOB Japan (see Chapter 16 for details on free on board and other terms of payment).

ABC Importing, which completes the application for a commercial letter of credit from its bank, is called the *applicant;* the exporter in Japan, XYZ International, is called the *beneficiary.*

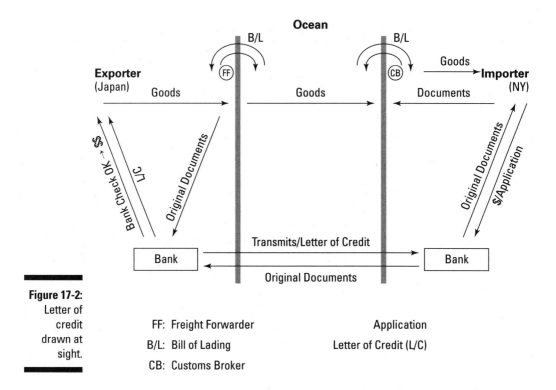

Figure 17-2:
Letter of
credit
drawn at
sight.

FF: Freight Forwarder   Application

B/L: Bill of Lading   Letter of Credit (L/C)

CB: Customs Broker

Here's how the transaction plays out:

1. ABC Importing applies for the letter of credit with its bank in New York.

Look at the application in Figure 17-3 and note the following:

1. The letter of credit number assigned by the importer's bank in New York

2. The advising bank in Tokyo, Japan

3. The name and address of the applicant, ABC Importing Company, New York

4. The name and address of the beneficiary of the proceeds of this letter of credit in Japan, XYZ International

5. The amount of the letter of credit (US$30,000)

6. The last date for presentation of documents for payment to the bank in Japan (May 15, 2012)

7. The last date for presentation of documents at the bank in New York (May 15, 2012)

8. A request by the importer to issue an irrevocable letter of credit in favor of the beneficiary (XYZ International), and the methods by which the letter of credit will be delivered

9. A description of the merchandise as it must appear on the invoice ("300 dozen of women's sweaters as detailed on order numbers 1234 and 1235")

10. Terms of sale, listed as FOB Japan

11. A listing of documents accompanying the draft submitted; these documents must be presented to the confirming bank in Japan: a commercial invoice (original and three copies), and a full set of original onboard ocean bills of lading marked "Freight Collect."

12. Latest date for shipment from the port in Japan

13. The fact that the importer has the right to either permit or prohibit partial shipments or transshipments. (If you prohibit partial shipments, the exporter must ship the entire order at one time; if you prohibit transshipments, the exporter must place the goods on the vessel that will deliver the goods to the port of destination — in other words, the goods can't be unloaded and placed on another vessel for shipment to the destination.)

The applicant (ABC Importing) takes this completed application and $30,000 to its bank in New York. ABC is giving the money to its bank for the purchase of the sweaters, together with instructions that the funds are to be released to the beneficiary (XYZ International) when the listed required documents are presented to the bank, prior to the expiration of the letter of credit. The required documents are the commercial invoice and the full set of onboard ocean bills of lading marked "Freight Collect."

Today, all banks allow you to complete the letter-of-credit application process online.

2. **The bank accepts this application and the proceeds for the letter of credit, and it sends the irrevocable letter of credit to the bank in Japan, requesting a confirmation.**

Figure 17-4 shows a copy of the negotiable letter of credit. The information on the application (refer to Figure 17-3) has been transferred to the negotiable letter of credit.

World Wide Bank
International Operations
P.O. Box 44, Church Street Station, NY, NY 10008
Cable Address: World Wide Bank

APPLICATION FOR COMMERCIAL LETTER OF CREDIT	1. Credit Number
2. Advising Bank Worldwide Bank/Japan 1 Maranouchi 2-Chomechiyodaku Tokyo 100 Japan	3. For Account of *Applicant* Name: ABC Importing Company Address: 89 Main Street City/State: New York, NY 10036
4. In Favor of *Beneficiary* Name: XYZ International Company Address: 13 Ginza City/State: Tokyo, Japan	5. Amount: U.S. $ 30,000 Thirty Thousand Dollars US 6. ❏ Presentation for negotiation. on or before 7. ❏ Presentation at World Wide Bank NY on or before Date: 05/15/08 Date: 05/15/08

8. Please issue an irrevocable Letter of Credit substantially as set forth and forward same to your correspondent for delivery to the beneficiary by:

❏ Airmail Only   ❏ Airmail with preliminary brief details cable   ◆ Full details cable

9. Available by beneficiary's drafts at   10. ❏ Sign on Chemical Bank NY for <u>100</u> % of invoice value _____ for _____ % of invoice value

11. Covering – *Merchandise must be described on the invoice as:*
      300 dozen of women's sweaters as detailed on order numbers 1234 and 1235

12. Terms: ❏ FAS_____   ❏ FOB <u>Japan</u>   ❏ C&F _____   ❏ CIF _____

13. Draft(s) must be accompanied by the following documents – Refer to Boxes Checked Below:
      ◆ Commercial Invoice, original and three copies
      ❏ U.S. Customs Invoice in Duplicate
      ❏ Marine Insurance Policy or certificate including war risks
      ❏ Airwaybill — consigned to World Wide Bank marked notify
      ◆ On Board Ocean Bill of Lading — Full Set Required, if more than one original has been issued to order of Chemical Bank marked notify applicant as shown above and marked <u>FREIGHT COLLECT</u>

14. OTHER DOCUMENTS: _____
_____

15. Shipment from: <u>Japanese Port</u>   17. Partial Shipment ❏ Permitted ◆ Prohibited
      to: <u>New York</u>   16. Latest: <u>04/30/XX</u>   Transhipment ❏ Permitted ◆ Prohibited

18. ❏ Insurance effected by applicant with <u>York Insurance Company</u> under Policy No. <u>123</u>

19. Documents must be presented to negotiating or drawee bank within <u>15</u> days, after shipment, but within validity of Letter of Credit *(if number of days left blank it will automatically be considered 21 days)*

20. Additional instructions if any: _____
_____

21. If credit is in foreign currency, *refer to box checked:*
      ❏ Foreign exchange is to be purchased for our account immediately
      ❏ Foreign exchange is not to be purchased at this time
22. If credit is at sight in foreign currency, *refer to box checked:*
      ❏ We do desire cable advice of payment to you by buying bank
      ❏ We do not desire cable advice of payment to by by buying bank
      This application is subject to the conditions on the reverse iside hereof, which is an integral part of this application

23.
Account with World Wide Bank: 123-000001

24. Company or Corporate Name: <u>ABC Importing Company</u>   Date: <u>April 20 2008</u>

Figure 17-3:
An
application
for a letter
of credit.

World Wide Bank
Trade Services Group
P.O Box 44, Church Street Station
New York, NY 10008

Issue Date: April 28, 2088
LC No.: T-341558

ADVISING BANK	APPLICANT
World Wide Bank - Tokyo Central P.O. Box 1279 3-1 Marunouchi 2 - Chrome Chiyoda-ku, Tokyo Japan	ABC Importing Company 89 Main Street New York, NY 10036
BENEFICIARY	AMOUNT: USD 30000.00
XYZ International Company Ltd. 13 Ginza Tokyo, Japan	(THIRTY THOUSAND AND 00/100 U.S. DOLLARS)

WE HEREBY ESTABLISH OUR IRREVOCABLE LETTER OF CREIDT IN YOUR FAVOR, DRAFT(S) TO BE MARKED "DRAWN UNDER CHAMICAL BANK, LETTER OF CREDIT NO. T-341558"

DATE AND PLACE OF EXPIRY: MAY 15, 2008 IN TOKYO, JAPAN

CREDIT AVAILABLE WITH ANY BANK
    BY: Negotiation of your draft(s) at sight drawn on Chemical Bank, accompanied by the documents indicated herein.

COVERING — MUST BE INVOICED AS:
    300 Dozen of Women Sweaters F.O.B. Japanese Port

DOCUMENTS REQUIRED:
    1. Commercial Invoice, Original and three copies
    2. On Board Ocean Bill of Lading — Full set required if more than one original has been issued, consigned to order of Chemical Bank, Marked NOTIFY applicant (as shown above) and "FREIGHT COLLECT"

PARTIAL SHIPMENTS: Not Permitted
TRANSHIPMENTS: Not Permitted
FOR TRANSPORTATION TO: New York
NOT LATER THAN: May 15, 2009

WE ARE INFORMED INSURANCE IS EFFECTED BY APPLICANT BY YORK INSURANCE COMPANY UNDER INSURANCE POLICY NUMBER 123.

DOCUMENTS MUST BE PRESENTED WITHIN 15 DAYS AFTER SHIPMENT, BUT WITHIN VALIDITY OF THE LETTER OF CREDIT.

ALL FOREIGN BANK CHARGES ARE FOR BENEFICIARY'S ACCOUNT
DRAFTS AND DOCUMENTS MAY BE FORWARDED TO US IN ONE AIRMAIL

THE AMOUNT OF EACH DRAFT NEGOTIATED, WITH THE DATE OF NEGOTIATION, MUST BE ENDORSED HEREON BY THE NEGOTIATING BANK. WE HEREBY AGREE WITH YOU AND WITH NEGOTIATING BANKS AND BANKERS THAT DRAFTS DRAWN UNDER AND IN COMPLIANCE WITH THE TERMS OF THIS CREDIT SHALL BE ONLY HONORED UPON PRESENTATION TO US, IF NEGOTIATED, OR IF PRESENTED TO THIS OFFICE (LETTER OF CREDIT DEPARTMENT, 55 WATER STREET, NEW YORK, NY 10041) TOGETHER WITH THIS LETTER OF CREDIT, ON OR BEFORE THE EXPIRY DATE INDICATED ABOVE.

IRREVOCABLE L/C

Authorized Signature

Figure 17-4:
A negotiable
letter of
credit.

3. **The bank in Japan presents the negotiable letter of credit to the beneficiary (exporter), XYZ International.**

   XYZ International is now in possession of a negotiable document that states that it will receive US $30,000 when the shipment of sweaters has been forwarded to the shipping company and placed onboard the vessel and when all required documents are presented to the bank in Japan before the expiration date. XYZ is a very happy exporter, because it knows that the money is in the bank.

4. **The exporter (XYZ) reviews all the conditions listed on the letter of credit.**

   XYZ contacts its freight forwarder to confirm that the goods can be shipped prior to the expiration date. If XYZ is not able to comply with one or more of the conditions, it will alert the importer (ABC) immediately, with a request to have the letter of credit amended.

5. **The exporter (XYZ) arranges with the freight forwarder to deliver the goods to the appropriate port of shipment.**

   When transferring the cargo to the freight forwarder, the exporter usually prepares the shipper's letter of instructions. The *shipper's letter of instructions* is just that — a letter from the shipper instructing the freight forwarder on how and where to send the export shipment. The instructions consist of the following:

   - The name and address of the exporter

   - The exporter's IRS employer identification number (EIN) or Social Security number (SSN) if no EIN has been assigned

   - The name and address of the person or company to whom the goods are shipped (known as the *ultimate consignee*)

   - The name and address of the authorized forwarder acting as the forwarding agent for the exporter

   - The name of the transportation company responsible for moving the cargo from the loading dock of the exporter to the point of shipment (known as the *inland carrier*)

   - The country in which the merchandise is to be consumed, further processed, or manufactured (known as the *final country of destination* or the *country of ultimate destination*)

   - The shipper's reference number with the freight forwarder

   - The date the shipment is sent to the forwarder

   - The method of shipment required

   - The numbers and kinds of packages (boxes, barrels, or cases) and any descriptive marks, numbers, or other identification shown on the packages

- The gross shipping weight (in pounds) of the commodities being shipped, not including the weight of the shipping container

- The selling price (or cost if not sold) of the number of items recorded in the quantity field when the vendor sold them to the purchaser

- Whether the shipper (prepaid) or consignee (collect) will pay freight charges; if the shipment is to be paid for cash on delivery (COD) by the consignee, specify the amount

- Any special instructions, such as a specific carrier to be used, special electronic mail notification, required certifications, and so on

- Instruction to the forwarder on how to dispose of the shipment in the event it proves to be undeliverable abroad

- An indication of whether the shipper wants to use an insurer chosen by the freight forwarder, if insurance is required; the insurance amount is usually 110 percent of the shipment value

6. **After the goods are loaded and placed onboard the vessel for shipment to New York, the freight forwarder completes the necessary documentation and receives the necessary documentation from the shipping carrier.**

   The key document returned to the forwarder is the original set of onboard ocean bills of lading, consigned to the order of the bank and marked "Notify Applicant — ABC Importing Company, New York."

   The bill of lading is the key document in this transaction. It serves as a receipt issued by the shipping company that a shipment has been received and loaded onboard the vessel for shipment to the port of destination (in this case, New York). The importer (ABC Importing) also requires the bill of lading in order to clear the goods through Customs and receive them from the shipping company.

7. **The exporter (or the freight forwarder) presents the documents, evidencing full compliance with the terms of the letter of credit, to the exporter's bank in Japan.**

8. **The bank reviews the documents to make sure they are in order and have been presented prior to the expiration date. If everything is in order, the bank releases the money to the exporter, XYZ International.**

   If the bank finds any discrepancies, the exporter's receipt of the money will be delayed. If the discrepancies aren't corrected, the confirming bank in Japan isn't allowed to release the funds. Here are the discrepancies that can cause delays:

   - Documents presented after the expiration date

   - Documents presented more than 21 days after shipment or other date as noted in the letter of credit

- Missing documents (such as bills of lading, inspection certificates, and so on)

- A difference between the description of the merchandise on the invoice and the description noted in the letter of credit

- A difference in the shipping terms from those specified in the letter of credit

- Unauthorized transshipment

- Shipment made after the date specified in the letter of credit

- Problems with the onboard bills of lading (for example, bills of lading that are improperly endorsed or improperly consigned or that state that the goods or shipping containers are damaged)

- Drafts and invoices not made out in the name of the applicant as shown on the letter of credit

 9. **The documents are returned to the importer (the applicant — ABC Importing) via its bank.**

 10. **The importer (ABC Importing) submits the documents to a *Customs broker* (an individual who is licensed to transact Customs business on behalf of others).**

 The Customs broker's responsibilities include the coordination of clearing the goods through Customs and arranging to have the goods delivered to the importer.

 11. **In order to have the shipping company release the goods to the Customs broker, the broker must give the original bill of lading back to the shipping carrier.**

 The shipping company releases the cargo only when the bill of lading is returned to them. Without the onboard ocean bill of lading, the shipping company will *not* release the cargo.

 12. **After the Customs broker receives the goods, the goods are transported and delivered to the importer (ABC Importing).**

The payment term *letter of credit drawn at sight* is so-named because the bank releases the funds to the exporter upon *seeing* the documents. Bank fees are the responsibility of the importer and are usually a percentage of the amount of the letter of credit. The percentage charge is based on the bank's policy and the relationship between the exporter and the bank.

When you're considering the letter of credit drawn at sight as a method of payment, keep in mind that it's extremely favorable to the exporter, because the exporter faces no risk. The exporter is guaranteed to get the money as long as the cargo is delivered to the carrier and documents are presented to the bank prior to the expiration date.

So, you may be wondering, what are the importer's risks of using this method of payment? The key is in the documents. The shipping company issues the bill of lading upon receipt of the goods. The goods arrive in a shipping container and are not individually inspected by the shipping company. In this example, the bill of lading will probably identify receiving one 20-foot container, which is said to contain 300 dozen women's sweaters. So it's possible that when the importer opens the container with the shipment, he could've received men's instead of women's sweaters, for example.

To minimize the risk of receiving the wrong goods, the exporter can arrange to have an independent inspection company inspect the goods. Inspection typically takes place at the manufacturer's or supplier's premises, at the time of loading, or at the destination during discharge or offloading. The inspection service then issues a certified certificate of inspection, which the importer adds to the letter of credit as a third required document. One of the major inspection services is SGS (Société Générale de Surveillance), 201 Route 17 North, Rutherford, NJ 07070; phone 201-508-3000; website www.sgs.com.

Time letter of credit

A *time letter of credit* is similar to the letter of credit drawn at sight (see the preceding section) with just one exception: With a letter of credit drawn at sight, the bank releases the funds to the exporter upon *seeing* the documents, but with a time letter of credit, the credit states that the payment is due within a certain *time period* after the bank accepts the documents (for example, 90 days after acceptance).

Using my earlier example of ABC Importing in New York and XYZ International in Japan, say the terms of payment are now a 90-day letter of credit. The process remains the same until you get to the point where the forwarder and/or exporter present the original documents to the bank. After the confirming bank accepts the documents, the bank is required to remit payment to the exporter in 90 days.

What if the exporter doesn't want to wait the 90 days for the money — can the exporter access the funds earlier? And what happens if the shipment arrives in New York 60 days after shipment, and the importer inspects the goods and realizes that the incorrect merchandise was shipped — can the importer instruct the bank not to remit payment? The answer to the first question is yes, and the answer to the second question is no.

The letter of credit that was issued was *irrevocable,* which means that it cannot be cancelled and the importer cannot stop the payment from being made.

On the other hand, because the money is guaranteed to the exporter in 90 days, the exporter has the right to go to the bank and borrow the money using the letter of credit as collateral. This process is referred to as *discounting* — the exporter discounts the letter of credit. Say the annual rate of interest on a secured loan is 12 percent (or 1 percent per month). In this case, the bank, upon request of the exporter, will remit the proceeds of the letter of credit *minus* the interest that would be due on the loan (3 percent).

Importers use discounting when they have an established line of credit with the bank. This approach may be used as an alternative to posting the original proceeds with the application for the letter of credit.

Exporter letter of credit checklist

Upon receiving the letter of credit, the exporter needs to carefully compare the credit terms with the terms of the original quotation, because if the terms aren't met, the letter of credit may be rendered invalid and the exporter may not get paid. If you're the exporter and you aren't able to meet the terms or you note any errors, you must immediately contact your customer and request that the credit be amended.

The following are points that you (as the exporter) need to evaluate when the credit is received and when the documents are being prepared. Make sure that

- ✔ The names and addresses of the buyer and seller are correct.

- ✔ The bank that issued the letter of credit is reputable and acceptable to you.

- ✔ The terms of the letter of credit are in accordance with your agreement. Will you be able to meet all the deadlines noted? Check with your freight forwarder to make sure that no unusual condition that could delay shipment is likely to arise.

- ✔ You and the buyer/importer are in agreement about partial shipments and transshipments. You may want to request that the letter of credit allow partial shipments and transshipments as a way of preventing some unforeseen last-minute problems.

- ✔ The descriptions of the merchandise, price, and quantity are correct.

- ✔ The terms of sale as noted are the same as in your original agreement.

- ✔ The letter of credit is transferable (if you aren't a manufacturer). A *transferable* letter of credit allows the beneficiary to request that the issuing bank (or another bank authorized by the issuing bank) make the funds from the credit available in whole or in part to one or more other parties. Funds can be transferred only when the bank issuing the letter of credit designates it as a transferable letter of credit.

Bill of exchange (or draft): Documentary collections

A *bill of exchange,* also called a *draft,* is similar in many respects to a check issued by a domestic buyer. As with checks that are used in day-to-day business situations, bills of exchange carry some of the similar risks: The check could bounce. The bill of exchange is an alternative method of payment to a letter of credit, and it's more advantageous to the importer while increasing risks for the exporter.

The process of using a bill of exchange is normally referred to as a *documentary collection.* In this transaction, the exporter entrusts the collection of payment to the exporter's bank, which sends documents to the importer's bank along with instructions for payment. Through the banks involved in the collection, funds are received from the importer and remitted to the exporter in exchange for the documents.

This method of payment involves the use of a draft that requires the importer to pay the face amount either on sight draft/documents against payment (SD/DP) or on a specified date in the future, known as sight draft/documents against acceptance (SD/DA).

Here are the key parties in a documentary collection:

- **Collecting bank:** Any bank, other than the remitting bank, involved in obtaining payment or acceptance from the importer (drawee)

- **Drawee:** The party, also known as the buyer or importer, that is presented with financial and/or commercial documents for the purpose of either payment or acceptance, in accordance with the collection instructions

- **Drawer:** The party, also known as the seller or exporter, that authorizes a bank (the remitting bank) to handle documents on its behalf

- **Presenting bank:** The collecting bank that presents the documents to the importer (drawee); usually the importer's bank

- **Remitting bank:** The bank that the exporter authorizes to carry out the collection on its behalf

Documentary collections are less complicated and less expensive than letters of credit. The importer is not obligated to pay for goods prior to shipment. The exporter retains title to the goods until the importer either pays the full amount of the draft or signs a letter of acceptance and agrees to pay at some specified future date. Similar to a letter of credit, the bank is responsible for controlling the flow of the documents, but the bank does not verify them or take any risks.

The bill of exchange is recommended for use only when the buyers and sellers have an established trade relationship. If you're an exporter, you need to be aware that you'll be taking on greater risks under this method of payment. The bank assists in obtaining payment, but it doesn't guarantee payment or verify the accuracy of the documents.

In the following sections, I cover the two main types of bills of exchange.

Sight draft/documents against payment

Sight draft/documents against payment (SD/DP) is similar to cash on delivery (COD) used in domestic transactions, except instead of being cash on delivery, SD/DP is cash on documents.

Here's how sight draft/documents against payment works (Figure 17-5 provides a visual representation of these steps):

1. **The importer forwards a purchase order to the exporter.**

   In the example from the earlier section "Letter of credit drawn at sight," ABC Importing in New York forwards an official purchase order, requesting the purchase of 300 dozen women's sweaters from XYZ International in Japan.

2. **The exporter (XYZ) confirms receipt of the order and prepares and ships the goods to the freight forwarder for loading onto the vessel for shipment to the port of New York.**

3. **After the goods have been loaded onto the vessel for shipment to New York, the shipping company issues the original onboard ocean bill of lading.**

4. **The exporter (XYZ) and freight forwarder present the original documents to the exporter's bank with instructions for obtaining payment.**

   Using the documents against payment collection method, the exporter (XYZ) gives the documents to its bank, which forwards them to the exporter's branch or correspondent bank in New York, along with instructions on how to collect the money from the importer.

   In this arrangement, the collecting bank releases the documents to the importer only upon payment for the goods. Upon receipt of payment, the bank transmits the funds to the exporter (XYZ).

5. **The importer (ABC) presents the documents (the original bill of lading) to the shipping company through its Customs broker in exchange for the goods.**

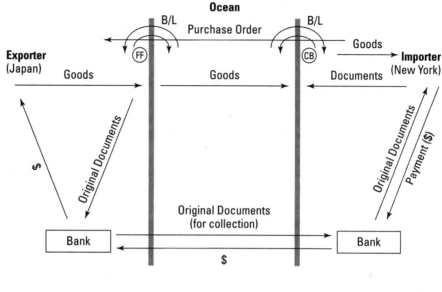

Figure 17-5:
Sight draft/
documents
against
payment.

FF: Freight Forwarder

B/L: Bill of Lading

CB: Customs Broker

Although this method is more advantageous to the buyer, the exporter has increased risk in this example. Even though the importer can't have access to the goods without payment, the exporter's risk is that if the draft is unpaid (that is, ABC Importing doesn't have the funds and rejects the shipment), the goods have to be returned or forwarded to another customer, and the exporter has to pay for that.

If you're an exporter, the sight draft/documents against payment approach is a high-risk one. I recommend it only when you and the importer have an established trade relationship and you're doing business with a buyer in a country that's politically and economically stable.

If you're the importer, keep in mind that the bank and the shipping company do not inspect the goods. Their responsibilities are only to issue, accept, and deliver the original documents. As with the letter of credit, the sight draft/documents against payment approach means taking a risk on the nature and quality of the goods. If you have any concerns, consider working with an inspection company (see "Letter of credit drawn at sight," earlier in this chapter).

Sight draft/documents against acceptance

With sight draft/documents against acceptance (SD/DA), the exporter extends credit to the importer through the use of a time draft. In other words, the exporter is requesting that payment be made at some time in the future (for example, 90 days).

In this situation, the documents are released to the importer upon acceptance of the draft and the importer's promise to make the payment at the designated future date. By accepting the draft, the importer becomes legally obligated to pay the invoice at a future date. At the due date, the collecting bank contacts the importer and, upon receipt of payment, transmits the funds to the exporter. (Figure 17-6 provides a visual representation of sight draft/documents against acceptance.)

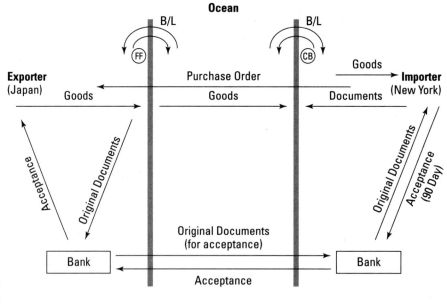

Figure 17-6:
Sight draft/
documents
against
acceptance.

FF: Freight Forwarder

B/L: Bill of Lading

CB: Customs Broker

In the earlier example, the exporter (XYZ International) agrees to sell the sweaters to the importer (ABC Importing) with payment terms of 90 days sight draft/documents against acceptance. The process is similar to the documents against payment approach (see the preceding section) with one major difference: When the documents are presented to the importer (ABC), the importer doesn't have to give the bank the money. Instead, the importer has to sign a letter of acceptance, agreeing to make the payment at some agreed-upon future date.

If you're an exporter, sight draft/documents against acceptance is an extremely high-risk option. If the buyer doesn't have the funds when approached by the bank for the payment, the unpaid bill just becomes another bad debt, and you're left with nothing.

Open account

The open-account payment method is a convenient alternative to the other methods. However, the importer must be well-established, have a long and favorable payment history, and have been deemed to be very creditworthy in order for this to work. Under the open-account option, the banks are eliminated from the process, and the exporter bills the importer, who is expected to pay under agreed-upon terms at some future date.

The open-account approach poses significant risk, and the lack of official documents and banking involvement make it difficult to legally enforce any claims. If you're an exporter, the process of pursuing these collections may be difficult and costly.

Consignment

International consignment sales follow the same procedures as consignment in a domestic transaction. If you're an exporter, you ship the goods to a foreign distributor, who's responsible for paying the exporter only if the goods are sold. You, as the exporter, retain title to the goods until they're sold, and payment is forwarded to you only after the goods have been sold and the distributor has received payment.

In the earlier example, XYZ International in Japan would forward the sweaters to ABC Importing in New York. ABC Importing would be obligated to remit funds to XYZ only if and when the goods are sold. And XYZ would retain title to the goods until ABC sells them.

The exporter has the greatest risk with the consignment method, with very limited control over the goods and a long wait before getting paid.

If you're thinking, "What exporter in his right mind would agree to such a thing?" you're not alone. Consignment is not widely used, but it is an option. Here's a situation in which it might be feasible: Say that XYZ, the exporter in Japan, has some really old, pre–World War II–style sweaters. The exporter doesn't think he'll ever be able to sell them, so he might take a chance, send them to ABC in New York, and tell ABC, "Give it a try, and if you sell them, send me the money." The exporter may make some money, and at least he doesn't have any inventory or holding costs.

Factoring in Foreign Currency Risks Due to Fluctuations

By definition, in any transaction, the importer and exporter always come from different countries and rarely use the same currency. Payments are usually made in either the exporter's currency or the importer's currency. In some rare situations, payment is made in some mutually agreed-upon currency that's foreign to both parties.

One of the risks involved with foreign trade is the fluctuation of exchange rates between currencies. If you're an exporter, you've agreed to accept payment in a foreign currency, and if the currency there is devalued, you'll lose money in the transaction. On the other hand, if the foreign currency increases in value, you'll make more money on the deal than you anticipated.

As the value of a currency increases in relation to the currency of another country, exports decline, and imports increase. On the other hand, as the value of a currency decreases in relation to the currency of another country, imports increase, and exports decline. Importers like a strong currency (in their own country), and exporters like a weak currency.

The risk due to the fluctuation in the exchange rate is always assumed by the individual who's either making or receiving the payment in a foreign currency. In other words, if you don't want any risks as an exporter, when you invoice your client, always do so in U.S. dollars. If you're an importer, always request that the supplier quote prices to you (and invoice you) in U.S. dollars.

If you're asked either to make a payment or to receive a payment in a foreign currency, consult an international banker before negotiating the sales contract. She can offer advice on exchange rate risks and recommend ways to minimize some of these risks. (To find an international banker, just go to your bank and ask for the international division.)

Noting Non-Cash Methods of Payment

A number of poor and developing countries want to acquire goods and products for which they don't have the convertible currency to pay for. If you're an exporter, here are the two main approaches to non-cash trade:

- ✔ **Barter:** Barter is the direct exchange of goods or services between two parties, with no money changing hands. Basically, instead of receiving cash for the products you send to the less-developed country, you receive products that are equal in value.

- ✔ The Department of Commerce says that barter in its various forms accounts for about thirty percent of the world's total business. The International Reciprocal Trade Association (IRTA) (www.irta.com/) recently announced that U.S. barter transacted through commercial barter brokers exceeds $9 billion annually. Over 450,000 U.S. businesses actively use organized barter.

- ✔ **Countertrade:** Countertrade is a non-cash method of payment that small to medium-size exporters don't normally encounter. A countertrade contract may say that the U.S. exporter will be paid in a convertible currency as long as the U.S. exporter (or an entity designated by the exporter) agrees to export a related quantity of goods from the importing country.

A *convertible currency* (also referred to as a *hard currency*) is one that's accepted by both residents and nonresidents for the payment of goods and services. A *nonconvertible currency* (also referred to as a *soft currency*) is one that usually has no value outside of the country that has issued it, and it more than likely will *not* be accepted by nonresidents for the payment of goods and services.

To see how countertrade works, say that South Africa wants to purchase 500 million U.S. dollars' worth of aircraft from Boeing, a U.S. company. The purchase may include a contractual agreement whereby Boeing would receive the US$500 million, as long as it agrees to identify customers for the equivalent quantity of goods to be exported from South Africa.

Chapter 18

Packing and Shipping with the Right Documentation

In This Chapter

▶ Understanding the role of a freight forwarder

▶ Identifying packing and labeling requirements for exports

▶ Obtaining cargo insurance on export shipments

▶ Identifying the documents required for exports

After you've received and accepted your export order, you need to coordinate shipment and get the goods into the hands of your customer. That sounds simple enough, but when you're getting your orders ready for shipment, you have to follow certain rules and regulations on packing, labeling, documentation, and insurance. If you want your goods to arrive in good condition and on time, following these requirements is essential.

In this chapter, I fill you in on all these requirements and help you get your products where they need to be when you need them to be there. *Note:* This chapter is mainly for exporters. If you're an importer, turn to Chapter 19, which addresses getting your goods through Customs.

Recognizing the Benefits of a Freight Forwarder

A *freight forwarder* is an independent company that acts as your agent in moving the cargo from its point of origin (in the United States) to its overseas destination. In the following sections, I go over the freight forwarder's services and explain how to find a freight forwarder.

Understanding what freight forwarders can do for you

Freight forwarders provide a valuable service to exporters. They coordinate the shipment of the goods from the factory, arrange to have the cargo loaded onto the vessel, and process the documentation on the shipment. Especially when you're new to exporting, having a freight forwarder you can trust helps ease the stress of sending your first shipments overseas.

Freight forwarders are familiar with

- ✔ U.S. export regulations (see Chapter 3)
- ✔ The import rules and regulations of the countries that the goods are being shipped to
- ✔ Alternative methods of shipping
- ✔ All the applicable documents connected with foreign trade

Whether you're shipping a small parcel via air, large crates by ocean vessel, or full container loads of goods, a freight forwarder can assist you in moving your cargo anywhere in the world at any speed that you need.

Freight forwarders also assist exporters by advising them about freight costs, port charges, consular fees, costs of special documentation, and handling fees. They do this as part of their price quote process for their prospective customers, so you don't have to worry about getting slammed with a charge you hadn't expected. Every charge you pay should be spelled out ahead of time, allowing you to budget and plan accordingly.

Freight forwarders can recommend proper packing so that the goods arrive in good condition, and they can also arrange to have the cargo export packed at the point of shipment or coordinate the packing of goods into a container.

When the order is ready for shipment, the freight forwarder coordinates the preparation of all shipping documents required by the foreign government, as well as those required as part of the payment process (see Chapter 17). They ensure that everything is in order.

Freight forwarders also arrange to have the goods delivered to the carrier in time for loading, prepare the bill of lading and any special required documentation, and forward all documents directly to the customer or to the paying bank, if applicable.

Export freight forwarders are licensed by the International Air Transport Association (www.iata.org) to handle air freight and the Federal Maritime Commission (www.fmc.gov) to handle ocean freight.

If you're exporting small parcels, then using the services of UPS International or Federal Express may be an easier option than working with a freight forwarder. In these situations, international shipping companies basically provide the services that would normally be provided by a freight forwarder. Use this option only when you're exporting small parcels, because the associated freight costs can be pretty high.

The documentation requirements imposed by foreign governments can, at times, be overwhelming. Just to get an idea, go to www.export.gov, click the I Want To link on the right-hand side of the page, click Find Country Information, click Trade Information Center–Country Database, select a region, and select a country. You'll be able to identify all Customs information and import documentation required in making shipments to the country you chose. A freight forwarder takes care of all this information and documentation for you.

Documents required for export shipments vary widely according to the country of destination and the type of product being shipped. Although there is a core set of documents with which every exporter should be familiar (covered later in this chapter), determining what additional documentation is necessary can be a frustrating process. There are a number of resources that help exporters make sure that they are sending out the right forms with their shipments. A reputable freight forwarder is always a good source of information about documentation. Express companies, such as Federal Express, UPS, and DHL, can also help. The most common documents are

- ✔ **Shipper's Export Declaration** (SED or Form 7525-V): The SED must be electronically filed at www.aesdirect.gov.

- ✔ **Consular Invoice:** If a consular invoice is required, copies are available from the Embassy or Consulate of the destination country. The Trade Information Center link http://export.gov/worldwide_us/index. asp can provide contact information for Embassies and Consulates around the country.

- ✔ **Certificate of Origin:** This document is only required by some countries. Special certificates are needed for countries with which the United States has special trade agreements, such as Mexico, Canada, and Israel. More information about filling out these special certificates is available from the Trade Information Center (i-800-USA-TRADE).

- ✔ **Additional documents**: These can include Commercial Invoice, Bill of Lading, Insurance Certificates, and Packing List.

Finding and choosing a freight forwarder

Freight forwarders are located in most metropolitan areas. Local business telephone listings often feature a freight forwarder or transportation section. Additionally, the National Customs Brokers and Forwarders Association of America (1200 18th St. NW, Suite 901, Washington, DC 20036; phone 202-466-0222; website www.ncbfaa.org) provides exporters with information on its members.

Privately operated forwarder listing services, such as the following, can also help you identify a local forwarder:

- ✔ **Directory of Freight Forwarding Services:** www.forwarders.com
- ✔ **Freightgate:** www.freightgate.com/directories/directories.tet
- ✔ **Freightnet:** www.freightnet.com
- ✔ **1800miti.com:** www.1800miti.com/links/warehouse/logistics/usa_dis_log.html

The criteria for choosing a freight forwarder are the same as for selecting a Customs broker (see Chapter 19). You want to identify a freight forwarder who has experience in the country where you anticipate doing business.

When you're establishing your relationship with a freight forwarder, the freight forwarder provides a contract that specifies the services that it'll perform and the terms and conditions of the relationship. You'll be appointing the freight forwarder as an agent to prepare documentation, so you have to provide it with a power of attorney for that purpose. Any mistakes that the freight forwarder makes will be *your* responsibility, as far as customers and government agencies are concerned.

Ask your attorney to review the agreement and make any appropriate modifications *before* you sign it.

Packing and Labeling Your Shipment

When you're packing a shipment for export, you need to be aware of the demands that may be placed on the package. The concerns include everything from weight and moisture issues to breakage and pilferage.

If your customer doesn't specify packing requirements, keep the following considerations in mind:

✔ Pack goods in a strong, sealed, and filled package when possible.

✔ If you can, pack and put your goods on pallets to ensure ease of handling.

✔ Make sure that packages and packing filler are made of moisture-resistant materials.

✔ Don't list the contents or brand names on the packages — you want to avoid possible pilferage.

Shipments via air require less heavy packing than ocean shipments. However, air shipments still need to be protected, especially if the items are packed in domestic containers, because they may still be subject to pilferage.

The marks and labels on export shipments need to meet shipping regulations, ensure proper handling, conceal the identity of the contents, and assist your customers in identifying shipments. The customer usually specifies export marks that need to appear on the cargo for easy identification. In addition to meeting your customer's requirements, you need to make sure the following marks appear on each carton you ship:

✔ **Your shipper's mark:** This is sort of like a return address. The shipper's mark, which identifies the exporter, can be used by the buyer for easy identification of the goods.

✔ **Country of origin:** If you're shipping from the United States, just put "Made in the U.S.A."

✔ **Weight marking (in pounds *and* in kilograms):** For a quick and easy conversion calculator, just go to www.google.com and type in *X* **pounds to kilograms** (where *X* is the number of pounds of your shipment). It'll tell you exactly how many kilograms your shipment weighs.

✔ **The number of packages and size of cases (in inches *and* centimeters):** For a quick and easy conversion, go to www.google.com and type in *X* **inches to centimeters** (where *X* is the number of inches). It'll tell you exactly how many centimeters your shipment measures.

✔ **Handling marks:** Handling marks are international pictorial symbols that are standard on shipments. For a complete list of them, go to www.in amarmarine.com/pdf/LossControl/Marks%20and%20Symbols.pdf.

✔ **Precaution markings:** These markings include stickers that say things like "This Side Up" or "Use No Hooks."

✔ **Port of Entry:** This is the city where your product will arrive in the country you're shipping to.

✔ **Labels for any hazardous materials:** These labels provide an important identification of packaged dangerous goods in transport, including items such as explosives, flammable liquids, gases, and so on.

Freight forwarders can supply you with the necessary information regarding these specific packing regulations.

Covering Your Assets with Cargo Insurance

Ocean or air export shipments need to be insured against loss, damage, or delay in transit. International agreements such as the Warsaw Convention and the Carriage of Goods by Sea Act limit the carrier's liability for international shipments, so you or the buyer needs to arrange for cargo insurance. The person responsible for making arrangements for cargo insurance depends on the term of sale (see Chapter 16). Consult an international insurance carrier or freight forwarder for more information on insurance.

If you're a small company, or if you're new to export and the terms of sales make you responsible for insurance, it'll probably be easier for you to insure the cargo under a freight forwarder's policy for a fee than to get a personal policy with an insurance company.

If the terms of sale make the foreign buyer responsible for the insurance, make sure that the buyer has obtained adequate insurance. If the buyer neglects to obtain coverage or doesn't have enough, damage to the cargo may force you to absorb a significant financial loss.

Nailing Down the Documentation

Although the actual purchase order from your overseas customer is the most important document you'll receive, you have to become familiar with many other documents before exporting your goods.

Because processing the documents for exporting goods can be a formidable task, you should seriously consider having a freight forwarder handle this portion of the transaction. Even if you hire a freight forwarder, you're responsible for the content of the documents that are prepared and filed. The freight forwarder prepares the documents based on information you provide.

The following documents are commonly used in exporting. Which ones you need to use depends on the situation, product, and government regulations of both the United States and the importing country. If you have questions about filing the correct documents for your specific situation, talk to a freight forwarder.

Commercial invoice

A *commercial invoice* (see Figure 18-1) is the first international document that you prepare as an exporter. It provides details that are included in many of the other documents.

Commercial Invoice

Date _____

Bill of Lading/Air Waybill No. _____

Invoice Number _____

Purchase Order No. _____

Terms of Sale (Incoterm) _____

Reason for Export _____

Shipper   Tax ID/VAT No. _____
Contact Name _____
Company Name _____
Company Address _____
City _____
State/Province _____
Postal Code _____
Country _____
Telephone No. _____
Email ID _____

Ship To   Tax ID/VAT No. _____
Contact Name _____
Company Name _____
Company Address _____
City _____
State/Province _____
Postal Code _____
Country _____
Telephone No. _____
Email ID _____

Sold To   Tax ID/VAT No. _____
Contact Name _____
Company Name _____
Company Address _____
City _____
State/Province _____
Postal Code _____
Country _____
Telephone No. _____
Email ID _____

No. Units	Unit of Measure	Description of Goods (Include Harmonized Tariff Number if known)	Country of Origin	Unit Value	Total Value

Additional Comments

Invoice Line Total	
Discount/Rebate	
Invoice Sub-Total	
Freight Charges	

Declaration Statement

Insurance	
Other (Specify Type):	
Invoice Total Amount	
Currency Code	

Shipper Signature / Title _____   Date _____

Total Number of Packages _____

Total Weight (indicate LBS or KGS) _____

These commodities, technology, or software were exported from the United States in accordance with the Export Administration Regulations. Diversion contrary to U.S. laws is prohibited.

Figure 18-1: The exporter prepares a commercial invoice.

The commercial invoice serves as a bill for the goods from the importer to the exporter, and it also serves as evidence of a transaction. Additionally, the importer uses the commercial invoice to classify the merchandise so that she can get the shipment cleared expeditiously through Customs and make sure that all duties and taxes have been accurately assessed.

A commercial invoice includes all the following required information:

- ✔ Complete name, address, and phone for both the exporter and *consignee* (the person actually receiving the shipment)

    The consignee is usually the importer, but the importer can have the goods shipped to another address or individual. The consignee is the person or company named in the contract as the person or company that the goods are being turned over to.

- ✔ Terms of sale (see Chapter 16 for details)

- ✔ Reason for export

- ✔ A complete description of the item:

    - What is the item?

    - What materials is the item made of?

    - What is the item used for?

- ✔ Harmonized Tariff Codes, if known; Customs uses this information to determine applicable duties and clearance requirements

- ✔ Country of origin (where manufactured) for each commodity

- ✔ Number of units, unit value, and total value (purchase price, in whatever currency the quote was made) of each item; if your shipment is just a sample shipment or one that has no commercial value, you still must state a nominal or fair market value on the commercial invoice

- ✔ Number of packages and total weight (in both pounds and kilograms)

- ✔ Shipper's signature and date

Consular invoice for exports

In some instances, certain countries require a *consular invoice* to control and identify goods. Consular invoices are normally purchased from the consulate of the country to which the goods are being shipped and usually have to be prepared in the language of that country. They also need to be signed by a representative of the importer's country at that country's embassy or consulate located in the United States. The consul charges a fee for this service.

You can get information about consular invoices and whether they're required in your particular situation by talking to your freight forwarder. You can also determine whether a specific consular invoice is required for any country by going to www.export.gov, clicking on I Want To on the right-hand side of the page, clicking on Find Country Information, clicking on Trade Information Center–Country Database, selecting the region, and selecting the country.

Shipper's letter of instructions

The *shipper's letter of instructions* (see Figure 18-2) is a letter from the shipper/exporter instructing the freight forwarder on how and where to send the shipment.

The information in this form enables the freight forwarder to process the shipment and prepare the required documentation. The information you provide on the form outlines the details of the agreement between the exporter and the importer for the specific sale.

Bill of lading

A *bill of lading* is a contract between the owner of the goods (normally the exporter) and the carrier of the goods. Here are the two types of bills of lading:

✔ **A nonnegotiable straight bill of lading:** The straight bill of lading is issued by the exporter. It pertains to the shipment of the cargo from the point of origin to the port of shipment. This document serves as evidence that the shipping carrier has received the goods and will be transporting them to the destination listed on the document.

To see a copy of this form, go to www.nebs.com, type 6225 in the product search box, and click "Go."

✔ **A negotiable shipper's order bill of lading:** The negotiable shipper's order bill of lading (see Figure 18-3), also known as a marine or ocean bill of lading, is prepared by the freight forwarder and issued by the steamship company. It covers ocean transportation. The importer needs this document as proof of ownership to take possession of the goods (see Chapter 17).

When I say that a bill of lading is *negotiable,* I mean that the goods being shipped can be bought, sold, or graded while they're in transit. The bill of lading is endorsed; just as a check can be endorsed from one party to another, a negotiable bill of lading can be endorsed from one party to another.

SHIPPER'S LETTER OF INSTRUCTION					
SHIPPER *(NAME AND ADDRESS INCLUDING ZIP CODE)*		INLAND CARRIER	SHIP DATE		PRO NUMBER
	ZIP CODE				
EXPORTER EIN NO.	PARTIES TO TRANSACTION				
ULTIMATE CONSIGNEE:					
INTERMEDIATE CONSIGNEE:					
FORWARDING AGENT:		POINT (STATE) OF ORIGIN OR FTZ NO.		COUNTRY OF ULTIMATE DESTINATION:	
SHIPPER'S REF NO.	DATE:	SHIP VIA			

SCHEDULE B DESCRIPTION OF COMMODITIES						VALUE
D/F	MARKS, NOS., AND KIND OF PACKAGES SCHEDULE B NUMBER	QUANTITY - SCHEDULE B UNIT(S)	SHIPPING WEIGHT (Kilos)	SHIPPING WEIGHT (Pounds)	CUBIC METERS	(U.S. dollars, omit cents) Selling price or cost if unsold

LICENSING NUMBER OR SYMBOL		ECCN (When required)		PAYMENT METHOD	
DULY AUTHORIZED OFFICER OR EMPLOYEE		Exporter authorizes forwarder named above to act as forwarding agent for export control and customs purposes.		C.O.D. AMOUNT	
SPECIAL INSTRUCTIONS:					
SHIPPER REQUESTS INSURANCE:		If shipper has requested insurance as provided for at the left hereof, shipment is insured in amount indicated (recovery is limited to actual loss) in accordance with provisions as specified in Carrier's Tariffs. Insurance is payable to shipper unless payee is designated in writing by shipper.		SHIPPER'S INSTRUCTIONS IN CASE OF INABILITY TO DELIVER CONSIGNMENT AS CONSIGNED:	

Shipper or his Authorized Agent hereby authorizes the above named Company, in his name and on his behalf, to prepare any export documents, to sign and accept any documents relating to said shipment and forward this shipment in accordance with the conditions of carriage and the tariffs of the carriers employed. Shipper guarantees payment of all collect changes in the event consignee refuses payment. The Company is to use reasonable care in the selection of carriers, forwarders, agents, and others to whom it may entrust the shipments.

Figure 18-2: The exporter prepares the shipper's letter of instructions and gives it to the freight forwarder.

Account Name and Logo Here (include phone, fax and OTI license number)	**BILL OF LADING**	
SHIPPER/EXPORTER (provide complete name and address)	BOOKING NO:	BILL OF LADING NO:
	EXPORT REFERENCES:	
CONSIGNEE (please provide complete name and address)	FORWARDING AGENT/ FMC NO:	
	POINT AND COUNTRY OF ORIGIN:	
NOTIFY PARTY (please provide complete name and address)	FOR DELIVERY OF GOODS PLEASE PRESENT DOCUMENTS TO:	

MODE OF INITIAL CARRIAGE	PLACE OF INITIAL RECEIPT	DOMESTIC ROUTING/EXPORT INSTRUCTIONS	
VESSEL NAME	PORT OF LOADING		
PORT OF DISCHARGE	PLACE OF DELIVERY BY CARRIER	FREIGHT PAYABLE AT	TYPE OF MOVEMENT

PARTICULARS FURNISHED BY SHIPPER

MARKS & NOS/CONT. NOS	NO. OF PACKAGES	DESCRIPTION OF PACKAGES AND GOODS	GROSS WEIGHT	MEASUREMENT

TOTAL NUMBER OF PKGS.

Liability Information
Clause 20 on the reverse side hereof limits the carrier's liability to a maximum of US$500 per package or customary freight unit by incorporation of the Carriage of Goods by Sea Act. To protect for a higher value, you may declare a higher value and pay the ad valorem freight charge or purchase cargo insurance.
Declared Value:
The shipper may increase the carrier's liability by declaring a higher value in the "Declared Value" box to the right and paying the additional charge that accompanies this.
Insurance:
The shipper may also purchase insurance on the goods listed on this bill of lading by indicating this in the box to the right and paying the additional premium.

DECLARED VALUE: $_____
If shipper enters a value, carrier's limitation of liability shall not apply and the ad valorem rate will be changed.

SHIPPER REQUESTS INSURANCE:
☐ Yes   ☐ No   *Must check one box!*
Amount: $_____

FREIGHT RATES, CHARGES, WEIGHTS AND/OR MEASUREMENTS SUBJECT TO CORRECTIONS	PREPAID	COLLECT

RECEIVED FOR SHIPMENT from the MERCHANT in apparent good order and condition unless otherwise stated herein, the GOODS mentioned above to be transported as provided herein, by any mode of transport for all or any part of the Carriage, SUBJECT TO ALL THE TERMS AND CONDITIONS appearing on the face and back hereof and in the CARRIER'S applicable Tariff, to which the Merchant agrees by accepting this BILL OF LADING.
Where applicable law requires and not otherwise, one original Bill OF LADING must be surrendered, duly endorsed, in exchange for the GOODS or CONTAINER(S) or other PACKAGE(S), the others to stand void. If a 'Non-Negotiable' BILL OF LADING is issued, neither an original nor a copy need be surrendered in exchange for delivery unless applicable law so requires.

BY _____
AS CARRIER

DATED _____

Figure 18-3:
A negotiable shipper's order bill of lading.

Air waybill

The *air waybill* is a bill of lading for cargo being shipped by air. It's a non-negotiable document, issued by the air carrier, that specifies the terms under which the air carrier will be transporting the goods to their destination.

Certificate of origin

Certain countries require a signed statement about the origin of the goods that are being exported. You can usually obtain a *certificate of origin* (see Figure 18-4) through organizations such as your local chamber of commerce.

A certificate of origin may be required even if the commercial invoice states that the goods have been made in the United States.

Inspection certificate

Some importers and foreign countries require that the goods be inspected by an independent inspection company prior to shipment. The purpose of the inspection is to attest that the goods are what you're specifying they are. Inspection certificates are issued by and obtained from the independent testing organization.

Dock and warehouse receipt for exports

The *dock and warehouse receipt* transfers accountability after the domestic carrier has delivered the goods to the port of shipment and left them with the international carrier (vessel or airplane) for export. The international shipping company issues this receipt after the ground carrier delivers the goods to the dock.

If you work with a freight forwarder, he'll prepare the dock receipt. When the goods are delivered, the receipt is signed by the shipping company and returned to the freight forwarder, who then returns the receipt to the exporter with the documentation and the freight forwarder's invoice for his services.

US Certificate of Origin

The undersigned _____
(Owner or Agent)

_____
(Name and Address of Shipper)

declares that the following mentioned goods shipped on _____

on the date _____ consigned to: _____

are the product of the United States of America.

MARKS AND NUMBERS	NO. OF PKGS BOXES OR CASES	WEIGHT IN KILOS GROSS	DESCRIPTION
Bill of Lading/Air Waybill No.:			

Sworn to before me

this _____ day of _____ 20 ____   _____
Signature of Owner or Agent

The _____

a recognized Chamber of Commerce under the laws of the State of _____ ,
has examined the manufacturer's invoice or shipper's affidavit concerning the origin of the merchandise and according to the best of its knowledge and belief, finds that the products named originated in the United States of North America.

Secretary_____

Figure 18-4:
A certificate
of origin.

Destination control statement for exports

The exporter is required to place the *destination control statement* on the commercial invoice, on the ocean bill of lading or air waybill, and on the shipper's export declaration. This statement notifies the carrier and all foreign parties that diversion contrary to U.S. law is prohibited. The destination control statement can be as simple as, "These goods are licensed by the Department of Commerce for export to [Name of Country]."

Insurance certificate

If the terms of sale on the transaction were cost, insurance, and freight (CIF; see Chapter 16), the exporter is responsible for providing cargo insurance against loss or damage while the goods are in transit from the point of origin until they arrive at the destination. The exporter issues a certificate of insurance that states the type and amount of coverage. For a sample certificate of insurance, go to www.unzco.com/basicguide/figure9.html.

Shipper's export declaration

The *shipper's export declaration* (see Figure 18-5) is a form used by the Department of Commerce to control exports and compile trade statistics. The exporter must prepare and submit this form to the Customs agent for shipments by mail valued at more than $500 and for shipments by any other means valued at more than $2,500. It's required regardless of value for any shipments being made under a validated export license (see Chapter 3). The shipper's export declaration is usually prepared and submitted to the authorities by the freight forwarder.

Export license

The *export license* is a document that the U.S. government requires for those items requiring a Validated Export License (see Chapter 3). The Bureau of Industry and Security (BIS) in the U.S. Department of Commerce is responsible for implementing and enforcing the Export Administration Regulations (EAR), which regulate the export and re-export of the majority of commercial items.

If you have any questions about these regulations, contact your local Department of Commerce official for assistance (see Chapter 3).

U.S. DEPARTMENT OF COMMERCE – Economics and Statistics Administration –U.S. CENSUS BUREAU – BUREAU OF EXPORT ADMINISTRATION

FORM **7525-V** (7-18-2003)   **SHIPPER'S EXPORT DECLARATION**   OMB No. 0607-0152

1a. U.S. PRINCIPAL PARTY IN INTEREST (USPPI)(Complete name and address)

ZIP CODE

2. DATE OF EXPORTATION

3. TRANSPORTATION REFERENCE NO.

b. USPPI'S EIN (IRS) OR ID NO.

c. PARTIES TO TRANSACTION
☐ Related ☐ Non-related

4a. ULTIMATE CONSIGNEE *(Complete name and address)*

b. INTERMEDIATE CONSIGNEE *(Complete name and address)*

5a. FORWARDING AGENT *(Complete name and address)*

5b. FORWARDING AGENT'S EIN (IRS) NO.

6. POINT (STATE) OF ORIGIN OR FTZ NO.

7. COUNTRY OF ULTIMATE DESTINATION

8. LOADING PIER *(Vessel only)*

9. METHOD OF TRANSPORTATION *(Specify)*

14. CARRIER IDENTIFICATION CODE

15. SHIPMENT REFERENCE NO.

10. EXPORTING CARRIER

11. PORT OF EXPORT

16. ENTRY NUMBER

17. HAZARDOUS MATERIALS
☐ Yes ☐ No

12. PORT OF UNLOADING *(Vessel and air only)*

13. CONTAINERIZED *(Vessel only)*
☐ Yes ☐ No

18. IN BOND CODE

19. ROUTED EXPORT TRANSACTION
☐ Yes ☐ No

20. SCHEDULE B DESCRIPTION OF COMMODITIES *(Use columns 22–24)*

D/F or M (21)	SCHEDULE B NUMBER (22)	QUANTITY – SCHEDULE B UNIT(S) (23)	SHIPPING WEIGHT (Kilograms) (24)	VIN/PRODUCT NUMBER/ VEHICLE TITLE NUMBER (25)	VALUE (U.S. dollars, omit cents) (Selling price or cost if not sold) (26)

27. LICENSE NO./LICENSE EXCEPTION SYMBOL/AUTHORIZATION

28. ECCN *(When required)*

29. Duly authorized officer or employee

The USPPI authorizes the forwarder named above to act as forwarding agent for export control and customs purposes.

30. I certify that all statements made and all information contained herein are true and correct and that I have read and understand the instructions for preparation of this document, set forth in the **"Correct Way to Fill Out the Shipper's Export Declaration."** I understand that civil and criminal penalties, including forfeiture and sale, may be imposed for making false or fraudulent statements herein, failing to provide the requested information or for violation of U.S. laws on exportation (13 U.S.C. Sec. 305; 22 U.S.C. Sec. 401; 18 U.S.C. Sec. 1001; 50 U.S.C. App. 2410).

Signature

Confidential – Shipper's Export Declarations (or any successor document) wherever located, shall be exempt from public disclosure unless the Secretary determines that such exemption would be contrary to the national interest (Title 13, Chapter 9, Section 301 (g)).

Title

Export shipments are subject to inspection by U.S. Customs Service and/or Office of Export Enforcement.

Date

31. AUTHENTICATION *(When required)*

Telephone No. (Include Area Code)

E-mail address

This form may be printed by private parties provided it conforms to the official form. For sale by the Superintendent of Documents, Government Printing Office, Washington, DC 20402, and local Customs District Directors. The **"Correct Way to Fill Out the Shipper's Export Declaration"** is available from the U.S. Census Bureau, Washington, DC 20233.

Figure 18-5:
The shipper's export declaration.

Packing list

The packing list (like the one at www.unzco.com/basicguide/figure7.html) is a document that lists the material found in each package. It indicates the following:

- ✔ The type of package
- ✔ The net weight (the actual weight of the goods)
- ✔ The legal weight (the weight of the goods plus any immediate wrappings that are sold with the goods)
- ✔ The tare weight (the weight of a container and/or packing materials without the weight of the goods it contains)
- ✔ The gross weight (the full weight of the shipment, including goods and packaging)
- ✔ The package's measurements (length, width, and height)

The packing list also shows the references (buyer's purchase order number and seller's order/invoice number) assigned by the buyer and seller.

Chapter 19

Getting Your Goods: Customs Requirements and the Entry Process

··

In This Chapter

▶ Understanding the process required to clear a shipment through U.S. Customs

▶ Looking at the role of a Customs broker

▶ Knowing which documents are required

▶ Dissecting how Customs inspects and values your imported goods

▶ Making sure your shipments arrive properly packed and labeled

▶ Understanding how import quotas may limit your ability to import certain items

··

*Y*ou've selected the products you want to import, identified the relevant rules and regulations, located a supplier, identified your target market, and found customers for the products. Now all that's left is getting the goods through the Customs maze and delivered to your customers.

When your shipment arrives in the United States, you (or your authorized agent) file the applicable entry documents for the goods with Customs at the port of entry. Imported goods are not legally entered into the United States until after the shipment has arrived, Customs has authorized delivery of the merchandise, and duties have been paid. Your job is to coordinate the examination and release of the goods by U.S. Customs (or hire someone to do that for you). In this chapter, I tell you how.

Understanding U.S. Import Requirements

The U.S. Customs import requirements are short and sweet, but navigating them is anything but easy. For your reference, here are the requirements:

- An individual may make his own Customs clearance of goods imported for personal use or business.

- The U.S. Customs Service does not require an importer to have a license or permit. Other agencies may, however, require a permit, license, or other certification, depending on the commodity.

- All merchandise coming into the United States must clear Customs and is subject to Customs duty unless specifically exempt.

- Customs duties are generally *ad valorem* — a percentage rate is applied to the dutiable value of the imported goods. Some articles, however, are dutiable at a specific rate of duty (so much per pound, gallon, and so on) or a combination rate (ad valorem and specific).

- The dutiable value of merchandise is determined by Customs. That value is basically the *transaction value,* the price the buyer actually pays the seller.

- Unless the item is free of duty, the tariff schedules provide three rates of duty for an item:

    - The rate for normal trading relations (General Column).

    - The rate for less-than-favorable countries (Column 2).

    - The rate for least-developing countries, which show a duty rate lower than the one presently accorded to most-favored nations. (This applies to items under the Generalized System of Preferences, Caribbean Basin Initiative, Israeli Free Trade Act, North American Free Trade Agreement, and Dominican Republic–Central America–United States Free Trade Agreement.)

Providing Evidence of Right to Make Entry

For goods to legally enter the United States, the bill of lading is required as evidence of ownership of the goods. Shipments arriving by air use an air waybill instead of a bill of lading. In most instances, the owner of the goods (or his representative) makes the entry.

You need to present the bill of lading to make the entry and get the goods through Customs. In some instances, the carrier can issue a document known as a *carrier's certificate,* which provides the particulars of a shipment and designates who may make a Customs entry on that shipment, for this purpose. (See `forms.customs.gov` for a sample of this certificate.)

When the goods are not imported by a common carrier — that is, you're hand-carrying them from a trip — your possession of the goods at the time of arrival is deemed sufficient evidence of the right to make entry.

You can provide evidence of right to entry yourself, or you can hire a Customs broker to do so on your behalf. In this section, I provide more info on each option.

Note: Every entry that's posted with U.S. Customs must come with a *surety bond,* a guarantee that any potential duties, taxes, and Customs penalties that may accrue will be paid. A surety bond also includes a provision for the payment of any increased duty that may be found after the goods have cleared Customs. You can obtain a surety bond through a U.S. surety company, or you can post the bond yourself in the form of U.S. money or government securities. If you hire a Customs broker to make the entry, the broker will use his surety bond to provide the required coverage.

Having the broker take care of the surety bond on your behalf is one of the primary reasons using a Customs broker makes more sense than trying to handle the entry yourself.

Making entry yourself

As an importer, you can make your own Customs clearance. You aren't required to use the services of a licensed Customs broker — you can visit Customs and arrange to clear the goods personally.

Entering your own goods may save you money because you don't have to absorb the broker's fees. But you still have to pay applicable duties and arrange for shipment. And you'll probably spend a significant amount of time going through the process, which is time-consuming when you're new to it.

Having others make entry on your behalf

You're allowed to designate another individual to arrange for Customs clearance on your behalf. People who arrange for Customs clearances for a living are known as *Customs brokers.* In order for a Customs broker to perform that function, you must provide her with a U.S. Customs Power of Attorney. You have to prepare and sign a Customs Form 5291 (see Figure 19-1) or a document that uses the same language as this form.

Department of the Treasury
U.S. Customs Service
19 CFR 141.32

POWER OF ATTORNEY

Check appropriate box:
- ☐ Individual
- ☐ Partnership
- ☐ Corporation
- ☐ Sole Proprietorship

KNOW ALL MEN BY THESE PRESENTS: That, ______________________________
(Full Name of person, partnership, or corporation, or sole proprietorship; Identity)

a corporation doing business under the laws of the State of ______________ or a ______________

doing business as ______________ residing at ______________

having an office and place of business at ______________, hereby constitutes and appoints each of the following persons

____
(Give full name of each agent designated)

as a true and lawful agent and attorney of the grantor named above for and in the name, place, and stead of said grantor from this date and in Customs Port and in no other name, to make, endorse, sign, declare, or swear to any entry, withdrawal, declaration, certificate, bill of lading, or other document required by law or regulation in connection with the importation, transportation, or exportation of any merchandise shipped or consigned by or to said grantor; to perform any act or condition which may be required by law or regulation in connection with such merchandise; to receive any merchandise deliverable to said grantor;

To make endorsements on bills of lading conferring authority to make entry and collect drawback, and to make, sign, declare, or swear to any statement, supplemental statement, schedule, supplemental schedule, certificate of delivery, certificate of manufacture, certificate of manufacture and delivery, abstract of manufacturing records, declaration of proprietor on drawback entry, declaration of exporter on drawback entry, or any other affidavit or document which may be required by law or regulation for drawback purposes, regardless of whether such bill of lading, sworn statement, schedule, certificate, abstract, declaration, or other affidavit or document is intended for filing in said port or in any other customs port;

To sign, seal, and deliver for and as the act of said grantor any bond required by law or regulation in connection with the entry or withdrawal of imported merchandise or merchandise exported with or without benefit of drawback, or in connection with the entry, clearance, lading, unlading or navigation of any vessel or other means of conveyance owned or operated by said grantor, and any and all bonds which may be voluntarily given and accepted under applicable laws and regulations, consignee's and owner's declarations provided for in section 485, Tariff Act of 1930, as amended, or affidavits in connection with the entry of merchandise;

To sign and swear to any document and to perform any act that may be necessary or required by law or regulation in connection with the entering, clearing, lading, unlading, or operation of any vessel or other means of conveyance owned or operated by said grantor;

And generally to transact at the customhouses in said port any and all customs business, including making, signing, and filing of protests under section 514 of the Tariff Act of 1930, in which said grantor is or may be concerned or interested and which may properly be transacted or performed by an agent and attorney, giving to said agent and attorney full power and authority to do anything whatever requisite and necessary to be done in the premises as fully as said grantor could do if present and acting, hereby ratifying and confirming all that the said agent and attorney shall lawfully do by virtue of these presents; the foregoing power of attorney to remain in full force and effect until the ______ day of ______, 19____, or until notice of revocation in writing is duly given to and received by the Port Director of Customs of the port aforesaid. If the donor of this power of attorney is a partnership, the said power shall in no case have any force or effect after the expiration of 2 years from the date of its receipt in the office of the Port Director of Customs of the said port.

IN WITNESS WHEREOF, the said ______________________________

has caused these presents to be sealed and signed: (Signature) ______________________________

(Capacity) ______________________________ (Date) ______________

WITNESS: ______________ ______________

Customs Form 5291 (120195) (Corporate seal) * (Optional) (SEE OVER)

INDIVIDUAL OR PARTNERSHIP CERTIFICATION *(Optional)

CITY ______________
COUNTY ______________ } SS:
STATE ______________

On this ______ day of ______ 19___, personally appeared before me ______________

residing at ______________, personally known or sufficiently identified to me, who certifies that ______________ (is)(are) the individual(s) who executed the foregoing instrument and acknowledge it to be ______________ free act and deed.

(Notary Public)

CORPORATE CERTIFICATION *(Optional)

(To be made by an officer other than the one who executes the power of attorney)

I, ______________, certify that I am the ______________

of ______________, organized under the laws of the State of ______________

that ______________, who signed this power of attorney on behalf of the donor, is the ______________

of said corporation; and that said power of attorney was duly signed, sealed, and attested for and on behalf of said corporation by authority of its governing body as the same appears in a resolution of the Board of Directors passed at a regular meeting held on the ______ day of ______________, now in my possession or custody. I further certify that the resolution is in accordance with the articles of incorporation and bylaws of said corporation.

IN WITNESS WHEREOF, I have hereunto set my hand and affixed the seal of said corporation, at the City of ______________ this ______ day of ______________, 19 ______

(Signature) (Date)

If the corporation has no corporate seal, the fact shall be stated, in which case a scroll or adhesive shall appear in the appropriate, designated place.

Customs powers of attorney of residents (including resident corporations) shall be without power of substitution except for the purpose of executing shipper's export declarations. However, a power of attorney executed in favor of a licensed customhouse broker may specify that the power of attorney is granted to the customhouse broker to act through any of its licensed officers or any employee specifically authorized to act for such customhouse broker by power of attorney.

NOTE: The corporate seal may be omitted. Customs does not require completion of a certification. The grantor has the option of executing the certification or omitting it.

☆GOVERNMENT PRINTING OFFICE: 1998 – 606-491 Customs Form 5291 (120195)(Back)

Figure 19-1: This form allows your Customs broker to act on your behalf when entering your goods into the United States.

A licensed Customs broker named in a Customs power of attorney may make entry on behalf of the importer. The Customs broker, on your behalf, prepares and submits documentation and sorts and releases the imported goods through Customs after paying the required sum of import duty. (For more on Customs brokers, see the next section.)

Working with a Customs Broker

Customs brokers are the only people authorized by the tariff laws of the United States to act as agents for importers in their Customs business. The Customs service licenses brokers, who are private individuals or firms, to do the following:

✔ Prepare and file the necessary Customs entries

✔ Arrange for the payment of duties

✔ Take steps to effect the release of the goods in Customs custody

✔ Represent the importer in Customs matters

The fees charged for these services vary according to the Customs broker and the services performed, but the general price for a routine entry is $75 to $100.

In addition to assisting in the entry process, Customs brokers can

✔ Help you decide which shipping routes are best for getting your goods in the shortest possible time

✔ Tell you which method of shipment is best for your goods and advise you on packing requirements for those goods

✔ Guide you on matters relating to international payments

When you're choosing a Customs broker, consider the following questions:

✔ **Do you have a specialized product line or type of import?** You may want to find a broker who either specializes or has a great deal of expertise in clearing your type of products. For example, numerous Department of Agriculture regulations apply to the importation of fruits and vegetables, and produce is perishable. Not every broker is experienced in handling these products.

✔ **How many ports will you use for your imports?** If you're importing through a large number of ports, look for a broker who has offices in those ports.

✔ **How connected is the broker?** You want to identify a broker who is fully automated with full connectivity not only to U.S. Customs but also to various web portals and cargo-tracking sites. Consider using a firm that participates in the Automated Broker Interface (ABI), which is a system that permits transmission of data pertaining to merchandise being imported into the United States.

✔ **What is the broker's general reputation?** The best sources of information about a broker's reputation are the broker's own customers. Ask for references — and be sure to contact them!

Looking at the Documents Required to Enter Goods into the United States

To make or file a Customs entry, the following documents are generally required:

✔ A bill of lading, airway bill, or carrier's certificate (naming the *consignee* — the person to whom the goods will be turned over — for Customs purposes) as evidence of the consignee's right to make entry.

✔ A commercial invoice obtained from the seller, showing the value and description of the merchandise.

✔ Entry manifest (Customs Form 7533; see Figure 19-2) or entry/immediate delivery (Customs Form 3461; see Figure 19-3).

CBP Form 3461 Entry/Immediate Release Delivery allows the importer or custom house broker to gain the immediate release of imported goods. While the goods may be removed from the port of entry, the release is considered to be "conditional" until the entry package has been filed.

When a shipment not exceeding $250 in value which is unconditionally free of duty and not subject to quota or to internal revenue tax arrives on a vessel of less than 5 net tons arriving otherwise than by sea, the inward foreign manifest on Customs Form 7533 may be presented in duplicate and used as an entry.

✔ Packing lists, if appropriate, and other documents necessary to determine whether the merchandise may be admitted.

The Customs broker is usually the one who prepares and submits these forms to U.S. Customs. If you're not using a broker, you have to prepare and submit the forms yourself — all the more reason to hire a Customs broker.

U.S. DEPARTMENT OF HOMELAND SECURITY
Bureau of Customs and Border Protection

Approved OMB No. 1651-0001
Exp. 12/31/2008

**INWARD CARGO MANIFEST FOR VESSEL UNDER
FIVE TONS, FERRY, TRAIN, CAR, VEHICLE, ETC.**

(INSTRUCTIONS ON REVERSE)

19 CFR 123.4, 123.7, 123.61

CBP Manifest/In Bond Number

Page No.

1. Name or Number and Description of Importing Conveyance	2. Name of Master or Person in Charge	
3. Name and Address of Owner	4. Foreign Port of Lading	5. U.S. Port of Destination
6. Port of Arrival	7. Date of Arrival	

Column No. 1	Column No. 2	Column No. 3	Column No. 4	Column No. 5
Bill of Lading or Marks & Numbers or Address of Consignee on Packages	Car Number and Initials	Number and Gross Weight (in kilos or pounds) of Packages and Description of Goods	Name of Consignee	For Use By CBP only

CARRIER'S CERTIFICATE

To the Port Director of CBP, Port of Arrival:

The undersigned carrier hereby certifies that _____ of _____

is the owner or consignee of such articles within the purview of section 484, Tariff Act of 1930.

I certify that this manifest is correct and true to the best of my knowledge.

Date _____ . Master or Person in charge _____

(Signature)

Previous Editions are Obsolete

CBP Form 7533 (05/00)

Figure 19-2:
The entry manifest form.

U.S. DEPARTMENT OF HOMELAND SECURITY
Bureau of Customs and Border Protection

Form Approved
OMB No. 1651-0024
Exp. 11/30/2008

ENTRY/IMMEDIATE DELIVERY

19 CFR 142.3, 142.16, 142.22, 142.24

1. ARRIVAL DATE	2. ELECTED ENTRY DATE	3. ENTRY TYPE CODE/NAME	4. ENTRY NUMBER
5. PORT	6. SINGLE TRANS. BOND	7. BROKER/IMPORTER FILE NUMBER	
	8. CONSIGNEE NUMBER		9. IMPORTER NUMBER

10. ULTIMATE CONSIGNEE NAME	11. IMPORTER OF RECORD NAME

12. CARRIER CODE	13. VOYAGE/FLIGHT/TRIP	14. LOCATION OF GOODS-CODE(S)/NAME(S)
15. VESSEL CODE/NAME		

16. U.S. PORT OF UNLADING	17. MANIFEST NUMBER	18. G. O. NUMBER	19. TOTAL VALUE

20. DESCRIPTION OF MERCHANDISE

21. IT/BL/ AWB CODE	22. IT/BL/AWB NO.	23. MANIFEST QUANTITY	24. H.S. NUMBER	25. COUNTRY OF ORIGIN	26. MANUFACTURER NO.

27. CERTIFICATION	**28. CBP USE ONLY**
I hereby make application for entry/immediate delivery. I certify that the above information is accurate, the bond is sufficient, valid, and current, and that all requirements of 19 CFR Part 142 have been met.	☐ OTHER AGENCY ACTION REQUIRED, NAMELY:
SIGNATURE OF APPLICANT **X**	
PHONE NO. DATE	☐ CBP EXAMINATION REQUIRED.
29. BROKER OR OTHER GOVT. AGENCY USE	☐ ENTRY REJECTED, BECAUSE:
	DELIVERY AUTHORIZED: SIGNATURE DATE

PAPERWORK REDUCTION ACT NOTICE: This information is to determine the admissibility of imports into the United States and to provide the necessary information for the examination of the cargo and to establish the liability for payment of duties and taxes. Your response is necessary. The estimated average burden associated with this collection of information is 15 minutes per respondent depending on individual circumstances. Comments concerning the accuracy of this burden estimate and suggestions for reducing this burden should be directed to Bureau of Customs and Border Protection, Information Services Branch, Washington, DC 20229, and to the Office of Management and Budget, Paperwork Reduction Project (1651-0024), Washington, DC 20503.

CBP Form 3461 (01/89)

Figure 19-3: The entry/immediate delivery form.

Deciphering the Types of Entry

When you submit the documents to have your imports released and entered into the United States, you have several entry options: immediate delivery, warehouse entry, foreign trade zones, and mail entry. I cover them all here.

Immediate delivery

An immediate delivery entry provides for immediate release of a shipment. It's used when an importer applies for a special permit for immediate delivery by filing a Customs Form 3461 (refer to Figure 19-3) prior to the arrival of the merchandise. If this application is approved, the shipment is released to the importer immediately after arrival.

This type of release is available only for the following types of merchandise:

- Merchandise arriving from Canada or Mexico
- Fresh fruits or vegetables arriving from Canada or Mexico
- Articles for a trade fair
- Tariff rate quota merchandise and, under certain circumstances, merchandise subject to an absolute quota (although an item that's under an absolute quota also requires that a formal entry be posted; for details, turn to "Identifying Import Quotas," later in this chapter)

You can arrange for an immediate entry with a Customs broker.

Warehouse entry

If you want to delay the payment of duties and entry of goods, you can arrange to have the goods stored in a bonded warehouse under a warehouse entry. A bonded warehouse is a facility under the control of Customs.

Technically, although the goods are stored in the warehouse, they haven't been entered into the commerce of the United States. If the goods are removed from the warehouse and exported out of the United States, the importer won't have to pay any duty. However, if the importer removes the goods from the warehouse and enters them into the commerce of the United States, the importer has to pay the duty rate that's applicable on the date he removes the goods from the warehouse.

While the goods are stored in the warehouse, they can, under Customs supervision, be cleaned, sorted, repacked, or changed in condition by a process that doesn't amount to manufacturing. If the items are exported after the goods have been modified, no payment of duty is required. If the items are modified and entered into the commerce of the United States, the importer is responsible for the payment of duty applicable to the goods in their modified condition at the time of withdrawal.

Goods can be stored in a bonded warehouse for up to five years.

Foreign trade zones

A U.S. foreign trade zone (FTZ) is an alternative to a bonded warehouse with one major exception: Goods stored in a foreign trade zone can be modified, and actual manufacturing operations can occur; further manufacturing is not permitted in a bonded warehouse. Also, there's no time limit on goods stored in a foreign trade zone.

As with a bonded warehouse, goods in the FTZ that are exported before entering the commerce of the United States don't require that a duty be paid. Goods modified or remanufactured in the zone and released into the commerce of the United States for consumption are subject to the payment of duty applicable on the final product in effect on the date of withdrawal.

 You can get more information on U.S. foreign trade zones from the Foreign Trade Zones Board, Department of Commerce, 1401 Constitution Ave. NW, Room 2111, Washington, DC 20230 (phone 202-482-2862; website `ia.ita.doc.gov/ftzpage/`). You can view the *Foreign Trade Zones Manual* on the Customs website at `http://www.cbp.gov/xp/cgov/trade/cargo_security/cargo_control/ftz/`. For the contact information for each FTZ project in the United States, go to `http://ia.ita.doc.gov/ftzpage/letters/ftzlist-map.html`.

Mail entry

In some circumstances, using a country's mail system (rather than a courier service, such as FedEx, UPS, or DHL) to import merchandise into the United States is to your advantage. Here are some of the benefits that mail entry offers to importers:

✔ Clearing goods through Customs is easy.

✔ You don't have to pay a Customs broker.

✔ You don't lose time trying to clear the parcel yourself.

✔ Shipping charges are less expensive than the cost of a courier service.

✔ No formal entry is required on duty-free merchandise, as long as the merchandise doesn't exceed the dollar limit.

You're allowed to import shipments that don't exceed $2,000 via postal system shipments. However, the following products are limited to imports of just $250:

✔ Articles of fur or leather; feathers and feather products; rawhides and skins

✔ Flowers and foliage, artificial or preserved

✔ Footwear; gloves; headwear and hat braids; millinery ornaments

✔ Billfolds and other flat goods

✔ Handbags; luggage

✔ Pillows and cushions

✔ Textile fibers and products; trimmings

✔ Miscellaneous articles of rubber or plastic

✔ Toys, games, and sports equipment

Here's how mail entry works: The exporter packages the goods and encloses a copy of the invoice in the package or securely attaches the invoice to the parcel. The exporter also attaches a Customs Declaration Form to the outer wrapping of the package, giving an accurate description of the contents and their value. Upon the package's arrival in the United States, a Customs officer prepares an entry for importations, and a letter carrier at the destination delivers the parcel to the addressee upon the payment of duty. A Customs process fee of $5 is assessed for each parcel for which documentation is prepared.

You can also send yourself goods from overseas. For example, say you're visiting Italy and you've found a manufacturer of quality costume-jewelry earrings. You purchase the earrings from the manufacturer and get a copy of the invoice. You then take the parcel to the nearest post office. Making sure that you enclose a copy of the invoice in the parcel, you seal the parcel, address it to yourself in the United States, and secure a Customs declaration form to the package. The declaration form says, "This package contains 1,500 pairs of costume-jewelry earrings. Value for Customs purposes: US$1,500." When the package arrives at the mail depot at the international airport where the goods arrive, a Customs officer inspects the parcel. The officer prepares a mail entry form and assesses any applicable duties. The parcel is then given to the postal service, which delivers the parcel and collects duty and a $5 Customs processing fee.

They're Here! The Arrival of Your Goods

Imported goods are not legally entered into the United States until the shipment arrives within the limits of the port of entry and U.S. Customs has authorized the delivery of the merchandise. This normally occurs when the importer (or the importer's Customs broker) files the appropriate documents.

To expedite the entry process, you can present Customs entry papers before the merchandise arrives, but entry won't take place until the merchandise arrives within the port limits.

The U.S. Customs Service doesn't notify you of the arrival of your shipment — the carrier of the goods usually makes this notification. Your responsibility is to make sure that you or your Customs broker is informed immediately so you can file the entry and avoid any delay in obtaining the goods. Stay in touch with the exporter and ask for an estimated time of arrival.

If imported merchandise isn't entered through Customs within five days of its arrival (exclusive of Sundays, holidays, or any authorized extension), Customs sends the goods to public storage or a general order warehouse to be held as unclaimed. The importer is responsible for any storage charges incurred while the merchandise is at the warehouse. If the goods remain unclaimed at the end of one year, the merchandise is sold at auction. If the goods are perishable, they may be sold sooner.

The U.S. Customs and Border Protection (CBP) has authorized EG&G/CWS Marketing and Rod Robertson Enterprises to auction off CBP general order merchandise and seized and forfeited property. Visit www.cwsmarketing. com for information on pending auctions, lists of items, dates and locations, and in-person and online bidding procedures.

Open Wide: U.S. Customs Examination of Goods

Prior to the goods' release, the port director designates representative samples of the imported goods to be examined by a Customs inspector under conditions that will safeguard the goods. This inspection ensures that you've met all the requirements on importing merchandise (see Chapter 3 for information on restricted merchandise and specific agency requirements).

For example, if you're importing fruits or vegetables, the goods are subject to inspection by the Department of Agriculture to make sure the items are safe for human consumption. Textiles and textile products are also considered trade-sensitive items. They may be subject to a higher percentage of examinations than other commodities.

In simple situations involving small shipments or certain classes of goods, such as bulk shipments, the inspector may examine the goods on the docks, at the container stations, at the cargo terminal, or at the importer's premises. The goods are then released to the importer. In other shipments, Customs may retain representative packages of the merchandise for appraisement purposes but release the remainder of the shipment. After the examination is complete, Customs releases the withheld packages to the importer.

The examination of goods determines the following:

- ✔ The value of the goods for Customs purposes and the goods' dutiable status
- ✔ Whether the goods are marked with their country of origin (the goods must be marked in a conspicuous place and in a legible and indelible manner to indicate the English name of the country of origin to the ultimate purchaser in the United States)
- ✔ Whether the goods have been correctly invoiced
- ✔ Whether the shipment may contain prohibited articles
- ✔ Whether other agencies' requirements have been met
- ✔ Whether goods in excess of the invoice quantities are present or whether a shortage exists

In this section, I cover how Customs determines the dutiable status of the goods that you're importing to the United States.

Determining the dutiable value of your goods

Unless specifically exempt, all merchandise coming into the United States is subject to a Customs duty. Customs determines the dutiable value of your merchandise, which is basically the *transaction value* — the price actually paid or payable for the merchandise when it's sold for exportation to the United States, plus amounts for the following items if they're not included in the price:

- The packing costs incurred by the buyer

- Any selling commission incurred by the buyer

- The value of any free or reduced-cost goods that are for use in producing or selling merchandise for export to the United States

- Any royalty or license fee that the buyer is required to pay as a condition of the sale

- The proceeds, accruing to the seller, of any subsequent resale, disposal, or use of the imported merchandise

These items are added only to the extent that each is not included in the price actually paid or payable, and they're added only if information is available to establish the accuracy of the amount.

If Customs can't use the transaction value, Customs has four alternative methods for determining dutiable value:

- **Transaction value of identical merchandise:** When the transaction value can't be determined, the Customs value of the imported goods being appraised is the transaction value of identical merchandise.

- **Transaction value of similar merchandise:** If merchandise identical to the imported goods can't be found or an acceptable transaction value for such merchandise doesn't exist, then the Customs value is the transaction value of similar merchandise.

  Similar merchandise is merchandise that's produced in the same country and by the same person as the merchandise being appraised. It must be commercially interchangeable with the merchandise being appraised. The identical or similar merchandise must have been exported to the United States at or about the same time as the merchandise that's being appraised.

- **Deductive value:** The *deductive value* is the resale price in the United States after importation of the goods, with deductions for certain items. Generally, Customs calculates the deductive value by starting with a unit price and making certain additions to and deductions from that price. The additions are for costs associated with packaging, and the deductions are for commissions or profit and general expenses, transportation and insurance costs, and Customs duties or federal taxes.

✔ **Computed value:** If Customs is unable to determine the dutiable value based on any of the preceding methods, Customs considers the computed value of the merchandise. The computed value consists of the sum of the following items:

- Materials, fabrication, and other processing used in producing the imported merchandise

- Profit and general expenses

- Any free goods, if not included in the preceding two bullets

- Packing costs

Deciphering your goods' dutiable status

Customs determines the goods' dutiable status according to the *Harmonized Tariff Schedule,* a technical document that classifies imported merchandise for rates of duty and statistical purposes. You can buy a copy from the Superintendent of Documents, Government Printing Office, Washington, DC 20402 (phone 202-512-1800; website www.gpo.gov). You can also access the document for free online at www.usitc.gov/tata/hts/bychapter/index.htm. (For more on the *Harmonized Tariff Schedule,* turn to Chapter 3.)

When goods are dutiable, the following rates may be assessed:

✔ **Ad valorem:** An ad valorem rate, which is the type of rate most often applied, is a percentage of the value of the merchandise. For example, if an item has a dutiable value of $10 and the rate is 10 percent ad valorem, the duty is $1.

Ad valorem is Latin for "to the value."

✔ **Specific:** A specific rate is a specified amount per unit of weight or other quantity, such as 5.9¢ per dozen.

✔ **Compound:** A compound rate is a combination of an ad valorem rate and a specific rate, such as 0.7¢ per kilo plus 10 percent ad valorem.

Rates of duty for imported merchandise may also vary depending on the country of origin. Most merchandise is dutiable under the most-favored-nation status, now referred to as normal trade relations (NTR). The applicable duty rates appear in the *Harmonized Tariff Schedule* in the General column under Column 1. (For a sample of the *Harmonized Tariff Schedule,* check out Table 19-1.)

Heading/ Subheading	Stat. Suffix	Article Description	Unit of Quantity	Rates of Duty		
				1		**2**
				General	*Special**	
4421.90.80		Clothespins: Spring-type		6.5¢/gross	Free (A+, BH, CA, CL, D, E, IL, J, JO, MA, MX, P, SG)	20¢/ gross
4421.90.85		Clothespins: Other	Gross	4.8%	Free (A+, AU, BH, CA, CL, D, E, IL, J, JO, MA, MX, P, SG)	35%

Table 19-1   Excerpt of the Harmonized Tariff Schedule (2008)

* A+ = Generalized System of Preference; AU = United States–Australia Free Trade Agreement; BH = United States–Bahrain Free Trade Agreement Implementation Act; CA = Goods of Canada, under the terms of general note 12 to this schedule; CL = United States–Chile Free Trade Agreement; D = African Growth and Opportunity Act; E = Caribbean Basic Economic Recovery Act; IL = United States–Israel Free Trace Area; J = Andean Trade Preference Act or Andean Trade Promotion and Drug Eradication Act; JO = United States–Jordan Free Trade Area Implementation Act; MA = United States–Morocco Free Trade Agreement Implementation Act; MX = Goods of Mexico, under the terms of general note 12 to this schedule; P = Dominican Republic–Central America–United States Free Trade Agreement Implementation Act; SG = United States–Singapore Free Trade Agreement

Merchandise from countries to which NTR rates haven't been extended is dutiable at the full rates you see in Column 2 of the *Harmonized Tariff Schedule.* (You may hear these countries referred to informally as the "least-favored nations.") Duty-free status is also available under various conditional exemptions, which are reflected in the Special column under Column 1 of the *Harmonized Tariff Schedule.* This column is for least-developing countries and shows a duty rate lower than those assigned NTR status. These rates are assigned under programs such as the Generalized System of Preferences (GSP), the Caribbean Basin Initiative (CBI), the Israeli Free Trade Act, the North America Free Trade Agreement (NAFTA), and the Dominican Republic–Central America–United States Free Trade Agreement (CAFTA-DR). It's your responsibility to show that the item you're importing is eligible for preferential duty treatment (if that is, in fact, the case).

In the following subsections, I cover the various preferential duty rates.

Generalized Systems of Preferences

The Generalized System of Preferences (GSP) is a program that provides for duty-free status for certain merchandise from less-than-developed independent and dependent countries and territories. The purpose of the GSP is to encourage the economic growth of these countries and territories. The United States enacted the GSP in the Trade Act of 1974. (The act occasionally expires and must be renewed by Congress to remain in effect. The Customs Service notifies the trade community of these expirations and renewals.)

You can find out whether an item is eligible under the GSP by identifying the Tariff Classification Code for the item found in the *Harmonized Tariff Schedule of the United States.*

Items that qualify under the GSP are identified by either an A or A* in the Special column under Column 1 of the tariff schedule. Items designated in this manner may qualify for duty-free status as long as the goods are being imported from the designated country. Certain countries listed with the A* may be excluded from the exemption — you see these exceptions as you browse through the *Harmonized Tariff Schedule,* or you'll be advised when you contact a commodity specialist team (see Chapter 3).

The list of countries and exclusions, together with the list of eligible items, can change from time to time. If you're looking at the tariff schedule, make sure you're viewing the latest edition. (The version at www.usitc.gov/tata/ hts/bychapter/index.htm is always current.)

You can also verify a country and product's participation in the program by asking the appropriate commodity specialist team at your local Customs office (see Chapter 3).

Here are the independent countries that can participate in the GSP: Albania, Angola, Antigua and Barbuda, Argentina, Armenia, Bahrain, Bangladesh, Benin, Bhutan, Bolivia, Bosnia and Herzegovina, Botswana, Brazil, Bulgaria, Burkina Faso, Burundi, Cambodia, Cameroon, Cape Verde, Central African Republic, Chad, Chile, Colombia, Comoros, Costa Rica, Côte d'Ivoire, Croatia, Czech Republic, Democratic Republic of the Congo, Djibouti, Dominica, Dominican Republic, Ecuador, Egypt, El Salvador, Equatorial Guinea, Eritrea, Estonia, Ethiopia, Fiji, Gabon, Gambia, Ghana, Grenada, Guatemala, Guinea, Guinea Bissau, Guyana, Haiti, Honduras, Hungary, India, Indonesia, Jamaica, Jordan, Kazakhstan, Kenya, Kiribati, Kyrgyzstan, Latvia, Lebanon, Lesotho, Lithuania, Macedonia, Madagascar, Malawi, Mali, Malta, Mauritania, Mauritius, Moldova, Mongolia, Morocco, Mozambique, Namibia, Nepal, Niger, Nigeria, Oman, Pakistan, Panama, Papua New Guinea, Paraguay, Peru, Philippines, Poland, Republic of Congo (Brazzaville), Romania, Russia,

Rwanda, St. Kitts and Nevis, St. Lucia, St. Vincent and the Grenadines, Samoa, Sao Tome and Principe, Senegal, Seychelles, Sierra Leone, Slovakia, Solomon Islands, Somalia, South Africa, Sri Lanka, Suriname, Swaziland, Tanzania, Thailand, Togo, Tonga, Trinidad and Tobago, Tunisia, Turkey, Tuvalu, Uganda, Ukraine, Uruguay, Uzbekistan, Vanuatu, Venezuela, Yemen, Zambia, and Zimbabwe.

And here are the non-independent countries and territories that can participate in the GSP: Anguilla, British Indian Ocean Territory, British Virgin Islands, Christmas Island (Australia), Cocos (Keeling) Island, Cook Island, Falkland Island (Islas Malvinas), French Polynesia, Gibraltar, Hear Island and McDonald Islands, Montserrat, New Caledonia, Niue, Norfolk Island, Pitcairn Island, St. Helena, Tokelau, Turks and Caicos Island, Wallis and Funtuna, West Bank and Gaza Strip, and Western Sahara.

Some products coming from a listed country may not be eligible to participate in the program. Check the *Harmonized Tariff Schedule* or contact the appropriate commodity specialist team at Customs if you're unsure.

Caribbean Basin Initiative

The Caribbean Basin Initiative (CBI) is a program similar to the Generalized System of Preferences (see the preceding section), except that this program is targeted toward countries that are part of the Caribbean Basin.

You can identify whether an item is eligible by identifying the Tariff Classification Code for the item found in the *Harmonized Tariff Schedule of the United States*. Items that are identified by either by an E or E* in the Special column under Column 1 of the tariff schedule may qualify for duty-free status as long as the goods are being imported from the designated country. Those items listed with the E* may be excluded from the exemption.

Here's a list of countries that participate in the CBI: Antigua and Barbuda, Aruba, Bahamas, Barbados, Belize, British Virgin Islands, Dominica, Grenada, Guyana, Haiti, Jamaica, Montserrat, Netherlands Antilles, Panama, St. Kitts and Nevis, St. Lucia, St. Vincent and the Grenadines, and Trinidad and Tobago.

Some products coming from a listed country may not be eligible to participate in the program. Please check the *Harmonized Tariff Schedule* or contact the appropriate commodity specialist team at U.S. Customs if you're unsure.

U.S.-Israeli Free Trade Area Agreement

The United States and Israel have implemented a free trade agreement intended to stimulate trade between the two countries. The agreement was amended in 1996 to add goods produced in the West Bank, Gaza Strip, and qualifying industrial zones.

Items identified by an IL in the Special column under Column 1 of the *Harmonized Tariff Schedule* may qualify for duty-free status as long as the goods are produced in Israel, the West Bank, Gaza Strip, or qualifying industrial zones.

NAFTA and CAFTA-DR

The North American Free Trade Agreement (NAFTA) and the Dominican Republic–Central America–United States Free Trade Agreement (CAFTA-DR) are agreements designed to stimulate trade between member countries.

NAFTA creates free trade among Canada, Mexico, and the United States. CAFTA-DR creates a free trade area that includes Costa Rica, the Dominican Republic, El Salvador, Guatemala, Honduras, Nicaragua, and the United States.

In the *Harmonized Tariff Schedule,* items designated with CA or MX in the Special column under Column 1 qualify for participation in NAFTA. Items designed with P or P+ in the Special column under Column 1 quality for participation in CAFTA-DR.

Looking at duty liabilities: Who owes what and when

The liability for the payment of duty becomes fixed when an entry for consumption (immediate delivery) or for warehouse (warehouse entry) is filed with Customs. (See "Deciphering the Types of Entry," earlier in this chapter, for info on both types of entry.) The person or firm whose name the entry is filed in — normally, the importer — assumes the obligation for the payment of duties.

When goods have been entered for bonded warehouse, liability for paying duties may be transferred to any person who purchases the goods and wants to withdraw the goods in his own name.

Paying a Customs broker doesn't get you off the hook in terms of your liability for Customs charges (duties, taxes, and other debts owed to Customs). If your broker fails to pay those charges on your behalf, you're still liable for them.

If you pay the broker by check, give the broker a separate check made payable to "U.S. Customs Service" for those Customs charges. The broker will deliver the check to Customs.

Considering Country-of-Origin Markings

U.S. Customs laws require that each imported item produced abroad be marked with the English name of the country of origin. The marking should be legible and located in a conspicuous place to tell the purchaser where the article was produced.

If the article isn't properly marked at the time the goods are imported, a marking duty equal to 10 percent of the Customs value of the article is assessed unless the article is exported, destroyed, or properly marked under supervision by U.S. Customs.

For a detailed list of items for which country-of-origin markings are not required, go to www.cbp.gov/linkhandler/cgov/newsroom/publications/trade/co_origin.ctt/markingo.pdf and go to pages 123 through 125. Or contact the U.S. Customs commodity specialist team (see Chapter 3).

Packing and Commingling: Making Sure Your Exporter Follows the Rules

When you import goods, the seller must pack the goods in a way that permits a U.S. Customs officer to examine, weigh, measure, and release the goods to you promptly.

To speed up the clearance of your goods through Customs, do the following:

- ✔ Receive from the seller an invoice or packing list that shows the exact quantity of each item of goods in each box, case, or other package.
- ✔ Make sure that the seller marks and numbers each package.
- ✔ Make sure that the marks or numbers appear on your invoice or packing list opposite the itemization of goods contained in the package that bears those marks and numbers.

Your goods will get through Customs faster if the packages contain goods of one kind only or if the goods are imported in packages with uniform contents and values.

Don't try to import a package that contains articles that are subject to different rates of duty and are packed in such a way that the quantity or value of each category can't be easily determined. The commingled articles will be subject to the *highest* rate of duty applicable to any part of the shipment, unless you manually segregate the goods under Customs supervision.

Your segregation of a commingled shipment is done at your own risk and expense. You have to do it within 30 days of the date of personal delivery or the date that Customs mails a notice to you telling you that the goods are commingled (unless Customs grants an extension). Bottom line: Do everything you can to avoid commingled goods.

Identifying Import Quotas

An *import quota* is a limit on the amount of merchandise that can be imported (into the United States) over a certain period of time. Although U.S. Customs administers the quota system, Customs doesn't have any authority to change or modify quotas, which are set by Congress.

There are two types of quotas:

- ✔ **Absolute quotas:** An absolute quota is a specific amount of a particular product that may be entered during a quota period. Some absolute quotas can be *global* (meaning a limit of a particular good coming from all countries). Other absolute quotas are allocated to specified countries (for example, the U.S. government may impose a quota of 1 million silk ties from Thailand during the first six months of a particular year). If goods arrive after the quota is closed, those imports in excess may be exported or warehoused for entry in a subsequent quota period.

- ✔ **Tariff rate quotas:** Tariff rate quotas allow for a specified quantity of goods to be entered into the country at a reduced rate of duty during a given period. However, quantities entered in excess of the quota for the period are subject to a higher rate of duty. For example, the U.S. government may impose a quota of 1 million silk ties for the first six months of the year at a duty rate of 5 percent; any quantities in excess of that are allowed to enter the country, but they have a duty rate of 40 percent.

You can get information on commodities subject to quota by contacting the Quota Staff, U.S. Customs Service, 1300 Constitution Ave. NW, Washington, DC 20229 (phone 202-927-5850; website www.cbp.gov/xp/cgov/trade/ trade_programs/textiles_and_quotas/guide_import_goods/ commodities.xml). Or you can contact a commodity team specialist (see Chapter 3).

The one category of articles that most start-up importers should be concerned about is textiles. If you decide to import certain textile products (such as cotton, wool, manmade fiber, silk blend, or other vegetable-fiber articles), be careful: If the quota period is closed, you won't be able to enter the goods into the United States. The goods will have to be either returned to the seller or warehoused at great expense. You can find information on textile quotas from the Committee for the Implementation of Textile Agreements, U.S. Department of Commerce (otexa.ita.doc.gov/).

Being Aware of Anti-Dumping and Countervailing Duties

Anti-dumping duties are taxes assessed on imported merchandise that's sold to purchasers in the United States at a price less than the merchandise would be sold in the manufacturer's home market.

Countervailing duties are taxes assessed to counter the effect of subsidies provided by foreign governments on goods that are exported to the United States. A *subsidy* is financial assistance that a country provides to a manufacturer in that country. Because the subsidy causes the price of the merchandise to be artificially low, U.S. manufacturers can't be competitive. If a U.S. manufacturer is a competitor in this kind of situation, the manufacturer typically asks the government to impose countervailing duties to counter the effects of the subsidy.

Before agreeing to purchase products, confirm whether that product is subject to any anti-dumping or countervailing duty order issued by the U.S. Department of Commerce. The rates of duty imposed on goods that are subject to one of these orders can be much greater than the normal rate of duty. For more information, contact your local office of the Department of Commerce or go to ia.ita.doc.gov/trcs/foreignadcvd/index.html.

When you negotiate a price with a foreign supplier, make sure you know the price that the supplier is selling the goods for in its own country. This information helps you evaluate your potential risk for punitive duties.

Part VI
The Part of Tens

The 5th Wave

By Rich Tennant

"They've been that way for over 10 minutes. Larry's either having a staring contest with the customer, or he's afraid to ask for the sale again."

In this part . . .

In the Part of Tens, I give you the keys to being a successful importer or exporter. With the information in this part — and some hard work — you'll be well on your way to starting a successful import/export business.

Chapter 20

Ten Keys to Becoming a Successful Importer

In This Chapter

▶ Identifying the keys to becoming a successful importer

▶ Understanding some of the major mistakes to avoid

▶ Reviewing the pitfalls to watch out for

*M*any small to medium-size manufacturing or services companies want to identify overseas suppliers so that they can lower their cost of goods sold and increase their profits. Entrepreneurs are excited by the thought of looking across international borders for business opportunities — many people see it as an exciting chance to travel and experience the satisfaction of working with people from all over the world.

Importing is not as easy as it may initially appear — in fact, it's a real challenge. You have to take the time to select the right product, understand the applicable rules and regulations, identify your customers, find out about different payment and shipping alternatives, and deal with the bureaucracy known as U.S. Customs. To help you do all these things successfully, this chapter gives you the ten keys to becoming a successful importer.

Familiarizing Yourself with Import Control and Regulatory Requirements

To avoid any problems in clearing your merchandise and getting it through Customs, you need to be familiar with U.S. Customs policies and procedures *before* actually importing your goods. U.S. Customs and Border Protection (CBP) does not require an importer to have a license or permit; however, other agencies — such as the Food and Drug Administration (FDA), the U.S. Department of Agriculture (USDA), and the Bureau of Alcohol, Tobacco, and Firearms (BATF) — may require a license or permit to import a specific product. Make sure you know what kind of license may be required to import your merchandise into the United States.

You also need to figure out whether the item you're importing is subject to any special requirements in terms of product specifications, testing, certification, marketing, labeling, packaging, and documentation.

The CBP website (www.cbp.gov) contains valuable information for new importers. You can also get assistance by contacting the appropriate commodity specialist team at your local district office at the U.S. Customs Service or by asking your *Customs broker* (a person you hire to assist you in clearing your shipments through Customs). For information on working with commodity specialist teams, check out Chapter 3.

Knowing How to Classify Your Products for Tariffs

The U.S. subscribes to the Harmonized Tariff Schedule of the United States (HTSUS) to classify goods for the purpose of assessing duties. The schedule's assigned tariff classification code impacts the rate of duty applied. Because duties can vary from product to product, you need to make sure that you know the proper classification to minimize duties and eliminate problems at the time your goods enter the U.S.

You can get assistance in finding the right code by talking to the commodity specialist team (see the preceding section). You can also request a written, binding ruling from CBP for the proper HTSUS classification and rate of duty for your merchandise. For more information on binding rulings, check out Chapter 3.

Checking Whether You Qualify for Preferential Duty Programs

You may be eligible to benefit from preferential duty programs such as the Generalized System of Preferences, the North American Free Trade Agreement (NAFTA), the Dominican Republic–Central America–United States Free Trade Agreement (CAFTA–DR), the Caribbean Basin Initiative, and so on. As an importer, if you don't take advantage of these programs, you may be subject to duties that you otherwise could've avoided, which makes the transaction more expensive for you. (For information on preferential duty programs, turn to Chapters 3 and 16.)

Researching Quota Requirements

Before you import certain commodities into the U.S., you need to research general quota information and quota requirements. An *import quota* is a limit on the amount of a certain commodity that can be imported into the U.S. during a specific period of time (see Chapter 19). There are two types of quotas:

- ✔ **Absolute quotas:** Absolute quotas usually apply to textiles but can, in some instances, apply to other goods. They limit the amount of goods that may enter into the commerce of the U.S. during a specific period. When that limit has been reached, no additional goods are allowed into the U.S.

- ✔ **Tariff rate quotas:** Tariff rate quotas permit a specified quantity of an item at a reduced rate of duty during the quota period. After that quota has been reached, the goods can still enter the country but at a higher rate of duty.

If the item you're importing is under an absolute quota and the quota has been closed, the goods that you import won't be allowed into the country. They'll either have to be returned to the seller or placed, at your expense, into a Customs-controlled warehouse until a new quota has been opened.

For more information on how to access quota information, turn to Chapter 19.

Checking the Reputation of Your Foreign Seller

You need to check the reputation, reliability, and financial status of your prospective trading partner. If your foreign seller has a questionable reputation, you'll want to select a method of payment that will protect the import against the sellers' nonperformance. (For more on methods of payment and their impact on you, check out Chapter 17.)

You can access information on the foreign seller through a U.S. Commercial Services program called the International Company Profile (http://export. gov/salesandmarketing/eg_main_018198.asp). Also, be sure to ask a prospective foreign seller for references and follow up with them over the phone.

Understanding Incoterms

As an importer, you have to understand the costs, responsibilities, rights, and obligations that accompany the use of a specific *Incoterm* (International Commercial Terms; see Chapter 16).

Every time a supplier submits a quotation for goods to you, the quotation must include a term of sale. If you don't understand the specific Incoterm, you may overestimate or underestimate the costs associated with the goods that you'll be importing.

Analyzing Your Insurance Coverage

Make sure you analyze the amount of insurance on your import transaction. Weather, rough handling of cargo by carriers, long distances, and other common hazards make it important that you determine the type, amount, and extent of coverage required. You need to make sure that you identify who'll be responsible for insurance against loss or damage while the goods are in transit.

If the foreign seller quotes using the term *CIF* (short for *cost, insurance, and freight*), the seller/exporter is responsible for obtaining the insurance. If any other shipping term is used, insurance is your responsibility; contact an international insurance carrier or your Customs broker for more information (see Chapters 17 and 18).

Don't assume, or even take the seller's word, that adequate insurance has been obtained. If the seller neglects to obtain adequate coverage, damage to the cargo may cause you a major financial loss, so make sure that the exporter/seller includes a certificate of insurance with all the other required shipping documents.

Knowing What's in the Purchase Contract

The purchase contract should include any issue deemed significant by either the buyer or the seller. Any purchase contract *must* deal with issues such as product acceptance, product warranties, and dispute resolution procedures. (For more on purchase contracts, turn to Chapter 6.)

Entering into an import transaction without a formal written purchase contract can expose you to many significant risks that you won't be able to exercise much control over.

Hiring a Customs Broker

You have the right as an importer to file a Customs entry on your own behalf. However, if you're a first-time importer, you'll want to consult a licensed *Customs broker,* a private business that handles the clearance of imported goods for you. Customs brokers are licensed by U.S. Customs and Border Protection (CBP). Importing procedures can be very complicated, and hiring a Customs broker can facilitate this process and minimize any potential future problems (see Chapter 19).

You can view a list of Customs brokers licensed to conduct business in a specific port by visiting the CBP website (www.cbp.gov/xp/cgov/tool box/contacts/ports/).

Staying on Top of Record-keeping

You have to comply with all record-keeping requirements of Customs. This includes keeping all documents relating to imports for a period of five years. Customs has the right to inspect the documents to determine whether you've complied with U.S. Customs laws. (For more on the kinds of records you need to keep, check out Chapter 19.)

Chapter 21

Ten Keys to Becoming a Successful Exporter

. . . .

In This Chapter

▶ Identifying the keys to becoming a successful exporter

▶ Understanding some of the major mistakes to avoid

▶ Knowing the pitfalls to watch out for

. . . .

You can get involved in exporting in numerous ways — from filling orders for a domestic supplier (such as an export management company) to exporting your own products. Many businesses — small, medium, or large — are excited about the idea of doing business internationally as a way to increase your sales and profits. *Remember:* Every U.S. manufacturer that does not currently sell its goods overseas can be a potential client for you.

Exporting is a challenge, and it isn't as easy as it may initially appear. You have to take the time to select the right product, understand the applicable rules and regulations in both the United States and the importing country, identify your customers, and find out about the different payment and shipping alternatives. However you choose to export, developing a detailed and thorough strategy is an important part of the planning process.

In this chapter, I cover the ten critical keys to becoming a successful exporter.

Identifying Your Market

If you're interested in exporting, you need to identify foreign export markets for your products. Without the right market, you won't be able to do any business. Thorough market research also helps you understand the economic, political, and cultural factors that will impact your ability to successfully sell your product. This kind of information is readily available through government agencies and business-related organizations such as foreign trade associations, chambers of commerce, and trade commission offices. (You can find more information on identifying your market in Chapter 8.)

Visit www.export.gov and register to become part of the user community. The site provides a wealth of readily accessible data at no cost, and it can assist you in identifying overseas markets for U.S. goods and services. The advantage of these resources is that they come from trade experts located in countries around the world. Because their expertise comes from hands-on involvement (as opposed to second-hand information), you can be assured that the data they provide is good.

Each individual market has different demands, and these demands can change. Changes in technology, lifting of trade barriers, and adjustments in import/export regulations are all factors that may impact the level and direction of international trade. These factors can have an influence, and you may need to consider adjusting your marketing and export strategies for the current situation.

Assessing Product Potential

As an exporter, you need to focus on what your product does and identify what needs it will satisfy in the foreign market. You also need to identify the strengths and weakness of your product in comparison to available competitive products. Take a look at Chapters 5, 8, and 9 to get information about selecting a product, assessing its potential, and developing an overall product strategy targeted toward your customer.

A product may be successful in the U.S., but that isn't any guarantee that it'll be just as successful in a foreign market. There may be no need for the product in the foreign country or the product may need to be modified.

Preparing a product for export requires not just knowledge of the product but also an awareness of many unique characteristics of each of the different markets you may be targeting. Cultural differences and local customs may also require product modifications in areas such as branding, packaging, and labeling. Awareness of and sensitivity to cultural differences are critical to a successful product introduction.

Different countries can have different product standards, and you need to understand the need to conform if you want to do business internationally. The U.S. Department of Commerce's National Center for Standards and Certification Information (NCSCI) provides this information for nonagricultural products; visit its website at `http://ts.nist.gov/standards/information/index.cfm`.

Familiarizing Yourself with Export Controls and Licensing Requirements

Exporting can expose your business to laws and regulations that you may not be familiar with. All kinds of different rules can impact your ability to successfully do business in foreign markets. One of these is U.S. export controls, which take the form of prohibitions, restrictions, and licensing requirements.

A key to being a successful exporter is being aware of these issues. Violation of these laws can have significant repercussions, from the government seizing your products to a denial of your privilege to export to fines and imprisonment. (For information on export rules and regulations, see Chapter 3.)

Investigating Import Controls

Before exporting your product to a foreign market, you need to identify whether the country you're exporting to has any import controls related to the sale of your product. These controls can include prohibitions, restrictions, or import licensing requirements, and they can be based on country of origin, product type, or product characteristics. Products that violate these controls are generally not allowed to enter the importing country.

Import documentation requirements and other regulations imposed by foreign governments vary from one country to the next. You need to be aware of the regulations that apply to your own operations and transactions. (For additional information, see Chapter 3.)

Understanding U.S. Export Laws

You have to be aware of your responsibilities when it comes to U.S. export laws. These laws are designed to make sure that U.S. exports go only to legally authorized destinations. For example, the Foreign Corrupt Practices Act prohibits a U.S. exporter from offering to pay a commission to a foreign government official, friend, or relative to get the business. The Anti-Boycott Act prohibits Americans from participating in foreign boycotts or taking actions that further or support such boycotts against countries friendly to the U.S. (For more on these laws, check out Chapter 3.)

Making Sense of Incoterms

As an exporter, you need to understand the costs, responsibilities, rights, and obligations that accompany the use of a specific incoterm.

Every time you prepare a quotation for a customer, the quotation must include a term of sale. If you fail to clearly identify the specific incoterm to your customer, it can lead to an overestimation or underestimation of costs associated with the goods that you'll be selling, which can ultimately lead to the loss of a sale.

Making Sure You Have the Right Insurance Coverage

You need to analyze the amount of insurance on your export transaction. Weather, rough handling of cargo by carriers, long distances, and other common hazards make it important that you determine the type, amount, and extent of coverage required. Also, make sure that you identify who'll be responsible for insurance against loss or damage while the goods are in transit (see Chapter 18).

If you quote to your customer and use the term *CIF* (short for *cost, insurance, and freight*), you're the one responsible for obtaining the insurance, and you must include a certificate of insurance with all the other required shipping documents that you send to the importer. If you're quoting with a term of CIF and you don't have an international insurance carrier, contact your freight forwarder (see Chapter 18) and discuss the option of using its cargo insurance policy.

If any other shipping term is used, the importer is responsible for securing the insurance.

Focusing on Foreign Market Risk and Methods of Payment

When you're selecting a method of payment in an export transaction, you need to identify the primary risk factors and then evaluate them to choose the one that's best for you. ***Remember:*** Getting an order is only one step in the process. You also have to make sure that you're going to get paid. Being paid in full and on time is critical to success, and the level of risk in extending credit is a major consideration (see Chapter 14).

Here are the two primary risk factors that you need be aware of:

- **Country risks:** Country risk factors include economic and political stability, the legal system, and the foreign exchange rate.
- **Commercial risks:** Commercial risk factors include company ownership/ management, financial performance, market share, and payment history.

Keeping Track of Documentation

Even though the actual purchase order you receive from your overseas customer is the most important document that you'll receive, you have to get familiar with many other documents before exporting your goods. A wide variety of documents are used in exporting; which of them is required in specific transactions depends on the requirements of the U.S. government and the government of the importing country (see Chapter 18).

Because the processing of these documents can be a formidable task, consider having a freight forwarder handle this portion of the transaction. Freight forwarders are specialists in this process. (See the next section for more on freight forwarders.)

Hiring a Freight Forwarder

An international freight forwarder acts as an agent on your behalf and assists in moving the cargo from the point of origin to the ultimate overseas destination. Freight forwarders are familiar with the import rules and regulations of foreign countries, U.S. export regulations, methods of shipment, and required documents relating to foreign trade.

A freight forwarder can assist you in preparing price quotations by advising on freight costs, port charges, consular fees, costs of special documentation, insurance costs, and handling fees. They recommend the packing methods that will protect the merchandise during transit or can arrange to have the merchandise packed at the port or put in containers. (For more information about the benefits of working with a freight forwarder and how to go about locating and choosing one, go to Chapter 18.)

If you use the services of a freight forwarder, you won't have to deal with many of the details involved with the exporting of your goods. Fees charged by forwarders are modest, and forwarders have access to shipping discounts. The experience and constant attention to detail provided by the forwarder is a good investment and a key to success.

Part VII
Appendixes

The 5th Wave   By Rich Tennant

"But rather than me just sitting here talking, why don't we watch this video of me sitting here talking?"

In this part . . .

1 give you references that you need when you're developing your import/export program. Here you find a general glossary of key international business terms, along with a listing of government resources. You also find info on how to use this book's CD-ROM.

Appendix A

Resources

· ·

Government Assistance Programs

Several federal, state, and local agencies offer programs to assist U.S. exporters. Some are guarantee programs that require the participation of a lender,
while others may provide direct loans or grants. All programs aim to improve
the exporters' access to credit by providing guarantees to financial institutions
to reduce their risk associated with loans to exporters.

The Export-Import Bank of the United States

The Export-Import (Ex-Im) Bank of the United States is an independent U.S.
government agency that facilitates the U.S. export of goods and services by
providing loans, guarantees, and insurance programs to exporters. The Ex-Im
Bank provides financing both pre- and post-export:

- ✔ **Pre-export financing:** Through the Ex-Im Bank's Working Capital
  Guarantee Program, lenders can provide financing to exporters for the
  purpose of purchasing or producing a product for export. If the exporter
  defaults on the loan, the Ex-Im Bank reimburses the lender the guaranteed
  portion of the loan.

- ✔ **Post-export financing:** The Ex-Im Bank provides commercial and political
  risk insurance. If the buyer fails to pay, Ex-Im Bank reimburses the
  exporter in accordance with the terms of the policy.

You can get specific information about the Ex-Im Bank's programs by
contacting the Business Development Group, Export-Import Bank, 811
Vermont Ave. NW, Washington, DC 20571 (phone: 202-565-3946; website:
www.exim.gov).

Department of Agriculture

The Commodity Credit Corporation (CCC) of the U.S. Department of Agriculture (USDA) provides several programs in financing the export of U.S. agricultural products:

- **Export credit guarantee programs:** The USDA administers export credit guarantee programs for commercial financing of U.S. agricultural exports. These CCC programs encourage exports to buyers in countries where credit is necessary to maintain or increase U.S. sales, but where financing may not be available without CCC guarantees.

- **Export Enhancement Program (EEP):** The EEP helps products produced by U.S. farmers meet competition from subsidizing countries, especially the European Union. Under the program, the USDA pays cash to exporters as bonuses, allowing them to sell U.S. agricultural products in targeted countries at prices below the exporter's costs of acquiring them. Major objectives of the program are to expand U.S. agricultural exports and to challenge unfair trade practices.

You can find more information on USDA programs by contacting the USDA, Foreign Agricultural Service, 1400 Independence Ave. SW, Washington, DC 20250 (phone: 202-720-3224; website: www.fas.usda.gov).

Small Business Administration

Small Business Administration (SBA) programs provide financial assistance to businesses interested in exporting but that may not be able to obtain trade financing. All applying firms must qualify as a small business under the SBA's size standards. The SBA defines a *small business* as any independently owned and operated business that is not dominant in its competitive area and does not employ more than 500 people.

- **Export Working Capital Program:** Under this program, a business can get a loan guarantee to finance the *working capital* (money needed to meet day-to-day operating expenses) needs associated with processing an order for a single- or multiple-export transaction. The purpose of this program is to assist businesses that are able to generate export sales, but need financial assistance to support these sales. The goal of the program is to ensure that qualified small-business exporters don't lose viable export sales due to a lack of working capital.

✔ **Export Express Program:** The Export Express Program assists small businesses in developing or expanding their export markets. The proceeds of these loans may be used to finance export development activities such as:

- Standby letters of credit when required as a bid bond, performance bond, or advance payment guarantee.

  A *standby letter of credit* is a letter of credit issued by the bank on behalf of its customer (the exporter) to serve as a guarantee to the beneficiary of the letter of credit (the importer) that the bank's customer will perform a specified contract with the beneficiary (that is, to make the shipment of the goods) and, if the customer defaults, the beneficiary may draw funds against the letter of credit as penalties or as payments. A standby letter of credit is also referred to as a *performance bond.*

- Participation in a foreign trade show.

- Translation of product brochures or catalogs for use in overseas markets.

- General lines of credit for export purposes.

- Service contracts from buyers located outside the United States.

- Transaction-specific financing needs associated with completing actual export orders.

- Purchase of real estate and equipment to be used in the production of goods or services for export.

- Term loans and other financing to enable small businesses, including export trading companies and export management companies, to develop foreign markets.

- Acquisition, construction, renovation, modernization, improvement, or expansion of production facilities or equipment to be used in the United States in the production of goods or services for export.

For more information on SBA programs, contact the SBA at 800-827-5722 or visit www.sba.gov. You can also contact your local SBA field office; look in the government pages of your local phone book or visit www.sba.gov/localresources/index.html to locate the office nearest you.

U.S. Customs and Border Protection

U.S. Customs and Border Protection operates 20 field operations offices in the United States that provide centralized management oversight and operational assistance to 327 U.S. ports of entry and 15 preclearance offices. For more information, you can contact U.S. Customs and Border Protection, 1300 Pennsylvania Ave. NW, Washington, DC 20229 (phone: 877-227-5511; website: www.cbp.gov). Here is the contact information for the field operations offices:

Atlanta, GA
1699 Phoenix Parkway
Suite 400
College Park, GA 30349
678-284-5900
www.cbp.gov/xp/cgov/toolbox/contacts/cmcs/cmc_s_atlantic.xml

Baltimore, MD
103 South Gay Street
Suite 715
Baltimore, MD 21202
410-962-6200
www.cbp.gov/xp/cgov/toolbox/contacts/cmcs/cmc_mid_atlantic.xml

Boston, MA
10 Causeway St
Room 801
Boston, MA 02222
617-565-6208
www.cbp.gov/xp/cgov/toolbox/contacts/cmcs/cmc_n_atlantic.xml

Buffalo, NY
4455 Genesee Street
Buffalo, NY 14225
716-626-0400
www.cbp.gov/xp/cgov/toolbox/contacts/cmcs/cmc_e_great.xml

Chicago, IL
610 S. Canal Street
Room 900
Chicago, IL 60607
312-983-9100
www.cbp.gov/xp/cgov/toolbox/contacts/cmcs/cmc_mid_america.xml

Detroit, MI
211 W. Fort Street, Suite 1200
Detroit, MI 48226
313-496-2155
www.cbp.gov/xp/cgov/toolbox/contacts/cmcs/cmc_w_great.xml

El Paso, TX
9400 Viscount Suite 104
El Paso, TX 79925
915-633-7300 Ext: 100
www.cbp.gov/xp/cgov/toolbox/contacts/cmcs/cmc_w_texas.xml

Houston, TX
2323 S. Shepherd #1300
Houston, TX 77019
713-387-7200
www.cbp.gov/xp/cgov/toolbox/contacts/cmcs/cmc_e_texas.xml

Laredo, TX
109 Shiloh Dr., Suite 300
Laredo, TX 78045
956-753-1700
www.cbp.gov/xp/cgov/toolbox/contacts/cmcs/cmc_south_texas.xml

Los Angeles, CA
1 World Trade Center
Suite 705
Long Beach, CA 90831
562-980-3100
www.cbp.gov/xp/cgov/toolbox/contacts/cmcs/cmc_south_pacific.xml

Miami, FL
909 S.E. 1st Avenue
Suite 980
Miami, FL 33131
305-810-5120
www.cbp.gov/xp/cgov/toolbox/contacts/cmcs/cmc_s_florida.xml

New Orleans, LA
423 Canal Street
Room 350
New Orleans, LA 70130
504-670-2404
www.cbp.gov/xp/cgov/toolbox/contacts/cmcs/cmc_gulf.xml

New York, NY
One Penn Plaza 11th floor
New York, NY 10119
646-733-3100
www.cbp.gov/xp/cgov/toolbox/contacts/cmcs/cmc_ny.xml

Portland, OR
33 New Montgomery St., Suite 1600
San Francisco, CA 94105
415-744-1530
www.cbp.gov/xp/cgov/toolbox/contacts/cmcs/cmc_n_pacific.xml

San Diego, CA
610 W. Ash St
Suite 1200
San Diego, CA 92101
619-652-9966 Ext: 100
www.cbp.gov/xp/cgov/toolbox/contacts/cmcs/cmc_s_ca.xml

San Francisco, CA
33 New Montgomery St., 16th floor
San Francisco, CA 94105
415-744-1530 Ext: 221
www.cbp.gov/xp/cgov/toolbox/contacts/cmcs/cmc_mid_pac.xml

San Juan, PR
#1 La Puntilla Street
Office Room 203
San Juan, PR 00901
787-729-6950
www.cbp.gov/xp/cgov/toolbox/contacts/cmcs/cmc_pr-vi.xml

Seattle, WA
1000 2nd Ave
Suite 2200
Seattle, WA 98104-1049
206-553-6944
www.cbp.gov/xp/cgov/toolbox/contacts/cmcs/cmc_nw_plains.xml

Tampa, FL
1624 East Seventh Avenue
Suite 300
Tampa, FL 33605
813-712-6100
www.cbp.gov/xp/cgov/toolbox/contacts/cmcs/cmc_n_florida.xml

Tucson, AZ
4740 N. Oracle Road
Suite 310
Tucson, AZ 85705
520-407-2300
www.cbp.gov/xp/cgov/toolbox/contacts/cmcs/cmc_arizona.xml

Currency Index

Currencies fluctuate daily. For up-to-date currency conversion, check out
XE.com's Universal Currency Converter (www.xe.com/ucc).

Currency	Country
Afghani	Afghanistan
Ariary	Madagascar
Austral	Argentina
Baht	Thailand
Balboa	Panama
Birr	Ethiopia
Bolivar	Venezuela
Boliviano	Bolivia
Cedi	Ghana (prior to August 2007)
Colón	Costa Rica, El Salvador
Convertible mark	Bosnia-Herzegovina
Córdoba	Nicaragua
Cruzeiro	Brazil
Dalasi	The Gambia
Denar	Macedonia
Deutschemark	Germany (prior to 1999)
Dinar	Algeria, Bahrain, Bosnia-Herzegovina (prior to 1999), Gaza, Iraq (prior to 1994), Jordan, Kuwait, Libya, Sudan, Tunisia, Yugoslavia
Dirham	Morocco, United Arab Emirates
Dobra	São Tomé and Principe

(continued)

Currency	Country
Dollar	Anguilla, Antigua and Barbuda, Australia, Bahamas, Barbados, Belize, Bermuda, British Virgin Islands, Brunei, Canada, Cayman Islands, Cook Island, Dominica, Fiji Islands, Grenada, Guyana, Hong Kong, Jamaica, Liberia, Montserrat, Namibia, New Zealand, Puerto Rico, St. Kitts, St. Lucia, St. Vincent, Singapore, Solomon Islands, Trinidad and Tobago, United States, Zimbabwe
Dong	Vietnam
Drachma	Greece (prior to 1999)
Dram	Armenia
ECU	European currency unit
Emalangeni	Swaziland
Escudo	Cape Verde, Portugal
Euro	Austria, Belgium, Finland, France, Germany, Greece, Ireland, Italy, Luxembourg, Netherlands, Spain and Portugal (not used in other European Union countries)
Florin	Aruba
Forint	Hungary
Franc	Belgium (prior to 1999), Burundi, Comoro Island, Djibouti, France (prior to 1999), Guinea (Conarky), Liechtenstein, Luxembourg (prior to 1999), Madagascar, Monaco, Rwanda, Switzerland
Franc CFA	Central Cameroon, Central African Republic, Chad, Congo, Ecuatoria Guinea, Gabon, Guinea-Bissau
Franc CFA west	Benin, Burkina Faso, Ivory Coast, Mali, Niger, Senegal, Togo, West African States
Franc CFP	French Polynesia, New Caledonia
Gourde	Haiti
Gulden	The Netherlands (prior to 1999), Netherlands Antilles, Suriname
Karbovanetz	Ukraine
Kina	Papua New Guinea
Kip	Laos
Kobo	Nigeria
Korun	Czech Republic, Slovakia
Krone	Denmark, Norway
Krona	Sweden

Currency	Country
Króna	Faroe Islands, Iceland
Kroon	Estonia
Kwacha	Malawi, Zambia
Kwanza	Angola
Kuna	Croatia
Kyat	Myanmar
Laari	Maldives
Lat	Latvia
Lek	Albania
Lempira	Honduras
Leone	Sierra Leone
Leu	Moldava, Romania
Lev	Bulgaria (prior to 1999)
Lira	Cyprus, Italy (prior to 1999), Malta, Turkey, San Marino, Vatican City
Litas	Lithuania
Livre	Lebanon
Loti	Lesotho
Maloti	Lesotho
Manat	Azerbaijan
Markka	Finland (prior to 1999)
Metica	Mozambique
Millim	Tunisia
Naira	Nigeria
New Cedi	Ghana
New Dinar	Iraq
New Lev	Bulgaria
New Sheqel	Gaza, Israel
New Dong	Vietnam
Ngultrum	Bhutan
Novo Kwanza	Angola
Nuevo peso	Mexico, Uruguay

(continued)

Currency	Country
Ougiya	Mauritania
Pa'anga	Tonga
Para	Yugoslovia
Pataca	Macao
Peseta	Spain (prior to 1999)
Peso	Argentina (prior to 1991), Chile, Colombia, Cuba, Dominican Republic, Guinea-Bissau (prior to May 1997), Mexico, Uruguay
Peso Uruguayo	Uruguay
Piso	The Philippines
Pound	Cyprus, Egypt, England, Falkland/Malvinas Islands, Gibraltar, Guernsey, Ireland (prior to 1999), Isle of Man, Jersey, Northern Ireland, Scotland, St. Helena, Sudan, Syria
Punt	Ireland
Quetzal	Guatemala
Rand	South Africa
Renminbi	China People's Republic
Rial	Oman, Yemen
Riel	Cambodia
Ringgit	Brunei, Malaysia
Rubel	Belarus
Ruble	Georgia, Kazakhstan, Kyrgyz Republic, Russia, Tajikistan, Turkmenistan, Uzbekistan
Rublis	Latvia
Rufiya	Maldive Island
Rupee	India, Mauritius, Nepal, Pakistan, Seychelles, Sri Lanka
Rupiah	Indonesia
Schilling	Austria (prior to 1999)
Sent	Estonia
Sente	Lesotho
Sentimo	Philippines
Sheqel	Israel
Shilin	Somalia
Shilling	Kenya, Tanzania, Uganda

Currency	Country
Sol	Peru
Som	Kyrgyz Republic, Tajikistan
Sucre	Ecuador
Taka	Bangladesh
Tala	Western Samoa
Tanga	Kazakhstan
Toea	Papua New Guinea
Tolar	Slovenia
Toman	Iran
Tugrik	Mongolia
Vatu	Vanuatu
Won	DPR Korea, Republic of Korea
Yen	Japan
Yuan	People's Republic of China, Taiwan
Zaire	Zaire (renamed the Democratic Republic of Congo in 1997)
Zlote	Poland

Appendix B

Multilingual Cross-Reference for International Shipping Terms

● ●

*T*his appendix lists several pages of common shipping terms in English, Spanish, French, and German. Keep it handy if you do business with the major players in Western Europe.

English	Spanish	French	German
Acceptance	aceptación	acceptation	Annahme
Accepted bill	letra aceptada	traite acceptée	Angenommener Wechsel
Acceptor	aceptante	accepteur	Akzeptant
Ad valorem duty	impuesto ad valorem	impôt ad valorem	Wertsteuer
Advance	anticipo	acompte	Vorleistung
Advice of arrival	aviso de llegada	avis d'arrivée	Empfangsanzeige
Advice of dispatch	aviso de expedición	avis d'expédition	Versandavis
Advice of shipment	aviso de embarque	avis d'embarquement	Verschiffungsanzeige
Air waybill	carta de porte aéreo	lettre de voiture aérienne	Luftfrachtbrief
Arbitrage	arbitraje	arbitrage	Arbitrage
Arbitration clause	cláusula de arbitraje	clause d'arbitrage	Kompromissklausel
Average	avería	avarie	Havarie
Balance of trade	balanza comercial	balance commerciale	Handelsbilanz
Bank	banco	banque	Bank

(continued)

English	Spanish	French	German
Bank charges	gastos bancarios	frais de banque	Bankspesen
Bank check	cheque bancario	cheque de banque	Bankscheck
Bearer certificate	título al portador	titre au porteur	Inhaberpapiere
Beneficiary	beneficiario	bénéficiaire	Empfänger
Bill/draft	giro	effet/traite	Ziehung/Wechsel
Bill draft	efecto	effet	Wechsel
Bill of exchange	letra de cambio	lettre de change	Wechsel
Bill of lading (B/L)	conocimiento de embarque	connaissement	Konnossement
Bonded warehouse	depósito aduanero privado	entrepôt douanier privé	Privates Zollager
Broker	corredor	courtier	Makler
Buyer (purchaser)	comprador	acheteur	Käufer
Calibration	calibración	étalonnage	Kalibrierung
In cash	al contado	comptant	Bar Kassa
Certificate of analysis	certificado de análisis	certificat d'analyse	Analysenzertifikat
Certificate of origin	certificado de origen	certificat d'origine	Ursprungszeugnis
Certificate of weight	certificado de peso	certificat de poids	Gewichtsbescheinigung
Certification	certificación	certification	Autorisierte
Chamber of Commerce	cámara de comercio	chambre de commerce	Handelskammer
Change	cambio	change	Wechsel
Charter party	póliza de fletamento	charte partie	Charterpartie
Check to bearer	cheque al portador	cheque au porteur	Inhaberscheck

English	Spanish	French	German
Clean B/L	conocimiento embarque limpio	connaissement net	Reines Konnossement
Clean draft	remesa simple	remise simple	Einfache Rimesse
Clear goods through Customs	despachar mercancías en aduana	dédouaner des marchandises	Waren verzollen
Clearance through Customs	despacho aduanero	dédouanement	Zoll-klarierung
Cleared goods	mercancías despachadas	marchandises dédouanées	Abgefertigte ware
Clearing house	cámara de compensación	chambre de compensation	Abrechnungsstelle
Commercial agent	agente comercial	agent commercial	Handelsagent
Commercial bill/trade bill	efecto comercial	effet de commerce	Handelswechsel
Community tariff	arancel comunitario	douanier commun	Gemeinschaftszölle
Community transit	tránsito comunitario	transit communautaire	EG-Transit
Confirmed letter of credit	carta de crédito confirmada	lettre de crédit confirme	Bestätigter Kreditbrief
Confirming bank	banco confirmador	banque confirmatrice	Bestätigende Bank
Consignee	consignatario	consignataire	Konsignatar
Consular certificate	certificado consular	certificat consulaire	Konsularische Bescheinngung
Consular fee	tasa consular	taxe consulaire	Konsular gebnhr
Consular invoice	factura consular	facture consulaire	Konsulatsfaktura
Container	contenedor	conteneur	Container

(continued)

English	Spanish	French	German
Contract of carriage	contrato de transporte	contrat de transport	Frachtvertrag
Contract of sale	contrato de venta	contrat de vente	Verkaufskontrakt
To credit an account	abonar en cuenta	créditer un compte	Gutschreiben
Credit report	informes de crédito	renseignements de crédit	Kreditauskunft
Crossed check	cheque cruzado	cheque barre	Gekreuzter scheck
Customer	cliente	client	Kunde
Customs	aduana	douane	Zoll
Customs agent	agente de aduanas	agent des douanes	Zollagent
Customs authorities	autoridades aduaneras	autorités douaniers	Zollbehörde Guarantee
Customs charges	gastos de aduana	frais de douane	Zollgebnhren
Customs declaration	declaración aduanera	déclaration en douane	Zollderdeklaration
Customs duties	derechos aduaneros	droits de douane	Zollzätze
Customs inspection	inspección aduanera	contrôle de douane	Zollkontrolle
Customs nomenclature	nomenclatura arancelaria	nomenclature douanière	Zollnomenklatur
Customs tariff	arancel de aduanas	tarif douanier	Zolltarif
Customs warehouse	depósito aduanero	entrepôt de douane	Zollager
Date bill/time bill	efecto a fecha fija	effet a échéance fixe	Festterminlicher wechsel
Date of acceptance	fecha de aceptación	date d'acceptation	Akzeptdatum
Date of payment	fecha de pago	date de paiement	Zahlungstermin

English	*Spanish*	*French*	*German*
Date of presentation	fecha de presentación	date de présentation	Eingangsdatum
Defect	defecto	default	Gebraurchshinderkiche
Deferment of payment	aplazamiento de pago	sursis de paiement	Zahlungsstundung
Delivery order	orden de entrega	bon de livraison	Lieferschein
Demand bill/ sight bill	efecto a la orden	effet d'ordre	Wechsel auf order
Docker	estibador	débardeur	Dockarbeiter
Documentary credit	crédito documentario	crédit documentaire	Dokumentenakkreditiv
Documentary draft	remesa documentaria	remise documentaire	Dokumentäre rimesse
Drawback exports	exportación temporal	exportation anticipée	Bevorschusste ausfuhr
Drawee	librado	tire	Bezogener
Drawer	librador	tireur	Aussteller
Due date	fecha de vencimiento	date d'échéance	Fälligkeistermin
Duty-free warehouse	depósito franco	dépôt hors douane	Freilager
Endorsement	aval	aval	Aval
Endorser	endosante	endosseur	Indossant
Exchange permit	permiso de cambio	permis de change	Devisengenehmigung
Export duty	impuesto a la exportación	taxe à l'exportation	Ausfuhrabgabe
Export firm	casa de exportación	maison d'exportation	Exportfirma
Export license	licencia de exportación	licence d'exportation	Ausfuhrlizenz
Exporter	exportador	exportateur	Exporteur
Extra charges	gastos extraordinarios	frais supplémentaires	Extrakosten

(continued)

English	Spanish	French	German
Floating policy	póliza flotante	police d'abonnement	Laufende police
Freight paid	flete pagado	fret paye	Fracht bezahlt
Goods clearance certificate	certificado despacho mercancía	congé des douanes	Erledigungsbeschinigung
Guaranteed bill	letra avalada	traite avalisée	Avalwechsel
Harbor dues	derechos portuarios	droits de quai	Hafengebnhren
Holder	poseedor	détenteur	Inhaber
Import duty	derechos de importación	droits d'importation	Einfuhrzoll
Import license	licencia de importación	licence d'importation	Einfuhrlizenz
Importer	importador	importateur	Enfuhrhändler
Insurance certificate	certificado de seguro	certificat d'assurance	Versicherungszertifikat
Insurance policy	póliza de seguro	police d'assurance	Versicherungspolice
Insurance premium	prima de seguro	prime d'assurance	Versicherungsprämie
Interim certificate	resguardo provisional	certificat intérimaire	Zwischenschein
Irrevocable credit	crédito irrevocable	crédit irrévocable	Unwiderruflicher Kredit
Issuing bank	banco emisor	banque d'émission	Emissionbank
Joint cargo service	servicio de grupaje	service de groupage	Sammelladungsverkehr
Landing certificate	certificado de descarga	certificat de déchargement	Löschschein
Letter of complaint	carta de reclamación	lettre de réclamation	Beschwerdebrief
Loading charges	gastos de carga	frais de chargement	Ladungskosten
Maintenance	mantenimiento	maintenance	Instandhaltung

English	Spanish	French	German
Manifest	manifiesto de carga	lettre de chargement	Ladungsmanifest
Manufacturer	fabricante	fabricant	Fabrikant
Maritime insurance policy	póliza de seguro marítimo	police d'assurance maritime	Seever Sicherungspolice
Mate's receipt	recibo de abordo	reçu de bord	Steuermannsschein
Notice of loss	aviso de siniestro	avis de sinistre	Shadensanzeige
Notifying bank	banco avisador	banque de notification	Anmeldende Bank
Official exchange rate	cambio oficial	change officiel	Amtlicher Wechselkurs
Open a credit	abrir un crédito	ouvrir un crédit	Einen Kredit Eröffnen
Order check	cheque a la orden	cheque à l'ordre	Orderscheck
Other countries	terceros países	tiers pays	Drittländer
Owner of the goods	propietario de la mercancía	propriétaire de la marchandise	Eigentnmer der gnter
Partial shipments	envíos parciales	expéditions	Teilverschiffungen
Payable at sight	pagadero a la vista	payable a vue	Zahlbar bei Sicht
Payable cash	pagadero al contado	payable comptant	Zahlbar in bar
Payable to order	pagadero a la orden	payable à ordre	Zahlbar an order
Payer	ordenante	donneur d'ordre	Auftraggeber
Payment	abono	dépôt	Gutschrift
Payment order	orden de pago	ordre de paiement	Zahlungsanweisung

(continued)

English	Spanish	French	German
Port regulations	reglamento portuario	ordonnance de port	Hafenordnung
Presenting bank	banco presentador	banque présentatrice	Vorzeigende Bank
Price list	lista de precios	liste des prix	Preisverzeichnis
Pro forma invoice	factura proforma	facture fictive	Proformfaktur
Promissory note	pagaré IOU	billet à ordre	Solawechsel
Provisional invoice	factura provisional	facture provisoire	Vorfaktura
Purchasing contract	contrato de compra	contrat d'achat	Kaufvertrag
Quality	calidad	qualité	Qualität
Rates in force	tarifas en vigor	tarifs en vigueur	Geltende Tarife
Receipt	recibo	quittance	Quittung
With recourse	con recurso	avec recours	Mit regress
Without recourse	sin recurso	sans appel	Ohne regress
Remitting bank	banco remitente	banque remettante	Übersendende Bank
Sale invoice	factura de venta	facture de vente	Verkaufsfaktura
Sample	muestra	échantillon	Muster
Sample fair	feria de muestras	foire d'échantillons	Mustermesse
Seller	vendedor	acheteur	Verkäufer
To send on consignment	enviar en consignación	envoyer en consignation	Konsignieren
Shipped B/L	conocimiento recibo a bordo	connaissement reçu à bord	Bordknnossement
Shipper	cargador	chargeur	Befrachter
Shipping company	compañía naviera	compagnie de navigation	Schiffahrtsgesellshaft
Shipping documents	documento de embarque	documents d'embarquement	Verschiffungsdokument

English	Spanish	French	German
Sight bill	giro a la vista	traite à vue	Sichtwechsel
Sole agent	agente exclusivo	agent exclusif	Alleinvrtreter
Storage charges	gastos de almacenaje	frais de magasinage	Lagerspesen
Table of par values	tabla de paridades	table de parités	Paritätentabelle
Tariff exempt	exención arancelaria	exemption droits de douane	Zollfreiheit
Tariff quota	cuota arancelaria	quota d'importation	Zollkontingent
Tax base	base imponible	assiette de l'impôt	Steuerbemessungsgrundlage
Temporary importation	importación temporal	franchise temporaire	Vorübergehende einfuhr
Time bill	letra a plazo fijo	traite à échéance fixe	Terminwechsel
Trade directory	anuario comercial	annuaire du commerce	Handelsadressbuch
Transit dues	derechos de tránsito	droits de transit	Transitzölle
Traveler's check	cheque de viaje	chèque de voyage	Reisescheck
Valve for Customs purposes	valor en aduana	valeur en douane	Zollvert
VAT	IVA	TVA	Mehrwersteuer
Warehouse	almacén	magasin	Lager
Warehouse warrant	certificado de depósito	certificat de dépôt	Lagerschein
Waybill	carta de porte	lettre de voiture	Frachtbrief
Wholesaler	mayorista	grossiste	Grosshändler

Appendix C

About the CD

*N**ote:* If you are using a digital or an enhanced digital version of this book, this appendix does not apply. Please go to `http://book support.wiley.com` for access to the additional content.

Using the CD that accompanies this book couldn't be easier. You can pop it into pretty much any Mac or Windows computer made in the last ten years as long as that computer has an optical drive capable of playing good, old-fashioned CDs. If you're the hesitant type, check out the following system requirements.

System Requirements

Make sure that your computer meets the minimum system requirements shown in the following list. If your computer doesn't match up to most of these requirements, you may have problems using the software and files on the CD. For the latest and greatest information, please refer to the ReadMe file located at the root of the CD-ROM.

- ✔ A PC running Microsoft Windows or Linux with kernel 2.4 or later or

   A Macintosh running Apple OS X or later
- ✔ An Internet connection
- ✔ A CD-ROM drive

If you need more information on the basics, check out these books published by John Wiley & Sons, Inc.: *PCs For Dummies* by Dan Gookin; *Macs For Dummies* by Edward C. Baig; *iMacs For Dummies* by Mark L. Chambers; *Windows XP For Dummies* and *Windows Vista For Dummies,* both by Andy Rathbone.

Using the CD

To install the items from the CD to your hard drive, follow these steps.

1. **Insert the CD into your computer's CD-ROM drive.**

   The license agreement appears.

   Note to Windows users: The interface won't launch if you have autorun disabled. In that case, choose Start⇨Run. (For Windows Vista, choose Start⇨All Programs⇨Accessories⇨Run.) In the dialog box that appears, type **D:\Start.exe**. (Replace *D* with the proper letter if your CD drive uses a different letter. If you don't know the letter, see how your CD drive is listed under My Computer.) Click OK.

   Notes for Mac Users: When the CD icon appears on your desktop, double-click the icon to open the CD and double-click the Start icon. Also, note that the content menus may not function as expected in newer versions of Safari and Firefox; however, the documents are available by navigating to the Contents folder.

   Note for Linux Users: The specifics of mounting and using CDs vary greatly between different versions of Linux. Please see the manual or help information for your specific system if you experience trouble using this CD.

2. **Read through the license agreement and then click the Accept button if you want to use the CD.**

   The CD interface appears. The interface allows you to browse the contents and install the programs with just a click of a button (or two).

What You'll Find on the CD

The following sections are arranged by category and provide a summary of the software and other goodies you'll find on the CD. If you need help with installing the items provided on the CD, refer to the installation instructions in the preceding section.

The software programs on the CD fall into one of the following categories:

✔ *Shareware programs* are fully functional, free, trial versions of copyrighted programs. If you like particular programs, register with their authors for a nominal fee and receive licenses, enhanced versions, and technical support.

✔ *Freeware programs* are free, copyrighted games, applications, and utilities. You can copy them to as many computers as you like — for free — but they offer no technical support.

✔ *GNU software* is governed by its own license, which is included inside the folder of the GNU software. There are no restrictions on distribution of GNU software. See the GNU license at the root of the CD for more details.

✔ *Trial, demo,* or *evaluation* versions of software are usually limited either by time or functionality (such as not letting you save a project after you create it).

Software

You'll find the following software on your CD:

✔ **Adobe Reader:** Adobe Reader is a freeware program that allows you to view, but not edit, Adobe Portable Document Files (PDFs).

✔ **OpenOffice.org:** OpenOffice.org is a free multi-platform office productivity suite. It is similar to Microsoft Office or Lotus SmartSuite, but OpenOffice.org is absolutely free. It includes word processing, spreadsheet, presentation, and drawing applications that enable you to create professional documents, newsletters, reports, and presentations. It supports most file formats of other office software. You should be able to edit and view any files created with other office solutions.

Additional resources

These documents should be helpful as you set up and run your import/export business:

✔ **Distributor and Agency Agreement Outlines:** This document provides two outlines — one for distributors and another for agents — that you can use in your discussions with other companies.

✔ **General Business Plan Outline:** This document gives you a template for developing your business plan.

✔ **Glossary:** Key terms you need to know in the import/export business.

✔ **International Trade Commission Offices:** A listing of trade commission offices around the world.

Government forms

The following list summarizes all the documents on the CD:

CBP Form 17: ATPA Declaration

CBP Form 19: Protest

CBP Form 26: Report of Diversion

CBP Form 28: Request for Information

CBP Form I-68: Canadian Border Boat Landing (Permit Sample)

CBP Form I-95: Crewman's Landing Permit

CBP/ATC Form 101, Event Application

DHS Form I-193, Application for Waiver of Passport and/or Visa

CBP Form 214: Application for Foreign-Trade Zone Admission and/or Status Designation

CBP Form 214A: Application for Foreign-Trade Zone Admission and/or Status Designation

CBP Form 214B: Application for Foreign-Trade Zone Admission and/or Status Designation Continuation Sheet

CBP Form 214C: Application for Foreign-Trade Zone Admission and/or Status Designation Continuation Sheet

CBP Form 216: Application for Foreign-Trade Zone Activity Permit

CBP Form 226: Record of Vessel Foreign Repair or Equipment Purchase

CBP Form 243: CCFR Event Application

CBP Form 247: Cost Submission

CBP Form 255: Declaration of Unaccompanied Articles

CBP Form 262: Request for Printed Material

CBP Form 300: Bonded Warehouse Proprietor's Submission

CBP Form 301: Customs Bond

CBP Form 301A: Addendum to CBP Form 301

CBP Form 306: Sensitive Security Information (SSI) Document Receipt

CBP Form 339A: Annual User Fee Decal Request - Aircraft

CBP Form 339C: Vehicle Application

CBP Form 339U: Update Transponder Information

CBP Form 339V: Annual User Fee Decal Request - Vessel

CBP Form 349: Harbor Maintenance Fee Quarterly Summary Report

CBP Form 350: Harbor Maintenance Fee Amended Quarterly Summary Report

CBP Form 400: ACH Application

CBP Form 401: Automated Clearinghouse Credit Enrollment

CBP Form I-408: Application to Pay Off or Discharge Alien Crewman

CBP Form I-418: Passenger List – Crew List

CBP Form 434: North American Free Trade Agreement Certificate of Origin

CBP Form 434A: North American Free Trade Agreement Certificate of Origin Continuation Sheet

CBP Form 442: Application for Exemption from Special Landing Requirements

CBP Form 442A: OVERFLIGHT Pilot/Crewmember Personal Information Release

CBP Form 446: NAFTA Verification of Origin Questionnaire

CBP Form 449: Certificate of Origin - ATPDEA

CBP Form 450: United States-Caribbean Basin Trade Partnership Act (CBTPA) Certificate of Origin

CBP Form I-510: Guarantee of Payment

DHS Form 590, Authorization to Release Information to Another Person

CBP Form I-736: Guam-CNMI Visa Waiver Information

CBP Form I-736 Guam-CNMI Visa Waiver Information – Korean

CBP Form I-736 Guam-CNMI Visa Waiver Information – Japanese

CBP Form I-736 Guam-CNMI Visa Waiver Information – Simplified Chinese

CBP Form I-736 Guam-CNMI Visa Waiver Information – Traditional Chinese

CBP Form I-760: Guam Visa Waiver Agreement

CBP Form I-775: Visa Waiver Carrier Agreement

CBP Form 823F: FAST Commercial Driver Application - Mexico

CBP Form 823S: SENTRI Application

CBP Form 1300: Vessel Entrance or Clearance Statement

CBP Form 1302: Inward Cargo Declaration

CBP Form 1302A: Cargo Declaration - Outward with Commercial Forms

CBP Form 1303: Ship's Stores Declaration

CBP Form 1304: Crew's Effects Declaration

CBP Form 1400: Record of Vessels Engaged in Foreign Trade Entered or Arrived Under Permit to Proceed

CBP Form 1401: Record of Vessels Engaged in Foreign Trade Cleared or Granted Permit to Proceed

CBP Form 3078: Application for Identification Card

CBP Form 3124: Application for Customs Broker License

CBP Form 3124E: Application for Customs Broker License Exam

CBP Form 3171: Application-Permit-Special License Unlading-Lading-Overtime Services

CBP Form 3173: Application for Extension of Bond for Temporary Importation

CBP Form 3227: Certificate of Disposition of Imported Merchandise

CBP Form 3229: Certificate of Origin

CBP Form 3299: Declaration for Free Entry of Unaccompanied Articles

CBP Form 3311: Declaration for Free Entry of Returned American Products

CBP Form 3347: Declaration of Owner: For Merchandise Obtained in Pursuance of a Purchase or Agreement to Purchase

CBP Form 3347a: Declaration of Consignee When Entry Is Made by an Agent

CBP Form 3461: Entry/Immediate Delivery

CBP Form 3485: Lien Notice

CBP Form 3495: Application for Exportation of Articles under Special Bond

CBP Form 3499: Application and Approval to Manipulate, Examine, Sample, or Transfer Goods

CBP Form 4315: Application for Allowance in Duties

CBP Form 4455: Certificate of Registration

CBP Form 4457: Certificate of Registration for Personal Effects Taken Abroad

CBP Form 4609: Petition for Remission or Mitigation of Forfeitures and Penalties Incurred

CBP Form 4630: Petition for Relief from Forfeiture

CBP Form 4632: Lien Holder Financial Statement

CBP Form 4811: Special Address Notification

CBP Form 5106: Importer ID Input Record

CBP Form 5125: Application for Withdrawal of Bonded Stores for Fishing Vessel and Certificate of Use

CBP Form 5129: Crew Member's Declaration and Instructions

CBP Form 5297: Power of Attorney

CBP Form 6043: Delivery Ticket

CBP Form 6478: Application for CBP Approved Gaugers and Accredited Laboratories

CBP Form 7501: Instructions

CBP Form 7501: Entry Summary with Continuation Sheets

CBP Form 7507: General Declaration Agriculture, Customs, Immigration and Public Health

CBP Form 7509: Air Cargo Manifest

CBP Form 7512: Transportation Entry and Manifest of Goods Subject to CBP Inspection and Permit

CBP Form 7512A: Transportation Entry and Manifest of Goods Subject to CBP Inspection and Permit

CBP Form 7514: Drawback Notice (Lading/FTZ Transfer)

CBP Form 7523: Entry and Manifest of Merchandise Free of Duty, Carrier's Certificate and Release

CBP Form 7533: Inward Cargo Manifest for Vessel under Five Tons, Ferry, Train, Car, Vehicle, etc.

CBP Form 7551: Drawback Entry

CBP Form 7551 Instructions

CBP Form 7552: Delivery Certificate for Purposes of Drawback

CBP Form 7552 Instructions

CBP Form 7553: Notice of Intent to Export, Destroy or Return Merchandise for Purposes of Drawback

CBP Form 7553 Instructions

I-94: Arrival/Departure Record

I-94W: Visa Waiver Arrival/Departure Record

Commercial Gauger and/or Laboratory Agreement

Canadian Customs Invoice

Certification of Origin Sample

Form e370 - Application to Transact Bonded Carrier and Forwarding
Operations (Canada)

Harmonized Tariff Schedule

Statement of Origin Sample Forms — Australia (4)

Troubleshooting

I tried my best to compile programs that work on most computers with the
minimum system requirements. Alas, your computer may differ, and some
programs may not work properly for some reason.

The two likeliest problems are that you don't have enough memory (RAM)
for the programs you want to use, or you have other programs running that
are affecting installation or running of a program. If you get an error message
such as `Not enough memory` or `Setup cannot continue`, try one or
more of the following suggestions and then try using the software again:

- ✔ **Turn off any antivirus software running on your computer.** Installation
  programs sometimes mimic virus activity and may make your computer
  incorrectly believe that it's being infected by a virus.

- ✔ **Close all running programs.** The more programs you have running,
  the less memory is available to other programs. Installation programs
  typically update files and programs, so if you keep other programs
  running, installation may not work properly.

- ✔ **Have your local computer store add more RAM to your computer.** This
  is, admittedly, a drastic and somewhat expensive step. However, adding
  more memory can really help the speed of your computer and allow
  more programs to run at the same time.

Customer Care

If you have trouble with the CD-ROM, please call Wiley Product Technical
Support at 800-762-2974. Outside the United States, call 317-572-3993. You can
also contact Wiley Product Technical Support at `http://support.wiley.
com`. Wiley will provide technical support only for installation and other
general quality control items. For technical support on the applications themselves, consult the program's vendor or author.

To place additional orders or to request information about other Wiley
products, please call 877-762-2974.

Index

John Wiley & Sons, Inc.
End-User License Agreement